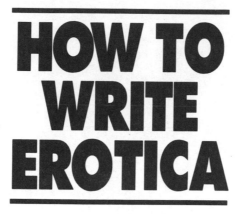

HOW TO
WRITE
EROTICA

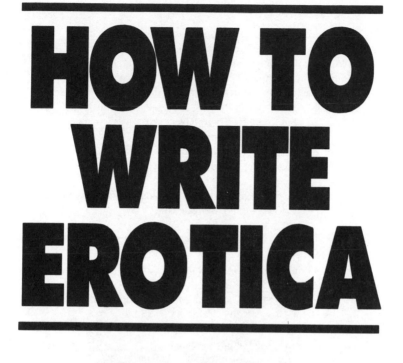

HOW TO WRITE EROTICA

VALERIE KELLY

THREE RIVERS PRESS / NEW YORK

Published by Three Rivers Press,
a division of Crown Publishers, Inc.,
201 East 50th Street, New York, New York 10022.
Member of the Crown Publishing Group.

Random House, Inc. New York, Toronto, London, Sydney, Auckland
www.randomhouse.com

THREE RIVERS PRESS and colophon are trademarks of Crown Publishers, Inc.

Printed in the United States of America

Library of Congress Cataloging-in-Publication Data
Kelly, Valerie.
How to write erotica / by Valerie Kelly.
Includes index.
1. Erotica—Authorship. I. Title.
HQ460.K45   1986   808´.02   86–7539

ISBN 0-517-58729-7

10 9 8 7

CREDITS

26   "Mothers Need Love Too." Copyright © 1981 by Blueboy, Inc. All rights reserved. Used by permission of *Video X* magazine.

29   "Video Foreplay." Copyright © 1981 by Blueboy, Inc. All rights reserved. Used by permission of *Video X* magazine.

35   "Confessions of a Breast Erotic" by Darien Lynx. Copyright © 1981 by American Art Enterprises, Inc. All rights reserved. Used by permission of American Art Enterprises, Inc.

39   "Keli's Bath." Copyright © 1981 by American Art Enterprises, Inc. All rights reserved. Used by permission of American Art Enterprises, Inc.

43   "Valene." Copyright © 1981 by American Art Enterprises, Inc. All rights reserved. Used by permission of American Art Enterprises, Inc.

44   "Stood Up." Copyright © 1981 by American Art Enterprises, Inc. All rights reserved. Used by permission of American Art Enterprises, Inc.

49   "A Lesbian Love Story" by Valerie Kelly. Copyright © 1981 by American Art Enterprises, Inc. All rights reserved. Used by permission of American Art Enterprises, Inc.

69   "How to Get Laid" by Lee Ann Hays. Copyright © 1982 by Lee Ann Hays. All rights reserved. Used by permission of Lee Ann Hays.

77   Video box cover copy for "Joys of Erotica, vol. 4." Used by permission of Video Cassette Recording, Inc.

How to Write Erotica *is dedicated to all those who supported my writing aspirations along the way and to all those who inspired me, especially C.L., and to all those would-be writers out there who may have finally found a genre to suit their interests and talents.*

C O N T E N T S

. Introduction   1
*The World of Erotica • The Adult Market as a
Training Ground • The Politics of Porn • How It
Began for Me • Life in the Business*

PART ONE
THE MARKETPLACE FOR PRINT EROTICA

1   The Marketplace for Erotic Fiction   25
*Letters • The Short-Short • The Long Short Story •
The Erotic Novel • The Erotic Romance Novel •
Poetry*

2   The Marketplace for Erotic Nonfiction   68
*Articles • Video Box Cover Copy • Paperback Cover
Copy • Advertising Copy • Public Relations Material •
Collateral • Reviews*

3   Writing for Special Markets   88
*Fetish Markets • New Trends • The Gay Male Market
• The Gay Female Market*

PART TWO
HOW TO WRITE PRINT EROTICA

4   The Basic Formula   121
*Plot • Character • The Setting • The Climax • Point of
View • The Denouement*

5 Telling Your Story 147
Knowing Your Reader • Tense • Active vs. Passive • Pacing • Focusing • Creating Emphasis • Writing and Reading

6 Making It Sexy 164
Writing Seductively • Creating Sensual Images • Using Buzz Words • Describing the Scene

7 Finding Your Material 174
Turning Your Experiences into Erotica • Avoiding Misinformation and Checking Your Facts • Where Not to Get Material

8 Getting Your Story Published 195
Deciding Where to Send Your Work • Query Letters and Cover Letters • Preparing to Submit Your Manuscript • Writing to Fit • Knowing Hardcore from Softcore

PART THREE
HOW TO WRITE EROTICA FOR THE SCRIPT MARKET

9 Writing Fantasy Phone Calls 209

10 The Marketplace for X-Rated Video Scripts 216
Understanding the X-Rated Video Industry • Selling Your Spec Script

11 The Basic Formats for X-Rated Video Scripts 226
The Mini Script • The Midi Script • The Maxi Script • The Full-Length Script • Writing to Specifications • Script-Writing Basics

12 Writing a Video Treatment, Outline and Script 236
Outlines and Treatments • Beginning a Script • What to Do and What Not to Do in Your Script

Afterword: Exercises to Get You Started 262

APPENDIXES

Appendix A: Magazines That Publish Erotica   272
Appendix B: Video Distributors/Producers   275
Appendix C: Recommended Reading   278
Appendix D: Sensual Words   282

Glossary   286

Acknowledgments   311

Index   312

INTRODUCTION

The World of Erotica

Welcome to the world of erotica. Don't be afraid. The water is warm, the atmosphere friendly. All those who would shake their fingers at you in admonition will not be present.

As a writer, you will find everything you need to practice your trade in this book: from the bare essentials of how to construct a stimulating and creative sentence, to detailed instructions about crashing the marketplace. Examples of each format are included so that there will be no doubt left in your mind as to what shape your work will take before it is ready to break print. However, this book is not geared only toward your writer self. You will also learn a great deal about today's sexuality and how it is portrayed in the adult literature of the eighties. As a reflection of our times, erotica and pornography serve to reveal both a sexually repressed public and one that is yearning for increased freedom of sexual expression.

There are many reasons why a person would buy this book. Possibly you are not a writer at all, but simply curious about how erotica is written; how one constructs a fantasy that kindles a reader's imagination. You may be seeking a better understanding of the world of pornography. Perhaps you want to know what writers of pornography are really like, what they do all day and if their fantasies are also erotic for them or if they treat the subject as they would any other. Some of you will actually sit down and write your own erotica for publication, but this book speaks to all of you.

There are those who will cock an eyebrow when you tell them what you write, and those who will tease you for spending your time dreaming up erotic fantasies to sell. Just smile sweetly and ask them if they can think of a more enjoyable way to spend one's time. The worst of the lot are those who will claim it's a sin to indulge in the world of erotica at all. Answer them by asking, "What could be sinful about writing about something wondrous, that feels so good." We were created as sexual beings and were meant to enjoy our sexuality.

Lifting sex above the purely physical and elevating it to the emotional and spiritual plane will be your job as writer. We don't fornicate; we make love. Discovering the subtle yet essential differences between the two will make you good at your work.

A word about words: Not that many years ago words like *damn* and *shit* were replaced in books and movies with *darn* and *shoot*. Expletives were deleted from everything public. Today, however, adults realize that these are only words, after all, with only as much power as we give them. Sexually explicit words and phrases have been slow in catching up and they are still commonly euphemized. With one exception. In the world of fiction, the writer is free to express ideas with any words seen fit.

However, the literary public can only stand so much verbal abuse, and the more you clutter your prose with explicit language, the more pornographic your critics will find you. The more you linger in your love scenes, the more graphic or X-rated your work becomes. Using explicit words was once just cause for burning books. Now, with a more enlightened and interested public, we have not only sexier reading material, but also an onslaught of books and magazines whose sole purpose seems to be the exploiting of the "dirty word" market. Dirty words are used just for the sake of using them, as when a child first learns to swear.

Words are magical. When strung together they can bring images to life in the reader's mind. These so-called illicit words and phrases can be employed in a sensitive, special and sparing way, and you can learn how to do it.

Although your primary objective may be to enhance your writing vocabulary, other benefits come of exploring inventive word use. Words are treasures and writing eloquently is a skill that can improve your life, professionally, personally, socially and in many other ways.

I'm making a big deal out of this because for the purposes of erotic writing you will have to allow yourself the freedom to express your ideas with the most descriptive and precise words possible, passing over only the archaic and those with defamatory connotations. *Fag*, for example, once a widely used term, is now considered derogatory and has been replaced with the term *gay*. When *fag* or *faggot* is found in men's magazines, it is used by one homosexual to another, in much the same way as a black person might call a black brother *nigger*, while a white person would not.

Feminists don't like it when women are referred to as *girls*, when men are not called *boys*, but *men* or *guys*. In the world of adult magazines, women are almost always referred to as girls, even if they're over fifty. Not because they are looked down upon as children, and not because they are symbols of children as sex objects: they are called girls because they have that girlish quality of curiosity about their bodies and an eagerness to explore anything that feels good. A girl is interested in what makes her different from a boy, and her willingness to "play doctor" can be read as unabashed sexual abandon. Every woman has the capacity to be a girl in bed, if she wants to be. It does not mean she isn't grown up, isn't a woman. It means at that moment she is more uninhibited, more of a pussycat, a nymphet, a scamp. I hope you don't get hung up in dogmatic rhetoric when you're reading this book.

What about the personal dilemma of whether or not to indulge in the writing of pornography? There are plenty of arguments against pornography in society. Yet pornography has existed, in one form or another, as long as history has been recorded. Archeologists have dated cave drawings of human genitalia at 30,000 B.C. and even earlier. Clay sculptures of figures with protruding phalluses or breasts go back to the Neolithic age, 9000 B.C. to 7000 B.C. In the 5th and 4th centuries, B.C., erotic vase painting was common in Greece, and sex acts were visually and graphically illustrated. Dialogue from the plays of Aristophanes reveals an en lightened sense of sexual humor. Neither was he timid in assaulting sexual sensitivities. In the staging of his play *Lysistrata,* for example, the male characters all have erections in the last act because their mates and mistresses refuse to put out. And this was in 411 B.C.

Sexual imagery and symbolism have been prominent in architecture, from the sculptured facades of India's great buildings, depicting couples during copulation, to the men's houses of New Zealand (equivalent to our city hall) where the lintel, or doorway, is sculptured as the spread legs of a woman, symbolizing threshold and passage. Perhaps much of the literature has not survived, but erotic art and architecture certainly imply an interest in sexuality, if not an obsession with it. The evidence of erotica in society exists in almost all countries over the centuries. Since there is little likelihood that we in the 1980s will do away with graphic sexual exploitation and pornographic literature in any or all of its various and sundry forms, let us go on to what we can do about it to make it more palatable to the majority.

At its very worst, pornography gives a lopsided view of sex and a bad impression of females. At its best it educates and enlightens people to the possibilities of enjoyment. Erotica does not cause pain, in and of itself, nor has it ever been proven to have a definitive link to sex crimes.

Yet, in its present state, it is far from being a positive influence for our society. Although I do feel we're fumbling our way along on the right track.

As a writer of "adult" material, it is your responsibility to free erotic literature from the heavy burden of its bad reputation—which some of our early magazine pornography surely deserved—and to develop a new language, a new form, which will enlighten the reader and celebrate the joys of sex. It is important to distinguish between erotica and pornography. Erotica celebrates sexuality, sex with caring, sex as expression and communication between lovers, sex as a release of emotions, as a solution to alienation and loneliness. Pornography exploits and often degrades sexuality. It shows sex for the purposes of objectifying it. Sex imposed upon one by another, sex with violence or humiliation and sex performed without feeling. With the attention and nurturing of a few sensitive writers, we can help implement the growth of sexual writing into acceptable literature. You can be at the forefront of this movement. You can help bring about change.

Sex is admittedly a touchy subject. Many novelists still "stop the action at the bedroom door" in the interest of good taste, or because they happened to be writing during an era when it was not acceptable in literature. Other writers venture into erotic scenes and suffer for it the wrath of the self-righteous. Even with all the nonsense over this tantalizing subject matter, well-written erotic literature has found an audience. The reader who curls up with Anaïs Nin's *Delta of Venus* or Harold Robbins' *Dreams Die First* does not skip over the sexually explicit passages. We are not afraid to enjoy erotica in the privacy of our imagination. The problem is sharing this side of ourselves with others.

Lonnie Barbach, Nancy Friday, Gail Greene, Shere Hite, Erica Jong, Darryl Ponicsan, Philip Roth, D. M. Thomas and many others have broken down the bedroom doors. We can go inside now and explore that one important aspect of our being that continues to be the most multifaceted, perplexing, convoluted, labyrinthine and mysterious of all, and which is a force that drives us out of control at times and yet brings us as much ecstasy as any other earthly thing. As a writer, you can relay these impressions and sensations to others. You can illuminate this dark and murky corner and exalt its wonders.

The Adult Market as a Training Ground

Writing erotica can improve your writing skills. Any kind of writing you do will make you a better writer: journal writing, letter writing, it all counts. If you want to be a published writer: you will explore all possible fields and eventually discover how difficult it is to sell stories. The prime difference between erotica and all other markets is the easy accessibility for the new writer. The quickest place to sell a short story today is the adult newsstand magazine, because there are so many of them which use fiction and comparatively so few writers competing for that space.

Regular mainstream magazines, such as *McCall's*, *Redbook* and *Cosmopolitan*, use far less fiction per issue and are literally besieged with submissions. In 1984, 36,000 stories were submitted to *Redbook* magazine. Of these, 50 were purchased. That's 720 to 1 against your being published in *Redbook*.

In the world of adult entertainment, in print and in video you'll come up against far less competition. In some cases, your story will be considered against four or five others. And increasing your odds is the fact that adult magazines have many more slots for fiction than do mainstream magazines. For example, *Penthouse Variations* uses approximately two dozen "letters" and ten full-length short stories per monthly issue, while *Esquire* and *Mademoiselle* use one story each per month.

Short fiction is currently the most accessible market for sexually oriented material. Another huge and growing adult market is in X-rated video. This medium is ideal for learning to write crisp, concise, dramatic dialogue, and could serve as a foundation for future television and screenplay work.

When you write short fiction and short video scripts, you improve your skills at handling story line and drama, and since you have little space in which to develop your story, you learn one of the most important lessons in writing: brevity. You learn to develop characters quickly and to create vivid dialogue. The more short stories you write, the more all of your writing will improve. At the same time, you can sell these stories and scripts to support yourself while you develop other areas of interest.

This field can be a training ground. It can be a terrific elementary school for writers, with the bonus that it pays you as you learn.

Even though the adult erotic market is among the easiest to break into and write for it is still important that you write well. Most of the time you'll have no editor to change your work (and no time-consuming rewrites), even if you need one. So get out your dictionary and use it. Now plug in the ol' Selectric. If you've never sold a thing, this is the place you can break into print. There is no market as accessible as this one.

A final word: Reading and writing erotica has to be done with a sense of the absurd, with a smile. Sex is wondrous, but it can't be taken totally seriously. Sex is a lark. It's a lavish short vacation that doesn't cost a dime and is available to anyone at the touch of a hand. Good loving sex is the best medicine for anything from a bad mood to a heartbreak.

So think of yourself as the deliverer of the word—and the good word is SEX. Sex can make you happy, get you high, make you forget your troubles and improve your life. Sex with love is the ultimate super-high. Writing about it can be almost as much fun as doing it.

The Politics of Porn

Sex and politics are connected in ways we can only begin to understand. A certain political theory advocates change by revolution, overthrowing the party in power and creating a new one. Another approach to change is to infiltrate the current system and to bring it about from within. This process is much slower, but in the long run, often more effective.

An organization as powerful and widespread as the current pornography network is almost impossible to overthrow. Its leaders are well connected and its advocates are fully supportive of the status quo. Like its sister, prostitution, it seems to be part of all societies. The best we can hope for is not the abolition of all pornography, but an adjustment in its content.

Few people would argue that sex itself is a bad thing. What feminists and others object to, and rightly so, is the perversion of sex, the exploitation of a natural function into a means of making money, the process of which turns women into objects or victims and men into insensitive users or macho studs.

There is a severe shortage of adult material which celebrates equal sexuality. I could list the books on one page and count the magazines on one hand. To date, however, promoting a healthy attitude about sex has not been one of the purposes of the publishing industry.

As more devoted writers infiltrate the industry and take the pen out of the hands of the uncaring, the amount of quality material will grow. Eventually we could create new publications based on the healthy view of equal sexuality, which in time would find a wide market as more people become exposed to this upgraded sensibility.

Perhaps this view is idealistic, but writers have to be idealistic because we are the dreamers for society. We have to point the way.

In its earliest stages, the magazine pornography business was underground and could safely and successfully propagate any warped, insensitive myths it deemed profitable, without opposition. In the 1950s, the business split up, and one element surfaced, trying to go legitimate by publishing a slew of nudist magazines. Photos of men, women and children frolicking in the sun, playing volleyball, swimming naked were put together with some rough copy advocating nudism and nudist camps (which, incidentally, were thriving at the time).

Then Hugh Hefner came on the scene with his revolutionary concept: a newsstand publication with a nude centerfold. In its own way, this breakthrough changed the face of pornography as well as that of so-called legitimate publications. Even if Hefner's magazine had maintained its original innocence and integrity, no one could have predicted or controlled the changes this open door would permit.

Our position on the literary nonacceptability of pornographic images was weakened in the face of this seemingly harmless celebration of the female form. On the positive side, we were allowed to enjoy prurient drives we had held closeted before then. On the negative side, this inroad to a brand-new, heretofore forbidden market was turned into a superhighway. As decadent and scandalous as we might have found *Playboy* back then, it is nothing compared to what those who came later have done with this relatively innocuous beginning.

Where pornography once had been mostly confined to teenagers snickering over French postcards in an alley, now it became an ominous ogre which threatened children and perverted men into thinking of women as objects. This change in attitude was mainly caused by the fact that pornography grew very fast. (We're experiencing a similar phenomenon currently with the video boom.) Men who once owned warehouses and drove trucks went into the girlie magazine business eager to capitalize on the fortunes to be made. They knew they needed pretty girls, photographers, pasteup artists and printers. The going phrase where writers were concerned was: "Anyone can write this stuff."

The main purpose for each magazine was to get the pictures to the public. Men wanted to see women nude or semi-nude. It didn't matter if the photographs were in black and white or color or how much the magazine cost. With this hungry market of sexually repressed baby-boomers, pornographers sprang up everywhere, especially in the larger cities, like New York, Chicago and San Francisco. But the biggest little boomtown was (and still is) Los

Angeles—the San Fernando Valley, home of the Valley Girl. The sunshine state offered cooperative weather conditions, a looser morality and a constant influx of nubile, albeit naive, young girls.

While *Playboy* pretenders invaded newsstands nationwide, the underground element continued to exploit popular exotic subjects and got into trouble. Bestiality, S&M, water sports, incest and especially child porn brought the nastiness of the industry to the attention of enough citizens that they were riled into political action.

Anti-porn activists called attention to the violent, obscene and abusive material of underground rags and demanded stricter laws. One of their main concerns was the presence of these publications in drugstores and supermarkets. Regulation proved to be difficult since there was the issue of freedom of the press, and it was hard to apply one rule to all forms of literature.

One result was legislation that required publications to have socially redeeming characteristics, especially when they were to be sold on public newsstands. Other new laws decreed that minors were not to be exposed to hardcore pornography. Adult bookstores were a direct outgrowth of this regulation, and this is where adult publications and newsstand "girlie" magazines had a final parting of the ways. What did this mean to the writer?

Formerly copy had been something to fill in the empty spots in the photo layout, or second-rights articles bought from irrelevant stock, but now it would take a place almost equal in importance to that of the pictorials. If you read the indicia in most sexually oriented magazines, you'll see something like this:

> . . . This magazine is published with the intent of informing and educating the adult public on various aspects of human sexuality. It is the belief of this publication that adults have the right to view and read such material. . . .

It doesn't matter if you're reading a magazine on the orgies of the suburban housewife, it is legally deemed socially relevant and educational. And with that stipulation, it is the written copy that lifts those exploitative photographs out of the realm of smut. Or at least, that is the premise of this argument.

For the newsstand magazines, there is another benefit to using articles and fiction. It gives the "straight" reader a legitimate excuse to buy the magazine. How many times have you heard a man say, "Oh, that. I just like to read the articles." Many a reader will not be embarrassed to have *Playboy* or *Penthouse* on the coffee table, but will still hide his adult, purely pictorial, material out of sight.

The pure hardcore adult store pornography still gets by with very little copy. This highly profitable market escapes some of the current flack from the public because it is a high-ticket item (some hardcore magazines sell for $75), and because it can only be purchased in an adult bookstore where no one under eighteen (or twenty-one, depending on the state) is allowed.

Some publication houses have been making breakthroughs toward a fairer, more sensitive view of sexuality and have the potential to educate and inform readers as well as to stimulate them. Couples are reading such publications together and using them as a basis for mutual intimate understanding. This appeal to both sexes is the goal of the new erotica, which will eventually, we hope, drive the old-style, denigrating pornography from the shelves.

Many writers of sexual material worry about their reputation. Although sexual activity is an aspect of life in which nearly all of us participate, talking and writing about it is still, unfortunately, often considered inappropriate behavior. And so the subject is hidden away with embarrassment and shame. This attitude is something you'll have to come to terms with yourself, but I can give you some ammunition.

The fact that hardcore pornography is saturated with negative imagery adds to the problem. Fortunately, it is gradually and subtly being undermined by our new form of erotica. Writers call it softcore or female-oriented or couple-oriented erotica because of its sensitive approach to sexuality, and because explicit sex acts are often between characters who care about each other. As this approach takes over the adult market, it will serve to legitimize verbal and graphic sexual expression. Men and women who have suppressed their own sexuality and denied their sexual cravings will have a voice to speak for them. A forum for couples will result, where each person can express desires to the other without shame, without feeling he or she is the only one in the world who wants to have a certain sexual experience. Ideas for new sexual adventures or positions, and sensitivity to another's needs will generate enthusiasm and set the stage for better, more honest, communication.

Men are aroused by female-oriented erotica because it appeals to their sensual side, their desire to please women rather than to pounce on them. It is tremendously satisfying for a man's ego to produce an orgasm in a woman (or to help to do so, depending on your philosophy), and gathering information regarding her physiology, psychology and sexuality aids him in this goal. "Tell me what you want" is a frequent request in the eighties and has more than taken the place of the old monster: "Slam-bam-thank-you-ma'am."

The archaic stereotypes of the macho man fucking just to get off, without kisses or foreplay, and the dispassionate woman who lies on her back counting the cracks in the ceiling will be all but obliterated in this new wave of mutual underbanding. These changes are a direct result of sex education. And just as psychologists, scientists and sex therapists are responsible, so are the writers of erotic material.

In a sense, erotica writers are giving people permission to admit to their sexual needs, problems, anxieties and questions. It is no longer a forbidden topic of conversation.

Discussing sexual needs or cravings can be an embarrassing or, at the least, a humbling experience. If the speaker is laughed at or put down, he might crawl back into his hole never to emerge again. Photographs and stories should help people to express their needs. Currently, hardcore pornography is severely lacking in sensitivity. Few women, when asked what is erotic to them, will point to a photograph of a girl on her knees having a man shoot his load in her face, and neither will most men. Unequal sex, sex forced by one on another, is for those who cannot love and those who have not yet learned to express their emotions and sexual needs in an adult way. Such attitudes are totally unacceptable to the rest of us.

Men who are attracted to women but cannot deal with them as people turn women into objects. They refer to their own lust as a bodily, not an emotional, function and to women as a conglomeration of physical parts. They are cunts with tits and asses, not human beings with much the same needs as men have. "Look at that cunt, boy, I'd like to fuck her." Never, "Look at that woman, boy, I'd like to get to know her."

Ironically, women have compounded the problem. In an effort to become equal, to take their rightful place at the side of man and not underneath him, women have imitated men in all respects, including, sadly, this one. It isn't only the men who go out on the prowl on Friday nights. Women have always been quick studies and in no time they caught onto the joys of multiple sex partners and one-night stands. A woman can now measure a man's status by the size of his penis without flinching, just as he measures hers by the size of her breasts. Women got even, or did they?

We are the casualities of the sexual revolution of the sixties. It was a time of changing values, questioning of authority and moral upheaval. In the confusion, definitions were somehow divorced from their roots.

Free love, which had originally been defined as the freedom to choose, came to mean casual sex; no-fault divorce became permission to desert one's family; the pill and legal abortion meant not only an increase in sexual freedom for women, but also an increased responsibility for women in making those moral choices which affected both sexes. The baby-boom generation, which was raised on a different set of values, was suddenly thrust into a world where having sex had become the ultimate goal, where nothing else meant very much any more, and where love, romance and intimacy were hopelessly lost in the shuffle.

The pendulum never stops in the middle. It headed toward the opposite extreme so that now we've returned to a mode of sexual repression without even realizing it. Sex without love turned out to be a fleeting high. This basic flaw was compounded and expanded by the scare tactics of "moral majority" groups and their media blitz on the epidemic of herpes, AIDS and other venereal diseases.

Other pro-family groups reminded career women of their biological time clock, urging them to begin having children and quit fooling around with careers. Marriage is on the upswing for the first time in two decades and divorce is on the decline. It would seem the adults of the postwar generation have had their fling and are returning to the traditional values of their parents. And yet nothing has changed. We are still confused. And we are still struggling with the conflict between wanting to be sexually free and yet feel loved romantically. One is gained at the cost of the other.

Both sexes got what they thought they wanted: intimate contact with multiple partners and no intimacy. And then what happened? Something was still missing. But now it wasn't so easy to identify. Sex, at least, was concrete, obvious. People knew when they were sexually frustrated, when their sexual expression was limited. So why, when the only limitations are self-imposed, are we still frustrated? What has eluded us this time?

Nobody really knows if men and women are basically monogamous or not. We're only guessing. The theory used to be that women were and men were not, because of women's nesting instinct.

That theory begins with the premise that we're merely following through with our genetic heritage. Our primitive male ancestors were intent on fertilizing as many young, healthy females as possible and the females relied on one partner at a time, for the sake of the children. Are we still creatures of caves?

Other theories propose that those of both sexes simply outgrow their partners. And if marital vows or children don't keep them, they go on to the next in the progression.

The closest we can come to a solution is to make a personal decision and let the world go its way. With all the misinformation and soap-box evangelists around, this solution isn't as easy as it sounds. If one chooses to remain single in a world that's turning married, one is going against the tide. Free love and open sexual expression with more than one partner have become for some the symbols of the destruction of family life, of "the American Way."

Pornography, erotica and sex in advertising are necessary in our culture because they address our need to express our sexual nature. Denying the power of sexuality, our sexual attraction and attractiveness, by obliterating literary and graphic publications would only serve to push the pornography industry underground again, where it would thrive. To blame pornography for our interest in it is backwards. We need to use our interest in it to mold the new form of erotic material which more accurately reflects our current sexual trends.

To make sexual expression a political issue, to confuse the enjoyment of it with sin or to judge a person's morality or ability to love by his sex life is a mistake. Sexuality is a personal issue, not a political one. It is an expression of emotion, not of morals. It is the inborn desire to reach out and make contact with another human soul. Having sex is a wonderful experience; making love to someone you cherish is a touch of heaven. To give sex more power than that is to grossly misunderstand it.

How It Began for Me

Anyone who has ever seen a newborn baby suckle her mother's breast knows the sexual instinct is already there. The baby's forehead sweats, her tiny fists tighten to the point of turning white at the knuckles and she pushes her face into her mother's flesh with verve and intensity. Feeding may be the first tangible demonstration of a child's sexuality.

I can't remember back quite that far. I can tell you I was onto the uses of sexual prowess as early as age two when I climbed up into my favorite uncle's lap, although I wasn't into producing erotica until a bit later.

I'd say it began in kindergarten. I couldn't write much more than my name at that time, but I was a heck of a good artist. My crude illustrations were quite recognizable to my peers and unfortunately to some of my teachers. Early on, I learned to disguise my more graphic representations in such clever ways that nobody knew what I was drawing. Even if they sensed the erotic influence, they couldn't tell why.

My first big hit as an erotic piece came disguised as a farm scene. Dozens of versions of country farms sprang from my wooden easel. Since I was raised in the city and had never so much as been near a farm in my short life, my prolific output of rural barnyards baffled my parents and teachers. Farm after farm was turned out by this budding Picasso. Some had large barns with horses and cows, others had little houses with peaked roofs and smoking chimneys. All of them had one thing in common: a silo.

I constructed the silo first, always in pale tones of pink and yellow mixed with white. (Are you with me yet?) The silo was always the largest object in my picture. It dominated my farm like a steeple on a church. The silo rose straight up from the ground, almost touching the place where I painted a blue strip of sky with white smudges. Next I painted rings around my silo, and I finished it off with a nice round cap on its top, which slightly overlapped the rim.

Two haystacks always sat at the bottom of this structure, and lots of tall sand-colored weeds grew around on the ground. Can you picture it?

By now you've guessed I must have seen my father naked at some point before I entered school, and I must have owned a picture book with farm stories in it, because my renderings were pretty convincing on both subjects. I think now the rings around the circumference of the silo must have been folds of foreskin. The haystacks, of course, were the scrotum and the long strands of wheat or weeds must have been hair.

One day, I had done a particularly magnificent job with my farm scene. My ranch house had a quaint white picket fence with giant pansies growing in the front yard, and my beautiful silo, which I'd painted bright red this time for variety, stood tall and proud over a garden flourishing with strong brown wheat. The haystacks were ripe for bailing. I stood back and admired my masterpiece with pride, and beheld my silo with the ambivalent stirrings of sexuality.

I was not alone. Standing behind me was the vice-principal of our elementary school.

"Valerie," she said in that voice grown-ups use for children, "this is marvelous! What a wonderful farm."

I shuffled my feet and hoped she'd go away. She didn't. "Would you like to live on a farm?" she asked.

"No, ma'am." I avoided her glass-covered eyes and stared at the teardrop-shaped holes in my Maryjane patent leather shoes.

"Have you ever lived on a farm?"

"No, ma'am." I'd stumped her.

Without losing her fuchsia smile, she asked: "But then why did you choose to paint a farm?"

I shrugged my shoulders and tried hard to think up a lie, but it was already too late. The vice-principal was taking my picture down from its clips. I was cooked.

"I'll tell you what," she said, beaming. "I'm going to take this lovely painting and put it right up on my office wall, right behind my desk, so everyone who comes to visit me will see your wonderful work."

Mortified, I flushed beet-red, which my teacher mistook for pride. All I could think of was how many people went through the vice-principal's office every day. There was the captain of the Fire Department, the school nurse, the local police officers, my teacher, my friends, their parents. And all of them would see what I had painted. Eventually, one of them had to recognize the symbolism.

The vice-principal was in her sixties and had never been married. Maybe she'd never seen a real one before, how did I know?

She kept the painting over her desk the whole time I was in elementary school. Every time I was called into the office for not taking my Polio vaccine or for being tardy, I had to look at my painting, its paper curling and yellowing with age, the red silo fading into a telling pink from the sunlight that beamed through the office window. I'll tell you one thing, it cured me of that particular vice. I restricted my erotic drawings to small pencil sketches after that.

By the time I reached sixth grade, I realized I had exaggerated the proportions, just a tad—only Godzilla could have had such a big one—and my depiction of the scrotum was pretty rank. What has continued to perplex me over the years is how I knew it was supposed to stand straight up like that. Freud would know.

After the silo debacle I began to learn what all of us have to learn, unfortunately, to suppress my sexuality. I became a dual self, the outer self a good little girl with a pure heart, the inner self, a raging potential nymphomaniac eager for the chance to try out her equipment. Like a good little girl, I grew up and got married. It didn't take. I got divorced. Like a good little girl, I tried to support myself. It didn't take so well either. Somehow I wound up as a writer. From there it was a short leap to writing about the subject I liked best: sex.

Even before I wrote erotica for a living, sexual scenes had begun to creep into my "straight" material. Friends remarked on my ability to describe sexual scenes with grace and delicacy. And during one of those times when I was looking for work, as all writers, artists and actresses must constantly do, I saw a small ad in the L.A. *Times* that aroused my curiosity. It was for a writer/editor of "adult material." Although I had no experience in the field, I did have writing samples and made a bet with myself that I could get the job if I tried. I got it over twenty-six other applicants. Probably not because I was any better than the others, but because I'm a woman. For once, this worked for me instead of against. This publishing house was producing forty quarterly softcore adult magazines and ten annual specials, all supposedly written by female models and they only had men to write them. My boss accurately predicted that if they could get a woman to write these stories, the girls in the photographs would seem more real to their readers. But could a woman write raunch? I took some work home and proved I could.

When they called me back to give me the job, I almost refused. How could I take a job I couldn't even tell my own mother about? And then I figured, writers are always looking for unusual experiences; I'll do it for a lark. (Someday maybe I'd even write a book about it!) Little did I know then that the lark would last six years!

My first assignment, a one-page story, took me two weeks to write. I couldn't get it "hot" enough. But once I got the format down and established a rhythm to my stories, I became very fast and very good at it. Within that first month, I was turning out stories five at a time. After six months, I had written over two hundred short erotic stories and about a dozen longer ones. The first collection of my work, *The Sensual Review: The Best of Darien Lynx* (my first pseudonym), was published and I was a star, at least in the adult publications business.

Then I was stolen away by an entrepreneur who intended to publish a nationwide men's magazine which would be called *Ultra*. It would combine articles about art, music and theater with high-fashion photography and a touch of class. There would also be a centerfold-type layout and some softcore erotica.

Well, we didn't even get the title right. Someone else produced a magazine under that title before we got the first issue together. Then my boss sank into the pits of the lower line newsstand porn magazines, and alas, I with him. For a year, I edited and wrote three of these rags and then I quit. I had never intended to become part of the machine that degraded and exploited women and there was no way I could give air to my personal views in this position.

My next move was to freelance. By then I had picked up a few stray clients, in the adult business and outside of it, for advertising as well as fiction, and I learned how to play the game by my own rules and get away with it. Since I had a portfolio stuffed with tear sheets and a reputation for quality work with a quick turn-around, it wasn't long before I had about a dozen publishers on my client list. I knew where I could pick up a quick buck or an easy job when I needed to make my rent or pay the dentist. And I attached myself to those rare customers who provided assignments on a regular basis and who paid on time.

Life in the Business

Since then, my career in erotica has had its ups and downs (so to speak). Overall, it has been fun and I've met many interesting characters for future novels. The people in this business are continually surprising because for the most part they're just like you and me. They aren't dirty old fat men in trenchcoats, slobbering over greasy typewriters. Instead, they're struggling screenwriters, playwrights, actresses, used car salesmen and lonesome cowboys.

When I began at the publishing house, my co-writers on the softcore side were an ex-playwright from off-Broadway, who happened to be very bright and erudite beyond the requirements of his job, and an ex-rancher/drifter from Texas, who really wore a cowboy hat and boots to work and whose horse packed 650 cc's. The only writer on the hardcore side (they have less copy in their magazines) was a twenty-seven-year-old Vassar graduate who could sling four-letter words like a trucker. One of my layout artists had worked formerly as a garage mechanic. He liked pasting down photographs and sizing chromes because it didn't get his hands dirty. Other writers are in this business because it's easy to make money and it doesn't cloud up one's mind, leaving the Muse free to peruse subjects for the next screenplay or poem.

The guys who run the publications could have come from anywhere, but for some inexplicable reason, most of them seem to hail from New York or Chicago, judging by their accents. I wouldn't worry about any similarity to those guys who used to be the pornographers. Since the Roaring Twenties or so, the old-time honchos have bought up strings of laundromats and clothing jobbers and gone into the franchise business. It could be it's easier to hide income when you're not being monitored.

The new bosses are quite a different breed. Many of them were once poor working class, though they've chosen to put all memory of poverty out of their collective consciousness. They came in for the fast buck and stayed to make sizable fortunes. One of my biggest clients, though I never work with him directly, drives his Rolls Royce to work when he gets bored with his Maserati. He used to own a warehouse. I think he was warehousing magazines and that's how he got involved.

Another man I know started in this business at age twenty-three and by twenty-eight was making a six-figure income. He told me he couldn't work for anybody else when he got out of college. He saw that no one was warehousing and packaging video boxes and took up the slack. Now he's got his own publishing business, adult video business, sex toy business, and several others, plus, he's about to enter the "straight" publishing world with a book on sex surrogates. It's this kind of entrepreneur who can do very well in this business.

When I first started expanding into the freelance porn market, I did think about the "bad guys." And when I'd made an appointment one day to meet a new client, I'll admit I was a little nervous. We'd arranged to meet in a parking lot behind the printing house, and I had been told to watch for a big black Lincoln. As the car pulled in, I studied the driver. The man behind the wheel, with his thick black hair, pock-marked face, and stone-cold expression, gave me cold chills. He sat chewing on a cigarette and looked straight in front of him, squinting from the smoke. I'd hit the big one. I was certain of it.

Cautiously, I approached the sedan. "Hi," I said weakly. "Get in," he replied without moving his lips. I let out a deep breath. "Oh, that's all right," I said. "It's such a beautiful day. I think I'll just stand out here." His expression did not alter, but his thick fringed eyebrows slowly joined in the center as he studied my face.

"On the other hand," I added, "maybe I could use a rest." I held my breath and took the passenger seat, but I left my door wide open. "Hot out today, isn't it?" I said, not daring to look him in the eye.

He reached over behind me to get something off the back seat. "There are ten sets here," he said. "I need them Monday."

Or else, I thought. "Fine."

"You can bring them to my office in Reseda," he added as he gunned the engine. I hopped out of the car, then stood clutching my work as I watched him peel away. An office in Reseda, I thought. Here I had already concocted a basement with one barred window, a hefty godfather lurking in the shadows and me in the one spot of light. If he didn't pay me for this work, what would I do? Nothing.

As it turned out, even though he looked ferocious this guy was a pussycat once I got to know him and became one of my best clients. He fell into this business in much the same way as I did—backwards. He was a paste-up artist and his work wasn't good enough for the advertising agencies. No ominous overtones. No hidden past: just a ruddy complexion and a shyness about smiling.

Suffice it to say that even though there may be some shady characters in the business, you'll probably never meet them. The guys you talk to will be family men of a different kind, the kind who mow their lawns on Sundays and fall asleep in front of the television set.

Most freelance writers do something else during the day, like work in a gas station or in an office. They write short stories or articles on the weekends and mail them in, or come in once a week or so to get assignments. Publishing houses tend to use the same writer over and over again, rather than look for new ones. So once you're in the door, you're in for life—or until you ask for more money.

Also, there's no jealousy between publishing houses, so a satisfied client may refer you to a colleague if you're looking for more work. I've gotten nearly all my jobs through referral. There's an endless supply waiting for you. All you have to do is go for it.

Naturally, just as it's best to live in Hollywood if you're a screenwriter or New York if you want to have your plays produced, you're better off if you live in a city which produces the material you wish to write. This applies to the smaller jobs as well as the larger projects such as feature and video scripts. The middle market, short stories and articles, is the exception. After you've established yourself, you can conduct your business by mail although it's still better to live within phoning distance. Everyone always wants things in by yesterday and you can't do that if your contact is in Boston and your home is in Denver.

The good news is you'll never need an agent for this material (not that one would handle you anyway), and that longer work, such as articles for *Forum* and *Sexology*, and long short stories (ten pages and more) for nationwide magazines can be written anywhere and mailed in. It's in the smaller jobs that you'll run into problems if you live in Podunk.

Having struggled through the trials and heartbreak of learning rules for writing children's books, formulas for sitcoms, structure for three-act plays, politics for screenwriting and patience for waiting on novels to be accepted, I can tell you without reservation that erotica is the easiest, most immediately satisfying, best-paying field for a new writer today. And that writer may as well be you.

PART ONE

THE MARKETPLACE FOR PRINT EROTICA

THE MARKETPLACE FOR EROTIC FICTION

There are many formats for erotica, probably more than I've listed here. Once you get pretty good at one or two, you should be able to slip into the others fairly easily. This chapter is just to familiarize you with the various types of jobs you will be doing if you choose to make a career, or even a lucrative hobby, out of writing erotic material.

Letters

The quickest way to get published is to send a "letter to the editor." Pick your poison, any magazine will do. *Penthouse, Forum, High Society,* they're always glad to have "real" letters from readers, which also happen to be grammatically correct and passably erotic. Letters can be a great training ground for you. There are also magazines which are predominantly letters, such as *Couples, Bedside Companion, Oui Letters, True Letters,* and so on.

Your approach will depend upon the column you're aiming for. You could ask Xaviera a question about your sexuality, or you could describe a personal experience in vivid detail for *Playgirl's* Erotica section, or you could make up a kinky story for "Kinky Korner." Space limitations are not important here. Take as long as you want as long as it's not over five typed, double-spaced, pages for a column in a newsstand magazine, or twelve pages for a letters magazine.

Now you know all readers don't send in letters this perfect, but they don't care if they get published either. *You do.* Why? Because once you have your stuff typeset and printed in a nationwide magazine, you have what we call in the trade a "tear sheet." Tear sheets are your passport to paying assignments.

Letters to the editor are really short stories. They have a main character—that's you (they are always told in first person)—they have a secondary character or two, a tiny plot and, of course, a climax (literally). The only key story element seldom found in letters is a jeopardy or obstacle the protagonist must overcome to get to the end. If you think of letters as little stories told to an intimate friend, you'll be on the right track.

Here are two examples of letters to the editor, published in *Video X* magazine (which is sold on the newsstand). The first one happens to have a minor obstacle for our heroine, which is completely explained by the end of the fourth sentence. Remember to write as if talking to a friend and not completing a college thesis, and you'll develop just the right speed, tone and rhythm for your story.

The conversational tone will make it appear as something other than what it is, a finished piece of fiction. You can use any means at your disposal to make your letter sound as real as possible.

Mothers Need Love Too

There is nothing unusual about my sex life. I'm divorced, have two children in junior high school and work as a secretary. I read in women's magazines about all of us girls getting laid all the time, going boating or dancing with handsome one-night stands. It never happens to me. After all, what man is going to want to date someone who has to make Spaghetti-O's before she goes out, and has to get home by ten to be sure everyone gets to bed OK. Besides, I'm not really promiscuous. All those modern diseases scare the hell out of me, and I don't trust any method of birth control short of total abstinence.

So why am I writing to you? Because this weekend something very special happened. I date this one guy. I have him for dinner with the kids once a week and on the other "date night" we go to a movie. Well, this time he said to me: "I want you to get a sitter for the kids and come over to my apartment. I'll cook dinner for you and we'll listen to some music." He was so masterful, I had to go along with it. We'd made love before, but only very quietly so as not to wake the kids and I was so paranoid, I couldn't climax.

Well, when I got there, he had the whole thing all set up. He's a painter, so his place is set up like a studio. His bed consists of a mattress laid flat in the middle of the living room floor. The bedroom is filled with huge canvases, stretched and painted.

As I walked in, I noticed the candle light right away. There was a board on the floor laid out with bread and cheese, little sauteed mushrooms, raw vegetables with sour cream, tiny Swedish meatballs, and chocolate brownies for dessert. There was white wine and a surprise—marijuana.

I was his slave that night, because I wanted to be. And I smoked the grass, drank the wine, and ate leisurely all night long. After an hour, I had all my clothes off and we both lay naked together, exploring each other's bodies. I had never experienced the luxury of lazy, drawn-out sex. It was always something done in a hurry, awkward and painful. And here I was, all wet and waiting for him, throbbing already in anticipation of his glorious penis, and yet he wasn't fucking me. He was waiting too.

He cupped my breast in his hand and talked about it, how beautiful it was. He teased the nipple with the tip of his tongue and sucked it gently. He ran his beautiful artist's fingers up and down my torso, lingering here and there. But the finest thing he did was lick the insides of my thighs. My skin is so soft and tender there and I could feel my pussy lips swell as he almost came near, then darted away.

And then he went down on me. Can you believe that at the age of thirty-three I had never experienced oral sex? At least not that end of it. He never asked me to "do" him, as other men had, but now he was eating me and not complaining, and not asking if that was enough. He just licked me and sucked me, drew his finger in and out of my cunt, as if he had all the time in the world.

His cock had grown large and was leaking. I tried to reach

for it, wanting badly to do something for him, but he wouldn't let me. Tonight was all for me.

He held one of my breasts in each of his hands, with thumbs on the nipples, and licked my pussy lips until they parted. Then he took my clit between his lips and tongue and sucked on it, at first gently, then harder. In my mind's eye, I could see my clit growing to enormous proportions, like a little cock. I could see his tongue at the bottom of it, causing it to grow, to expand, to get hot.

I was sweating, though I couldn't remember it being hot in the room. My neck felt red from heat. When I closed my eyes, it seemed my vagina was the largest part of my body, that it was all of me, and still growing by the minute. And I was so hungry, so hungry for the type of good loving he was giving me that I could almost taste my orgasm.

Then it began. My legs began to tremble, my pelvis lifted itself off of the mattress as if out of control. I wanted my cunt to inhale his tongue like a cock. I wanted to fuck his mouth with my clit. I thought of all those dirty words I had never said to him, wanting to be a lady.

But then I said them, "Fuck me!" I said, at first in a low growl, then a whisper, then in my real voice. But he wouldn't. He continued to eat and suck on me like a hungry animal.

Suddenly I began to orgasm. My clit made one last jab forward, my pussy lips opened to grab whatever was available, and my insides clamped together. I groaned so loudly, I startled myself. But I kept coming, and he kept sucking on me. My legs were closing in around his head now but he didn't mind, he didn't stop. Again I came. And again. And just when I thought I could not possibly take any more, he came into me and fucked me.

He rammed his hard cock into me as far as it would reach. My pussy was tight and hot from coming and it clamped down on him as if to keep him there forever. He buried his head into my neck but I searched out his mouth to kiss him and I tasted myself. It turned me on even more. I pushed my tongue down his throat and he sucked on that too.

It was wild. His body was hot and wet. I could feel the sweat on his back and ran my fingers around his crack with it, reaching as far as I could into him. I pushed his butt so that his pelvis came hard against mine, forcing his prick in deeper and deeper. And then he came, moaning with each thrust and release. "Oh, baby," he said, "I love you so much."

That turned me on as much as anything else he did that night. My body trembled as it came down from my orgasm. The tension gradually released. My cunt let go of his now softening prick. I felt wonderful.

I felt so good that I fell asleep. In his arms. Falling asleep in a man's arms was something I hadn't done since I was married, and something I missed very much. When I woke up at six a.m., I was angry with myself and him for forgetting everything like that. But when I got home, the babysitter didn't complain at all. She was glad to have made the extra money. And the kids thought it was funny, mommy tiptoeing in with shoes in hand like that. It was no big deal.

And that's why I wrote this letter. To say to all the other single mothers out there that it's OK for us to have sex lives too. And to all you guys there's a lot more to us "older women" than Spaghetti-O's and baby sitters. We're really good fuckers!

Video Foreplay

You're going to think this is madness, but I have a confession to make about my Beta-Max machine. He and I are lovers.

I'm thirty years old and the guys at the office call me a "10," though I've never been married. I was waiting to fall in love, which didn't happen until I was twenty-five and then one of those unfortunate things happened. I fell in love with "Mr. Wrong." When I met him he was a college professor, dashing and charming as he lectured us from his podium on the lecture-hall stage. I fell deeply in love the first time I saw his pale blue eyes flash.

He was older than me and divorced and embittered by life. He drank a lot, and I wasn't used to that. But I put up with everything to get next to the man. It wasn't hard to attract him. I used my thick blonde hair and full breasts to the max, accenting all my attributes with the right clothes and accessories. I weaseled my way into his life, seducing him all the way, and after six months of sexual bliss, he allowed me to move in with him. It went down-hill from there.

Within a year, we'd broken up. He coldly sent me away from his house and I found a little apartment in another city. But I never fell out of love.

Whenever a man walks by, I look for the professor, in his eyes, in his gait, his build. I can't shake him, and I can't fall for anyone else. They all pale by comparison. He was so brilliant and so interesting.

Finally, last year I gave up looking for a replacement and resigned myself to being single the rest of my life. I watched a lot of television, signed up for all those pay-TV channels and lost myself in a world of fantasy. Then I bought my Beta-Max.

My original idea was to purchase some favorite movies (with steel-gray-haired men in them), and I bought *Indiscreet,* some early Clark Gable movies, and anything that starred a handsome, gray-haired man who fell in love with the heroine. I was Ingrid Bergman, Susan Hayward, Claudette Colbert, whoever I needed to be to catch all that love and attention.

One night, in my local video store, I spotted a porn actor with gray hair and blue eyes. He was on the box cover of an erotic videotape doing unmentionable things to a pretty blonde. I bought it and took it home.

Soon I was buying others with the same guy in them and then I found other guys who attracted me. I didn't like the movies with just girls in them or where the girls vastly outnumbered the guys. I liked the more romantic ones, slowly paced, more sensual build-ups, with a story line. Soon the man behind the counter understood my tastes and helped me choose the tapes. He even let me preview a few, because a large collection can be quite expensive.

Now at night, instead of a handsome lover, I have my Beta-Max machine, loaded to the transistors with hot porn, hard-ons and people cumming and cumming and cumming. I fix myself a scotch on the rocks, light up a joint, and on the second drink I turn on my machine. Then it turns me on.

Sometimes I douse myself with men's cologne and let a cigar smolder in my ashtray. If the girl in the story has a vibrator, I get mine out too and copy her actions. Mine is a different kind, it straps onto the back of my hand. But I have a rubber dong too that I can insert at certain moments.

I stroke myself as the people in the story are getting warmed up to each other. When a girl bends over and runs her fingers up and down her crack, I bend over on my bed and imitate her, caressing myself, sometimes smoothing lotion around my sensitive areas. Then when the guy brings out his hard-on, I get real close to the screen. This makes his throbbing, hard prick much larger than life and I imagine myself touching it, licking it. I can't lick my dildo because it tastes like rubber, but sometimes I suck on my fingers instead. Sometimes I'll suck them, then push them into my cunt, then take them out and suck them some more. I'm getting so that my own juices turn me on as much as a man does.

During one 60-minute tape, I can usually come twenty times. Sometimes I turn it off though and go to sleep, then turn it on again at various times the next day to catch a few scenes. I'm hard all the time. I'm wet all the time.

The guys in the office must notice this, but they don't say anything. When one tries to ask me out, I make it clear I'm not interested in him. I have everything I need with my Beta-Max, and it'll never hurt me, be mean to me during a drunken rage, or throw me out on the streets. My Beta-Max is the ideal lover if you ask me.　　　　　—Call me "Ingrid"

Most magazines pay very little for letters, if at all. But they have an insatiable appetite for them, requiring dozens per month. Some magazines, specifically letters magazines, such as the ones I mentioned previously, will buy your letters by the batch on a monthly basis once you establish yourself with them as a writer who can produce. Send them a freebee or a tear sheet as a sample. Then, once they accept you, ask if you can send them more by assignment (your first choice) or on spec (without assignment).

One of the students in my How to Write Erotica class sent her "true-life" adventure story of incest by the seaside to a letters magazine called *Letters Magazine* and they bought it at their rate of four cents a word, or one hundred dollars. She was delighted, since it was her first piece of erotica and the science fiction she had been writing for eight years had never sold.

Letters magazines usually have categories to fill. If you notice that one magazine is long on group sex stories, but short on "straight" sex (one boy with one girl), you might want to choose group sex for your first attempt. If you do vary from their approach, at least make sure it fits into a category they use or you'll be wasting your time and theirs.

Now for what they *won't* buy. Here is a letter I submitted to *Chic Letters,* which had been buying from me at the rate of eight to twelve per month. This one was sent back. Take a look at it and see if you can guess why it was turned down. I'll give you a hint. I wasn't thinking of my reader. I was thinking of what a good time I was having writing the story and how funny the situation was that I created.

Transsexual

Last weekend, I had the scare and the time of my life. First, I got the scare then I decided there was nothing to be scared of.

I picked up what I thought was a chick at a bar. Beauty she was. Called herself Scarlet and had the biggest brown eyes and the thickest, juiciest cherry-colored lips and the most luscious, thick brown hair I'd seen on a dame in a long time. She wore a little T-shirt with her name spelled out in spangles across the front of it. And her cute little titties made points in it. Then she had shorts on, cut-off jeans, and high-topped boots.

She was a knock-out. I found her on Hollywood Boulevard. That should have made me suspicious. I know the gays hang out there. But I saw those little titties bouncing up and down and I thought for sure she was a broad. She wasn't.

We got to my hotel room and I already had a hard-on. I started kissing up on her, drinking in that sweet perfume, playing with her hair, and she started moaning and playing around with my cock. She pulled it out and made noises like she was real impressed.

I finally got her T-shirt off and there they were, real cute little ones, with hard, perky nipples. I licked and sucked on them like crazy.

I kept pulling on her jeans, but she kept pushing my hands away from there. That shoulda made me suspicious but I was too eager to keep things going, so I didn't pay it no mind.

Then she slid my pants down and started playing with my balls. Like tickling them. It felt so good I forgot about her sweet little pussy and just thought about my own cock.

She really knew what she was doing when she took that thing in her mouth too, boy. Finally, I'd had enough and I threw her down on the bed. Her expression changed suddenly and I knew I'd done something wrong. She tried to stop me, but then I was curious, and I ripped those little shorts off and what do you think I found between that babe's legs?

It was a pecker, a cute little pecker. She didn't have a hard-on. It just laid there to one side.

Scarlet started to cry, which made me look up at her face again. I didn't want her crying. I didn't know what to do. I felt a little bit repulsed by the fact that she was a he, but not all that turned off. My hard-on was still raring to go. I hadn't been discouraged.

I held her in my arms and rocked her and begged her to stop crying. I told her to be a good little girl and then realized what I was saying so I just shut the hell up.

Well, Scarlet cuddled up into my arms like the sweet little thing that she was and started telling me this long story about how she was a girl in a guy's body. I'd heard such tales before on TV and such, but it was weird to be holding this kind of person in my own arms.

While I was rocking her, I felt her little prick come up. Cute little thing it was, about a quarter the size of my monster. Her breasts got hard too, just like a girl, and I started fooling with them and sucking them and stuff.

Pretty soon I was just as turned on as I was before I found out she was a boy. And she went down on me just like she did before and I dug it. I mean, it almost added to the pleasure to know she was a guy.

She got me so riled, that I wanted pussy more than ever. It wasn't going to do it, just letting her suck me off, or even jack me off. I wanted cunt and I wanted it now. I must have said some of my feelings out loud like, because Scarlet heard me.

What she did is she bent over, like doggie style, and told me to stick it up her ass. I thought that would turn me off too, until I saw her ass from behind. Cute little thing, it was, hairless and round and fleshy like a chick's.

So I did it. I put a little spittle on my prick and I pushed it in past her little pink rim, real gentle like and I heard her give out a little cry.

I was used to grabbing onto boobs when I fucked in this position, but she didn't have much hanging down up there. And then I latched hold of this little cock of hers and I played with it while I was balling her.

Hey, it was all right. Like jacking off and fucking at the same time.

Scarlet was crying out all sorts of things. Her voice had gone down a few octaves since we discovered her little secret. And she was talking about how much she dug straight guys, how much she loved to have cock up her ass, and how good everything I did felt to her.

I was being real gentle with her little cock, but now I was getting loaded and ready to come and I must have pulled on her a little too hard because she bucked forward with a jerk and a little cry.

I said I was sorry and she said, let me do it and she grabbed hold of herself while I was balling her. This left my hands free to press in those fat cheeks of hers. I pushed them in around my cock and rammed her.

Then I came, I yelled out it felt so good, and while I was coming, I could hear Scarlet coming too. And I looked down just in time to see that little bugger squirt. Hell, it was great.

I can't say I cruise Hollywood Blvd. and look for transsexuals, but I don't turn them down neither.   —Phil

Many of us know a man who has found himself, to one degree or another, in this situation. And yet, you won't find an audience for this story. Why? Because people (usually men) who purchase erotica want to get aroused, and they don't want to feel foolish doing it. They also don't want to interrupt their rise to orgasm with a chuckle over a joke you put in just at the wrong moment.

There are exceptions to the rule that sex and humor don't mix. Humor can work when you've written your entire story tongue-in-cheek or when your character is funny all by herself. Her approach to sex, which is refreshing and laughable, is part of her sex appeal. In some cases a happy mix of witty remarks and playful sex works. These stories can be submitted to any magazine. Here is one that works. "Confessions of a Breast Erotic" will show you how to use humor with style. Not everybody I gave this story to got off on it, but most of them had a good time reading it. And those who are into big breasts and what to do with them got a special thrill. It isn't easy to combine humor and sex on the page, so if you're having problems with it, don't even try. If it happens naturally, let it happen and see if your characters can handle it.

Confessions of a Breast Erotic
BY DARIEN LYNX

Did you ever have a hard-on in your tit? No, I guess not. Well, I have. My name is Kit and guys who know me well call me "Kit the Tit" and other guys can guess what they're talking about. I have incredibly large breasts with fantastically sensitive nipples. I can come by my tits alone, and often do.

But not that often. Because guys these days are not into tits. I wish I'd been a grown-up when Jayne Mansfield was around, I mean those were the days of the "breast-erotic." A breast erotic, I learned from my shrink, is a woman who gets off on her tits. That is, she likes to have men get off on them, she likes them squeezed and pressed and licked and sucked and she likes it done a lot. Very often. Three times a day would not be too much.

I meet lots of guys who want to fuck, but not as many who are into tits like I am. Take the last guy for example. Oi! What a prude he was, that one. His name was Alvin, and I tried my darndest to call him Al or Vinnie, but he would have none of that. He insisted on being called Alvin, and this is important to the story, because you see Alvin had a lot of ideas like that.

Anyhow, this guy Alvin said he wanted to fuck me. Well, you know he didn't say it like that, first he invited me for coffee twelve times and finally over to his house for a drink and then he said something like: "Do you think we ought to do . . . you know."

Well, I knew, so I stripped and I couldn't wait to bring out my huge bazongas. I saved it till last, taking off every piece of clothing except my bra.

So just when I get ready to take it off and let them out, Alvin, bless his weak heart, turns the bedroom light off.

"Alvin, what are you doing?" I shrieked.

"We're going to bed, aren't we?" He said as he crawled over my body to lie on "his" side of the bed.

I turned the light back on.

"Alvin, don't you want to see my tits?"

"I can see them quite well," said he. "They fall over the top of that . . . thing you wear."

Well, I opened up the front hook of my bra and let those babies fall almost onto Alvin's little face.

"Oh, my sweet lord," he said. His eyes grew big and wide, and his mouth fell open. "They are rather large, aren't they."

"Don't ya just wanna suck them and mangle them?" I asked, grinning in anticipation.

"Oh, heavens no," he answered, shaking his head back and forth vehemently. "I wouldn't dream of it."

"Why not?" My voice cracked, I was so disappointed. "Alvin, don't you like tits?"

"Well," he began, sitting up slightly in the bed, "Mother says that men who suck on . . . those things . . . do it because they didn't get enough of mother's milk when they were children. She said I would never need to do that because I was weaned late."

My nipples shrivelled in disappointment. I resorted to pleading. "Alvin, I like having my nipples sucked. I like my huge boobs twisted and mangled and squished against my body. I want your tongue all over them."

"Gosh," he said.

"At least give it a try, Alvin, please?" I was clearly begging, but if he went for it, it would all be worth it.

I took one huge tit in each hand and surrounded his face with them.

"Mmmmghf," said Alvin.

I rubbed those huge knockers around his cheeks, smothering Alvin's little head, smashing my chest into his mouth. He fell back against the headboard. I straddled his body, putting my sweet pussy up against his chest. Poor Alvin, he didn't have a sucker's chance.

When he opened his mouth to speak, I shoved one boob in there. My nipple was as big as the ones you see on baby bottles and just as hard too. Alvin sort of kissed it, he really didn't know what he was supposed to do.

"Suck it, Alvin, please, just suck it."

He did. Whooooo! I nearly fell off the bed. "Harder, Alvin, hard as you can!"

Alvin's mother was dead wrong. He was a natural-born sucker. He sucked like he really expected to get milk out of me, and for a while, he was sucking so hard I thought he might do just that!

Now let me explain a bit what this "breast erotic" business is all about. Some women are so sensitive in their nipples that they can feel everything that happens to them there in their cunt. What I mean is, there's this line of nerves that goes down from the nipples to the vagina. So when someone sucks on my nipples, it's just as if he's sucking on the inside of my cunt. And man, if you don't think that feels terrific, well, you're just mistaken.

My left tit was getting sore, so I switched over to my right. Alvin didn't mind. His head was all hot and sweaty and his body was bucking around like a new colt. His hard-on was jamming into my thighs, but I wasn't ready for that yet. I wanted to come just once this way, as only a true "breast erotic" can.

That "connection" I spoke of made every suck turn into a vaginal contraction, and my dear, sweet pussy was getting all juicy and ready to come. My tits were getting harder and harder and the nipples were growing larger and larger and turning rich, wine red. I held each one and squeezed it like I was squeezing milk into Alvin's throat and I pushed those babies into his face.

And then I came. My pussy got hotter than a bull's ass at brandin' and I whooped and hollered like I was callin' in the pigs.

Alvin was a little excited too, I must say, and his poor throbbing cock was dripping all over my legs. So he took hold of me by my ample hips and lifted me clean off the bed and back down again, straight on his cock.

Wham! He went straight to the top of my cunt. Wham! My cunt took hold of him and let him and his cock know just what we were made of. I was already climaxing so Alvin came in during mid-show and don't think his happy prick didn't appreciate it.

Alvin took both tits and put them in his mouth and tongued them and sucked them. I thought I was in breast heaven.

He started coming. It made him thrash his head from side to side (and therefore let go of my tits). Not to be left out, I jumped off of him fast as a hen to a new rooster and wrapped that lovely, wet cock up in a tit-outfit. With one breast on each side of his cock, Alvin pushed it up and down, really enjoying the feel of them, and when he peeked over the tops, I grabbed his cock head with my mouth.

He came. He spurted that beautiful white lotion all over my neck and shoulders and I managed to get one squirt aimed at my titties. WOW! That felt good!

Alvin fell back, panting and wheezing. I used his rest period to smear his cum all over my boobs. They looked so slick and shiny that way. I rubbed cum all around the huge melons and then I put a little extra on the nipples, pulling them to a point.

One of them looked so good I had to have a little suck, so I did. My pussy said thank you. It grabbed hold of Alvin's knee and began slurping. Alvin gazed through a curtain of sweat and tears and evidently found this scene a turn-on, because his member began to come to life again.

"You can suck your own . . . breast?" he asked in amazement.

"I guess I was weaned early," I answered between slurps.

Alvin asked if he could fuck me while I was doing that. I of course said yes, and it was the beginning of a long breast-erotic relationship. But I'm not always that lucky.

If you're not into tits, stay away from girls like me. But if you really get off on sucking and handling gal's knockers, watch out for "breast erotics." My shrink says there's one of us in ten. You can recognize us by the way we give you a hug. It always feels as if we're hugging you with our bodies as well. Like we'll press our tits into your chest so there's no mistaking that they're real and hungry for a suck and a cock.

And man, once you latch onto a breast erotic chick, you give those babies loving care as often as you can, and you'll be as happy as a rooster in a new chicken coop.

The Short-Short

The short-short story is usually from one paragraph to five pages, or 1,250 words maximum. "Keli's Bath" (below) is one. Typewritten, it was four pages, a little on the long side. You'll find lots of these short-shorts in adult bookstore publications, although the current trend is toward shorter, three-paragraph stories. Short-shorts also appear as story lines for special photo layout sections in major newsstand magazines.

Keli's story was written for an adult store magazine called *Bust Parade,* and the model, Keli Stewart, happens to have large breasts which she is fondling in the photos in the layout. When the model is famous, or wants to be, you will use her professional name. Otherwise, it's part of your job to make up a name for her and/or a name for your story.

This example has a full story line, with a beginning, a middle and an ending.

Keli's Bath

Keli loves the feel of her breasts when they're wet and soapy, so the bathroom is her favorite spot for sexual activity. It also means she takes baths at odd times, whenever the urge overtakes her.

One day around noon, Keli was engaged in one of her two-hour soapy explorations, completely forgetting her appointment with the man from the gas company.

Keli liked to drain the water from the tub and cover herself with soap. The slick, pasty substance resembled cum and she'd spread it to every part of her body.

She smoothed the paste around her nipples, into the crease beneath each breast, along the arch of her neck, and then ran her soapy hand down the length of her body to her pussy. There she worked her way into the folds of her vulva.

Slowly, she slid her fingers in between the flaps of her pussy lips and worked her way upward toward her clitoris. Then she smoothed the soap over the little head of her clit, pressing in gently. She reached over and turned the water on and that's why she didn't hear the gas man knock on the open front door and then walk in.

Alan, a new man on the route, walked through Keli's house calling, "Anybody home?" When there was no answer, he shrugged his shoulders and began to look for the furnace. He checked the faucets in the kitchen and walked to the bathroom.

By the time he arrived, Keli was draped across the rim of the tub, creamy with soap and leaning back on one arm. Her head was thrown back and her fingers were rapidly working her clit.

Alan's jaw fell open and he dropped his tool box.

Keli was so close to coming, all she could think of was what a prick he was for interrupting her just then.

She stopped massaging her pussy and asked him what he was doing in her house. He stuttered a bit and explained his need to check out her faucets, see if the water heater was functioning as it should.

Then he said, "I guess I came at a bad time, but I have to say, you have the most beautiful tits I ever saw. And that soap, that soap looks just like cum."

Keli smiled. She was not an easy lay, and had therefore spent the last months alone with her vibrator. But this man was so cute and sweet. She began to wonder what his cock would feel like in her cunt or between her tits.

Alan's prick was beginning to fight the restraints of his uniform. He leaned against the door jam for support.

"Are you gonna check the faucets?" she asked, smiling.

He nodded, went to the sink and turned on the water. While he waited for it to get hot, he stole another glance at Keli.

"What about the tub faucet?" she asked. "I'm not sure if the hot works."

Alan turned the sink water off and reached over Keli's ample chest to turn on the hot water.

As he passed over her, she kissed his chest, unbuttoned a few buttons and kissed lower. Soon she was unbuckling his belt and kissing lower yet.

Alan almost fell into the tub.

"You're getting soap all over your nice uniform," she said.

Keli helped him take it off. Then she wet him down with water and covered him with the same soapy mixture that covered her. She smoothed his rough, tanned skin with creamy soap and worked over his whole body, saving the best for last. She took a handful of foam and wrapped it around Alan's balls, squeezing gently as she washed. Then she drew the soap up the shaft of his cock, pulling back his foreskin to wash the tip.

Alan pushed his firm cock between Keli's tits and moaned in ecstasy. Then Keli sat on the edge of the tub and Alan fucked her cunt. The soap blended in with his cum and hers. They climbed into the tub and made love on the hard, cold porcelain. Their groans during orgasm echoed in the tile room.

When it was over, Keli turned the water back on and they lay there, letting it soothe and cover them both.

"Guess what," Keli said. "The hot works." But Alan just groaned.

Most short-shorts will be written after the photos are selected, as was this one, so you can draw from them for your inspiration. Basically, I'm describing what Keli is doing in the photo set and adding a reason for her to do it and then a story element (the other character and his entrance on the scene) to make it into a complete piece of fiction.

Other adult store magazines which use short-shorts: *Geisha Girls, Leg Parade, Chunky Asses, Sappho, Lesbian Lovers, Big Mama, Legs & Lingerie,* and more of the same. These titles change when they stop drawing. Some titles, such as *Tip Top* (from the tip of her toes to the top of her hose), for the leg lover, have sustained production for decades. *Tip Top* is currently in its twenty-fifth year in print. Print runs for adult store magazines are usually small compared to newsstand magazines. A typical run of one issue is 5,000, and even at that, the publisher expects to dispose of a thousand or two through his mail-order outlets (when they don't sell out in the adult store chains).

Writing to pictures is something you must eventually learn to do. If you get a job in an adult magazine publication house, this task will be the major portion of your job. For each "package" you will receive twenty-two magazine flats, which will come together to form a forty-four-page magazine. A flat is a huge piece of white cardboard with blue lines on it. On the flat will be two pages of a photo layout, such as pages four and five, with black-and-white photographs already pasted down. Some flats will have color transparencies in their jackets fastened onto the boards with masking tape and instructions for sizing. There will be areas on the page with no photos in them and you will have to decide how much copy will fit into these blocks, or your art director will tell you.

You'll learn how to spec type once you get into the business. Don't let it frighten you if a prospective employer asks you if you know how to do it. It's easy to learn. The only thing you have to know here is that it means you are greatly restricted in the amount of copy you will be required to write, maximum as well as minimum.

For example, if Keli's story requires one blurb 15 picas wide and 20 lines deep, and two inserts (bold type, often "pull-outs" from your blurb), each 13 picas wide and 3 lines deep, you won't be able to go off and running with your fantasy. You're bound into copy blocks.

You are also restricted by the pictures themselves. If Keli is seated in a bathtub, you're not going to be talking about her tennis lesson. Sometimes the pictures inspire you and give you an angle to write on. Other times, they obstruct your progress by giving you a character you dislike and a situation that has no potential.

For a while, at one place I worked, they were breaking in a new photographer, and all his sets looked the same. Each model was given the same dull sequence of instructions. She was told to sit in a chair, then take off her blouse and sit in the chair, then take off her shorts and sit, again in the chair. How much can you say about a girl sitting in a chair?

Then there's always the blind photo editor who gives you a whole set of twenty photographs of a beautiful girl, none of which show her face. She's looking at the back of the set or at her feet. Maybe you can write for a girl with no face, but I can't.

My solution to these situations was to complain to the head art director, who complained to the art editor and photographer. Three months later, when the next flats came through, they were better. Meanwhile, I had to build a fantasy for the model out of almost nothing.

Here is an example of another type of short-short, the one-para-graph personality story. (That's one paragraph of story and three to five bold-type inserts to place on the following pages of the set.) All you have to do is make the girl seem like a real person. You won't have time to create an erotic fantasy for her.

You'll notice the titles of adult store magazines often refer to a certain part of the female anatomy or something a female wears or does. Most adult magazines are fetish oriented. That is, *Legs & Lingerie* is about just what it says, and *Bust Parade* concentrates on just what you'd think it would.

So the photo sets, as well as your story, will cater to this fetish by using words which describe the girl's involvement with the par-ticular fetish. For example, the following is from a magazine called *Strip Tease*. The girl in this particular layout is gradually taking off her clothing and modeling lingerie and a sundress.

Here is the story:

Valene

Hi. I'm Valene and I run a boutique on the west side. We sell pretty underthings, sundresses, bathing suits and stuff like that for discriminating women. And women who like to turn their men on. I thought I'd model a few of our outfits for you on these pages and give you some ideas for your Christmas list. I think my favorite is the silk outfit on the bottom left. It makes me horny when I sleep in it and it feels really nice against my skin. But men like the one on the right, the garter-belt-and-nylon routine. I guess they'll never get over that. It doesn't really matter what a girl wears as long as it suits her. That's where a good boutique salesperson shows her talent.

There's another place where I show my talent. And that is, of course, in the bedroom. By the time I get my man in bed, he's already warmed up and ready to screw, but I always make him wait.

Men like my pussy because there's so much there to play with, big juicy lips that swell up and react to his touch. I have a big clit too, which I love to show off to the right people.

I have a king-size bed because I like to have lots of room to screw around in, room for three if that's what I want.

The first paragraph is soft. It was set in 8-point type (large, reading size) and laid on the front page of the photo set as an introduction. The second, third and fourth paragraphs were set as inserts (in dark, bold type) and placed near photographs of what the copy describes. Most single-girl adult magazines will have this type of copywriting.

When the magazine is about lesbians or swinging or threesomes, or all three, you will have more story lines available to you. The photos will be pasted down in the order of seduction and you need only follow along, telling the reader why those people are doing what they're doing.

"Stood Up" is a story I wrote for an adult magazine called *Hers & Hers*. The photo layout showed two girls taking each other's clothing off and then making love. That's not much of a start but it's better than one girl sitting on a chair. Here is the story I made up for my characters.

Stood Up

We were over at Lynette's house waiting for our boyfriends to pick us up, but they called instead. Jerry said there was a real good game on and could they come over after. He said it might go into extra innings. It was already nine o'clock, so I said, "Forget it, Jer," and I hung up.

Lynette was real mad at me at first and we argued. She said, "What are you doing, Felice? I've been waiting all week to go out with Skip. I'm so horny!"

I told her we didn't need guys who take us for granted and that she should learn to be more independent. Then I told her what my cousin and I used to do when we got horny. Lynette was shy at first, but I could tell the idea excited her because she kept giggling.

I unbuttoned her dress and slid my hand inside to caress her tit. She really dug it. Then I lifted her skirt and saw she wasn't wearing any panties, which made it easier for me to eat her. I told her to put her leg over the back of the couch so I would have lots of room to tongue her pussy.

Lynette was getting restless. She wanted to do something with her hands and mouth too. So she pulled me down onto the couch and began to lick my nipples until they got big and hard. Then she stuck her finger in my cunt and wiggled it around. Before I knew it, she was on the floor, licking where her finger had been.

I smoothed her long hair as she licked and sucked. When she began to finger herself at the same time, I got really turned on. I was dying to come.

We went into her bedroom, but then the dumb phone rang. It was Skip, apologizing for Jerry's bad attitude. He said they'd been drinking beer and got carried away with the game.

Lynette was trying her darndest to concentrate on Skip's pleas for forgiveness, but I was driving her wild with my tongue and fingers. She kept telling Skip, "That's OK, I'll call you back later," but he was full of excuses.

Finally, she set the receiver down and paid full attention to what I was doing to her, leaving Skip alone in his misery.

Lynette reached for me and said, "Come here, you lusty nympho," and was down on me before I could react to her words.

I tried to stifle my moans of ecstasy, but soon I was moaning from pleasure. I heard Skip on the receiver calling out: "What's going on over there? . . . You got a guy there,

Lynette?" But neither of us had the composure to answer, or maybe we just weren't all that interested.

Lynette came hard while I was sucking on her pussy and I came when she finger-fucked me. Even though we were exhausted from all that sex, we still felt sort of horny. So we decided to go over and seduce the guys.

Boy, were they surprised to see us. Skip thought we were stoned or something because our eyes were glazed and we hadn't bothered to put our clothes back on. We'd just thrown our coats over naked flesh.

I jumped on Jerry and nearly knocked him over, tore off his jeans, and pulled out that delicious cock. Lynette took off all of Skip's clothes and hers too. We all made love in the same room. It was a turn-on watching them and doing it too. We didn't even think about how we had gotten stood up.

You can tell what the photos show by what I've written. There was actually a telephone being used in part of the set. But the latter part of the story was not in the pictures. There are no men in lesbian books. The reader doesn't mind reading about what his girls would like to do to a man, he just doesn't want to see that man. This way, he can dream that it might be him.

You will need to understand the difference between a hardcore publication and a softcore one. In hardcore there will be insertion, by penis, dildo or finger. However, if you examine the photographs more closely, you will find other ways to tell the difference. The difference is difficult to explain because each state has its own rulings and each magazine stand has its own way of dividing the various types. The typical way of handling the problem is: If a magazine dealer has all types of magazines (which is very rare), he may put his softcore, nationwide sex publications, such as *Playgirl, Playboy, Hustler* and *Penthouse,* in one section, his letters publications, such as *Forum, Letters* and *Penthouse Variations,* in another. The harder newsstand types, such as *Genesis, Cheri, Juggs* and all the video magazines will be together, as will his gay male rags, such as *Mandate, Skin, In Touch* and *Blueboy.* Still another shelf will house the newspaper type pornography, like *Screw, Swingers Digest* and *Impulse.* Then, if he handles the very hard stuff, it will be behind some kind of barrier. There you will find the pure sex magazines I refer to as adult-store material. The $25 all-color specials, the gay male stuff that shows them coupled, and the softcore (meaning no men in this context) all-girl magazines.

With hardcore, adult-store magazines (not newsstand), that is, those that do show couples having sex, writing to photographs is simplified because not only do you have more than one character on the page, you have a complete story line.

Quite often a hardcore set is a group of photos which were taken while a video was being taped. The actors have a loose script and story line to walk through, usually a variation on the old, "came to borrow some sugar" routine. All you have to do is explain what they're doing. Since this is hardcore, however, you have to use strong language. It's not a man at the door, it's a hunk, and not only does he have a cup of sugar in his hand but he's packing a thick, ten-inch cock in his trousers. The woman who answers the door is not a housewife who was just watching television, she's a horny wench who has spent her morning jacking herself off for lack of a big prick to tickle her pussy.

Usually, men are the best hardcore writers. Sorry if that sounds sexist, but it's true, probably because hardcore tends to be more violent, more aggravated. Softcore is for the beginners because it eases into the sexual situations like stepping into a very hot bubble bath. Shy people read, write and live this way. So if you can stand the heat, ignore this warning and jump in. Otherwise, take your time and work up to it through softcore writing.

Hardcore is quick, easy writing because all you'll be creating is a one- or two-sentence description of the photos, every fourth page or so. A typical hardcore blurb will read something like this:

> Big-busted Susie Sunshine digs hard dicks, the thicker, the better. Watch her gag on Mac's 9-incher. . . . Now he shoves his cock deep inside her ass and she loves every fucking inch of it.

Another type of adult-store hardcore magazine is a cross-breed. It doesn't cost $25 and come in full color like the specials. It costs $6 to $8 and is mostly black and white. These little magazines have two to five stories in them. Other than that, the assignment is

. You write the tale that makes sense out of the photos,
n the art director has mixed up the order.

ompleted one where the art director put "come shots" at
three places throughout the story. Naturally, my heroine was quite
impressed with her man's capacity for multiple orgasms. Use mistakes to your advantage.

The Long Short Story

A full-length fiction piece will be ten to twenty pages long, typewritten. You must write the first one "on spec." You can send this story in cold, or query first. If you have published before, you can include tear sheets. To find out which magazines use fiction, browse through those at your local newsstand. Most do. They use fiction to fill in the gaps between their "hard" news. Some have larger gaps than others.

Cavalier, Eros, Genesis, Gent, Penthouse, Stag, Swank and *Cheri* all use fiction. There are plenty of others. Letters and forum-type magazines use lots of fiction, six to twelve stories per issue, in addition to their letters.

If you haven't written a story yet, choose one of these publications and aim straight for it. It wouldn't hurt to choose several which use the same format, so you'll have a list of potential buyers for when you get rejected.

If you take rejection personally, quit now and avoid the pain. Writers can't afford to be overly sensitive and editors are not going to baby you. Once your story is in the mail, forget about it and write another one. Keep doing this until you lose track of how many are out there and until the checks start coming in and then it won't hurt so bad when one editor turns you down.

If you've already published a few stories and want to query first, write to the magazine of your choice and ask for an assignment. Tell the editor what you want to write about, don't expect him to come up with a story line for you.

An average first sale may net you about $150. As you increase your reputation (and skill), you may try asking for more. But most of the mainstream men's magazines have a budget to stick to and they won't pay any more than they have to. On the other hand,

$150 isn't bad for a ten-page story. Fifteen bucks a page should be enough to make it worth your while to knock some of these out.

Send the editor your story with a cover letter, a brief cover letter (see page 197 for a full discussion of cover letters). Save his eyes for your story. Give him ten days and then call him. But be nice. There is a six percent chance he really was in Palm Springs visiting a sick aunt and didn't have time to read your masterpiece. He probably will not call you, unless you completely blow him away with your tear sheets.

Here is "A Lesbian Love Story," first published in an adult men's magazine called *Lesbian Lovers*. You'll find more examples of this format in other chapters.

A Lesbian Love Story

Deborah McGraw was my Art History teacher at City College. I'll never forget the first time I saw her standing behind the podium, lecturing on the art of the eighteenth century.

I thought then that it was her knowledge of her subject which impressed me so deeply, but now I know better. She was beautiful, sensuous and had an odd way about her that was not really masculine, but stronger somehow than a really feminine woman.

Her short, straight hair was blonde still, with a strand of gray or two around her temples. Her eyes were chocolate brown, like a Rembrandt background. Her lips were full and colored a deep red. She wore simple tailored suits with silk blouses or scarves underneath. And she was quite tall. She towered above me when I stopped her after class on some pretense.

By mid-term, I knew it was the lady behind the professorial image that I was attracted to. But I guess she knew even before then, because it was she who made the first move.

Deborah invited me over for dinner. Oh, I wasn't the only one, she wasn't that forward. She invited several of us graduate students (all women, I noticed) and some of her colleagues as well.

Her maid served a beautiful dinner of swordfish, lobster

bisque and baked broccoli. The guests stayed for cocktails and conversation and by around ten o'clock, people began to make motions about going home. When I saw that most of the students had left, I picked up my coat and began to say thank you and goodnight but she stopped me. She said, "Please wait. I'd like to talk with you."

That was all she needed to say. Her long fingers on my arm as she spoke were enough to persuade me. Anything else she might have uttered would have been superfluous.

Finally the last guest made her departure and we were alone. I was suddenly scared, or at least I felt awkward. What would happen now?

Deborah sat down next to me on the couch and for the first time that evening I noticed she wasn't wearing a bra. For an older woman, she had magnificent breasts. They weren't large, but they sort of came to two little points. I was curious about the shape of her nipples.

As I suddenly realized that I was staring at her breasts while she was talking to my face, I flushed. Then I looked at her. She had stopped talking and now she smiled at me.

"You are a very beautiful girl, Laurie," she said.

I blushed again. "No, no, you're the one who is beautiful."

She laughed. "Tell me, what did you think of our guests?"

I wondered why she asked that. "Well, Susan and Margaret I know from class, Professor Raye seems nice. I've never had Dr. Eagan for anything."

"Did you notice anything . . . odd . . . about Dr. Eagan?" she asked.

"No, why do you ask?"

"How about Margaret? How well do you know her?"

"If you mean do I know she's gay, the answer is yes. She came onto me once." I was beginning to feel uncomfortable.

"I take it you didn't like that," said my teacher.

"I . . . I guess I didn't like her approach, but then I'm not gay, so what do I know?" Instantly, I felt like a dolt. Why was I saying such stupid things?

"You know what you like, I am sure. That shows in your painting." Deborah refilled my wine glass.

I was thrilled that she had noticed my work. Art History teachers didn't usually wander over into the studio art classes.

As I watched her walk to the kitchen for more wine, I noticed her gait. She had such a graceful walk, like a princess. Her long hostess skirt blew softly round the outline of her legs with each forward step. And her silk blouse clung to those pointed nipples.

Unconsciously I rubbed my hand on my crotch. Fortunately, she didn't see that. I pulled my hand away immediately. What was I doing? I had a boyfriend. Why was I getting all turned on by a woman?!

She came back into the room and when she sat down beside me this time, I noticed she sat a little closer. Then she threw her head back over the soft red cushions of her couch and allowed her blonde locks to caress the fabric. She looked beautiful with her neck stretched like that.

I followed the line of her neck down to her cleavage and noticed that one flap of her blouse had come open just slightly. I could see the thin line underneath her small breast.

As I looked at that line, my own breasts began to tingle. I felt my nipples harden. If I'd been stoned, I could have blamed all this on dope or booze, but I was all there and still feeling tremendously attracted to a female!

Then she caught me looking. She sat up and faced me, with a dreamy look in her eyes. I wanted to kiss her soft cheek, caress her lovely hair in my fingers.

She was smiling at me. I looked to my lap suddenly.

"I . . . I'm sorry, Dr. McGraw, but I . . ." I didn't know what to say. How would I apologize for something she didn't even know about? But she must have known, I was sure it showed in my face.

I looked at her again and found her still smiling, waiting for me to continue.

"I've never felt this way before," I said. "I feel sort of like the first time I was with a boy and I knew he was going to kiss me."

"What does that tell you?" she asked. She was so cool.

I took a deep breath and leaned back on the couch. I had no

idea what was going to happen to me, but I felt safe with her and I felt ready to allow things to flow between us.

Deborah reached into my blouse and very delicately cupped my breast. My hard nipple grew even more erect at her touch. My clit was throbbing between my legs and my pussy lips were wet already. My whole body had anticipated her touch and now it was ready for anything.

"Laurie," she whispered. "Would you like to come to bed with me?"

When I hesitated, she added: "You won't have to do anything you don't want to do."

So we went into the bedroom. It was beautifully decorated in mahogany and various types of wood. There were real prints on the walls, Zuniga, Picasso and one Degas.

She took me to the bed and slowly undressed me, beginning with my blouse. As she slipped the silk off my shoulders, she ran her long fingers over each bone and muscle, harder than a tickle but softer than a squeeze. She followed the line of my collar bone to the center of my throat, then traced a line down between my breasts. She bent forward slightly and opened her mouth to my nipple, not sucking it, but just barely holding it in her wet mouth.

When she released the nipple, it stood hard and stiff. She did the same thing to the other one. My legs wanted to melt.

She unbuckled my skirt and let it drop. Then she pulled down my pantyhose. I had left my shoes in the living room, so now all that was left were my panties. Deborah left them on.

She slipped out of her shoes and in her bare feet, she was just my height. With a swish, her skirt fell to the floor and revealed long, tanned, shapely legs.

Now she took her blouse off and when I saw her beautiful, tight tits with the huge, brown areolas, I nearly fainted. I wanted to touch them so badly, and I knew it would be all right to do it but I just couldn't.

She stepped closer to me, so close that her breasts were even with mine and just barely touching. I couldn't stand it. I pressed my chest into hers and our breasts squished against each other's.

What a turn-on that was! I still get a rush when I remember it.

We stood like that for a few minutes I think, just holding each other, trembling, sighing. I wanted to rock myself in her arms.

Finally she pulled back again and ran both of her hands over my hips and buttocks, without going inside my panties. Then she moved one hand around to the front and ran her finger between my pussy lips, still through the fabric.

"Oh, Laurie, you're so wet for me," she whispered.

I could barely stand by now, and my pussy was reaching for her finger. She was touching me so lightly, so delicately, it was almost frustrating. I wanted her. I wanted Deborah McGraw even though she wasn't a man, in fact, especially because she was a woman. I wanted this woman lying naked beside me. I wanted to suck her gorgeous brown tits and take her finger into my cunt.

Deborah moved me gently to the bed and laid me down. My knees were bent over the side of the bed and she was kneeling between my legs. I knew what was coming next. My boyfriend had done this routine many times.

But Deborah was so different in her approach, it was like a brand-new experience. As she parted my legs, she stroked the insides of my thighs. Her light touch raised goosebumps on my skin and sent tingles running up and down my spine. I still had my white silk panties on and she played lightly over them without going beneath.

Then she began to kiss my thighs, licking now and then. Light, gentle kisses, unlike any man I'd ever known. No stubble of a beard on this face, she was smooth as satin, soft as cotton.

She swept her large luscious lips up and down my legs with no hint of going further. Then just as I was letting myself relax and enjoy this sensual experience, she moved her lips over the line of my panties.

She kissed my crotch through the silk, blowing hot air through the weave of the fabric. My clit rose to attention.

She put her tongue out and pushed the panties into the

crevice between my legs. My pussy muscles reached out for her and tried to grab her tongue, but there was too much in the way. If this experience hadn't been so erotic, it would have been frustrating.

Now she licked the place where my legs joined my torso, the crease that was now marked by the elastic edge of my underpants. Her tongue was as strong as a finger and she pushed the fabric aside with it.

By now I was pushing my pussy up toward her in involuntary thrusts. Finally her tongue found its way into my pussy hole and I cried out in ecstasy.

Quickly she slipped my panties off and buried her head between my legs. She was all over the place at once.

She licked my clit, then my pussy lips, dug her tongue into my cunt for a minute and then was back on my clit. She ran her tongue between my clit and foreskin until I was buzzing down there, or felt like it.

Now her fingers were working too and she was jamming them up me, slipping easily through with my cum wetting the way. She looked up to me, but I could hardly control myself. I knew I looked pretty silly, getting all worked up about another woman. I knew my face was red with excitement and my tits were swollen and hard and my clit was a dead giveaway as well. But I just couldn't help it. And now, I knew it was too late to turn back, because I was beginning to orgasm.

It began at the center of my vagina, way up inside. It felt like a hot fire ball, increasing in dimensions until it filled my cunt with fire and flood. Then my clit burst into flames and grew inside Deborah's mouth so that it felt as large as a tomato and twice as red. Three fingers of her hand were being sucked on by my firm pussy muscles which tried to draw her in deeper and deeper.

I was writhing around on the bed like a cat in heat. My body was wet and flushed and all of my muscles were tense. My pussy began a series of spasms, clamping so tightly on Deborah's fingers that my whole body jerked up with each jolt.

I was moaning so much, I sounded as if I were crying. And Deborah was talking to me, urging me on.

"Come to me, come. Laurie, give it to me," she would say, over and over again.

It was the longest climax I had ever had in my life. I felt like a dishrag afterward, drenched but drained. And I was so thirsty.

Deborah anticipated me and brought in a cool glass of ice water. I drank the whole thing and smiled up at her. It was then I noticed her breasts again. I had been so wrapped up in what she was doing for me, that I had totally forgotten about her. Now I knew how a man felt when a lady gave him head. It seems you go out of this world someplace.

My body was exhausted, at least most of my body. But my clit was still hard and my pussy was making sucking motions and noises like it was anxious for more action.

I reached up for one of those lovely tits and Deborah slid down beside me on the bed. I could almost take the whole tit in my mouth. It was a wonderful sensation. No wonder men go wild over sucking boobs.

Every part of Deborah's body was appealing to me. The curve of her neck, which I had grown to appreciate earlier, became the target of my first homosexual kiss. Behind her ear, I found another little crevice for my lips and tongue. She smelled so good! Her hair was like wild flowers, her neck was sweetened by some exotic perfume. Her underarms smelled like baby powder and her pussy, oh what a sweet smelling pussy she had.

Her crotch hairs were blonde, not like mine, and they weren't coarse and wiry, they were soft, like a baby's hair. Her pussy lips were pink on the outside and got redder as they folded inside of her cunt. Her clit wasn't a small pearl like mine, it was long and red.

It was also extremely sensitive, so I had to be ever so gentle with it. I couldn't suck hard like I liked mine sucked, I had to just hold it in my mouth like a very tiny penis.

Deborah came almost immediately and then came again right after. Everything I did seemed to get her going. It was so easy. Not like my boyfriend, who can't come unless I suck him for a half an hour, until my jaw is aching and I've passed excitement and gone into weariness.

She was so easy to please that it was all I wanted to do, just please her, all night long.

And that's what we did.

In the morning, Deborah actually apologized to me. She said she was sorry she was such a maniac, but that she hadn't had sex in a very long time. Being a lesbian in a small college town can be a very lonely life.

I told her she would never have to worry about that again. And so far, three semesters later, that's still true. My boyfriend hasn't figured out why I need so much tutoring for a subject he considers a whiz, but I don't care if he does find out. Deborah is a much better lover than he is. She comes so easily, she makes me feel like some kind of terrific stud. And she eats me so well. Sometimes we fall asleep in that position, her head between my legs, her hot mouth on my pussy. And I have the neatest dreams.

I haven't bothered to think about whether I'm gay or not. I don't really care. What's important is that when two people love each other and love making love to one another, then they should be together. Age, sex, color, no boundary is big enough to keep true lovers apart.

The Erotic Novel

There are erotic novels masquerading as mainstream fiction in your local bookstore and on newsstands. These are heavy on story line, have sporadic love scenes and come to the market via legitimate publishers. It is as difficult to get one published as it is to get a regular novel published. You must sell your idea to a publisher, usually by writing the entire novel first (200 to 500 pages).

There's another type of "erotic" novel (and I use the word loosely here) which is published by adult-material houses. It is also found on the newsstand but the material is more explicit and this fact will be indicated in some way on the cover. Inside, the story will be light on plot and heavy on sex scenes. There won't be three pages together without some talk about the sex that is about to happen, has already happened or is happening. This stuff is hard-core. The original manuscript, typewritten, is 160 pages and the subject matter most often falls into one of four categories:

The Young Innocent Female.   She is just out of college or high school. She goes to the big city to make good and meets a horny boss, or similar rake, who takes advantage of her. She proceeds to enjoy it and later becomes the one who needs it.

The Captive Woman.   Here is another innocent victim who somehow is kidnapped into white slavery or some other weird situation and taken advantage of by an evil master, male or female, who makes her do things to earn her food.

The Horny Housewife.   Her husband is in prison or the service and she's got a hard-on. She goes after everything in pants and at least one thing in a skirt until her husband comes home and makes her pay (often with a lesbian show staged for his enjoyment).

Incest.   Father/daughter incest, the most common kind, is a rather sorry subject and one I'm sure most of us could live without. Sometimes it involves a mother and son from the son's point of view. A spin-off of this topic is the family-fest, where mom, dad, sis and brother are all in on the act, with maybe even a few uncles thrown in. Weird stuff.

There are some very old lines still floating around which have animals and/or children in them. As far as I've been able to find out, no one is writing these anymore and few publishers are producing them. They are reprints from an earlier, pre-enlightened age: the stone-age of sexuality.

Something you should know about all of these books (probably you'll be relieved to know) is that there is no market for them right now. Publishers have realized that all these stories sound the same. They are mostly recovering old editions, changing the titles and authors' names, and sometimes the character's names. When they are buying, they pay between $400 and $600 each, which at 160 pages comes out to $3 a page or so. That's more than Anaïs Nin got, but a whole novel is a lot of work! And you're not exactly turning out a classic in literature.

The Erotic Romance Novel

If it's been a long time since you've perused a romance novel, you might want to take another look. They've changed! I remember as recently as five years ago reading a book from a popular line that was not only filled with typos and misspellings, but told a ludicrous, completely unbelievable story with a ridiculous gothic-type heroine and a stereotyped macho hero. I forced myself through it (never ignore a potential money market), but only once.

There is a whole slew of new romantic lines, each one vying for that quarter-billion-dollar market of voracious fans. And they're all doing well. For years, romance novels have sold when all other fiction was struggling. Romantic fiction consistently takes a fifty percent share of the paperback market.

In 1980, a few daring publishers stretched their horizons to check the torrid waters of passion press. Where yesterday's heroines were chaste virgins of twenty and heroes seldom accomplished more than a goodnight kiss at the climax, readers were hungry for steamier stories, the hotter, the better.

You may have heard the theory that romance novels are the female version of pornography. Its premise is that since men are into visual stimulation, they want pictures of sexy girls in erotic poses, whereas women, being more introverted and sentimental by nature, are into words. Women prefer to use their imaginations to form their own erotic visuals. So men buy photo-filled sex magazines and women read romance novels and everyone gets what they need. Or do they?

The husband comes home from a long day at the office, after jacking off in the john at lunch break over the latest *Playboy* centerfold (ask him if you don't believe me), and the wife finishes up her latest edition of *Silhouette Intimate Moments* just in time to make dinner. He's looking at her, wondering if her panties look anything like the ones he saw in the *Playboy* ads. She's looking at him, wondering if he still loves her and if he does, will he tell her so after the kids go off to bed. Could it be that our reading habits are widening our already monstrous gender gap?

Well, ours is not to reason why, right? The only thing we care about is that there is a market here for erotica and we're going to jump into it head first.

Here's an example of what happened when one publisher broke down the bedroom door. Silhouette, a division of Simon & Schuster, got there first with the most and has kept their lead. In their first year, 21 million Silhouette Romances were sold. They were so impressed with their own success, they went into deeper waters with their *Special Edition* in 1982, featuring a greater degree of sensuality than ever before.

Not satisfied yet, three months later they introduced *Silhouette Desire,* their hottest baby. But wait, we're still not finished with this daring firm. After doing extensive reader research and finding no enemies among the masses, *Silhouette Intimate Moments* arrived. With its longer format and increased adventure angle, the love scenes took an even greater portion of the story.

Simon & Schuster doesn't have a monopoly here by any means. Other publishers have developed new romance lines or resuscitated old ones: Dell Publishing has *Candlelight Ecstasy* and *Candlelight Ecstasy Supreme,* the Berkley Publishing Group has *Second Chance at Love* and Bantam has *Loveswept. Superromance,* from Worldwide Library, is a lengthier version of the little passion pulp, and even the old standard Harlequin Romances are in on this trend with their *Temptation* and *Superromance* lines. Historical romance lines were always pretty hot.

What this all means to you, dear writer, is a brand-new market, easily accessible because the readers have voracious appetites for new approaches to the same old tired love story. I'll give you an example of what's been overdone already so you won't waste your time, but first let's look at the characters in these little love stories.

One of the most important changes romances have undergone is probably a direct result of the baby-boom kids growing into middle age. The publishing houses are trying to reach today's woman with contemporary settings and heroines. The heroine in today's romances is not a nineteen-year-old virgin. She is older, wiser, more experienced and she has a good job. She's twenty-eight to forty, believe it or not, and she cares about something other than getting married. Although, when she meets the hero, this idea comes promptly to mind. He is, of course, the one she's been waiting for and who is much more suitable for her than the one she left behind. (This woman has a past!)

The hero is not so much of a pure cad anymore, and though he's still devilishly magnetic, he doesn't have to be perfect. In fact the publishing houses like a flaw or two, both in his physical make-up and in his personality. All flaws are done away with, however, when the end comes near. He is gentle, always a perfect lover and an expert in his career field, very successful on all levels. And of course, he's madly in love with the heroine from the word go.

Regency romances, gothics and historicals involve extensive research and a knowledge of the period. They are more complex than the smaller contemporary romance novels referred to as category lines. Category novels will be a much easier conquest for the new writer and many of them have erotic scenes. Category romances are written with a formula. I took about a dozen of them, folded the corners down on hot pages and found they occurred at a similar frequency and were of similar duration in the various novels of each line. Each line is different, however, so you'll have to do some homework before you set to work. A short-cut would be to write the publisher with your SASE and ask for a "tip" sheet.

This is what Berkley Publishing said *not* to do in your *Second Chance* novel:

> The heroine is too often a journalist, photo-journalist, actress, artist, writer, archeologist, travel agent, or is connected with a resort hotel.

This tip lets out all the stories I had in mind. The person who said, "Write what you know," obviously didn't have to make a living as a writer.

In regard to sex, Berkley states that it's OK for the hero and heroine to make love before they get married, and that you can describe each scene sensuously, but don't you dare use any of those words. Make it poetic and exciting. They also ask for a steady build-up in sexual tension throughout the book.

Publishers' tip sheets are often so meticulously detailed that they almost write the story for you. If you can write a story at all, you should be able to make a play for this market. If you are still queasy about the hardcore erotica business, you might want to gingerly ease yourself in with one of these.

There are two excellent books that I know of which will give you the details. They are *How to Write a Romance and Get It Published,* by Kathryn Falk, and *Writing Romance Fiction for Love and Money* by Helene Barnhart. Each how-to book has a chapter devoted solely to sensuality and how to achieve it on the page, where you'll find the opposite advice from what I've given you for erotica. The reason is your readership.

When someone buys a sex magazine, they buy it for the sex, not for the story. As you've seen when you've read my examples, stories written for adult magazines are usually very light on plot and heavy on love-making. Well, in a romance novel, the romance comes first, then the characters, then the story, then the sex. Different priorities, you see.

I took three books from the same line and folded down the sex pages. The first kiss or intimate brush of the fingers occurred in the first chapter or close to it. Thirty pages later comes the passionate make-out scene, then two or three love scenes later, the lovers got five pages to play it to the finish without interruption.

Another problem you may run into is vocabulary. You're going to need a whole new list of sensual adjectives for romance books because these scenes call for some clever avoidance of clinical terminology. Each house has a different degree of evasiveness, and the writers within those lines also differ in their approach. Some are so vague it's hard to tell whether the writer is talking about the ocean or the heroine when she says waves were cresting.

However, these scenes do have something in common with the erotica we've been learning about. There is the same constant build-up of sexual tension. The heroine is always thinking about her hero in a sexual way, even when she's trying not to. Unlike the nymphets in sex books, this woman is not always ready to get laid. She requires seduction, even if she's sex-starved, which is often the case. Because romance heroines are still "good girls," they don't have sex in between true loves, like normal people do. They wait until they fall in love with the next Mr. Right.

Passion takes a different course, and because we have two hundred pages instead of twenty to follow it, our heroine takes her sweet time with each tender moment. (By the way, I should warn

you these characters never have "normal" names like Susan or Joe.
They are instead Lanceford, Layne, Lucas, Lindsay, Jordan, Elton,
Ravenna, Hadley, Brenton, and so on.) I've written an example
based on the mood of the stories I've read. This is how one of the
early scenes might go:

> Morgana glanced out the window to see what Jordan was
> doing to her gazebo. He had taken that moment to wipe his
> brow with his tanned forearm and she couldn't help but no-
> tice the beads of sweat glistening on the back of his thick
> neck. His shirt sleeves were rolled up tightly, binding his
> shoulders and exposing the brown bulges of his biceps. Try as
> she might, she could not return to her chores. She was hypno-
> tized. Yet the longer she watched him, the harder she found it
> to breathe. She had twisted the dishcloth in her hands until
> her fingers burned. When she looked down to see what she
> had done, she saw her nipples had hardened, making peaks of
> cotton in her crisp apron.

Hey, hot stuff, right? It may seem tame after what we've been
through, but to the romance crowd, wet dreams are made of anticipation, foreplay, lust and finally, full-on passion. They want sex,
all of it, all the way, but they want it slow and sensual. They want
a hundred and eighty pages of foreplay and a five-page payoff at
the climax.

The name of this game is: How to talk about sex without mentioning it. In a way, it's a little like the videotape blurbs you'll read
about in Chapter 2. You're disguising your meaning with euphemisms. The difference is you've got a sophisticated reader here.
She's an enthusiastic reader, she's educated, she's smart, and she
knows what she wants. You won't be able to fake it with a bunch
of ordinary words; she's after the big, plush ones. The seasoned
romance writer uses terms such as *luminous with desire, tumes-
cent swelling, mind-drugging kisses, languorous strokes, frenzy of
need, hardness of passion* and the ever-faithful *stirring in her loins
she couldn't identify.* You get the idea.

Along that same line, the description can get fairly graphic
above the waist. It's all right for men and women to have nipples
and the woman is allowed to have breasts, but never tits or boobs,

please! When you get down yonder, however, you're in unfriendly territory. These women have no private parts at all. They're sort of like Barbie dolls. They have V's, mounds, triangles, areas between their legs, fiery centers and depths of passion, but no pussies or clits. The men are equally endowed with euphemisms and lacking in sex parts. They have hidden fires, manhood, a bulge, a surge of passion or a hardness of flesh, but no cock and balls. If you thought coming up with twenty-five words for breast was hard, you're in for a real problem here.

In the romance novel the attitudes of the two lovers are all mixed in with their foreplay. This area is another point where romance differs from pure erotica. Whereas, in a straight sex story, all the lovers are thinking about is what they're doing, in a romance, they've got all sorts of other things on their minds. Often the underlying turmoil is enough to interrupt the love-making altogether.

Take for example this next scene with Jordan and Morgana, which I have also created just for you. Imagine that earlier on, certain story elements were established. Jordan is in love with Morgana, but thinks she may be using him to get her proposal through his firm. He's suspicious of her motives and yet overwhelmingly drawn to her poetic magnetism and lavender eyes. Morgana cares deeply about her proposal—it was all she had before she met this cool customer—but now she's in love and confused. She wants the proposal to be considered separately from their personal relationship, but her lovesickness keeps getting in the way. She hates Jordan for putting this business between them, and yet. . . .

In a romance, each person has to respect the other or the deal's off. So somehow, before Jordan gets Morgana in his clutches, he's got to believe she's good at the core and the same thing goes for her. You may not be able to get all that into one scene, but with a bit here, a bit there, eventually you'll get the effect you're after. Let's try writing an arousing, erotic scene with no naughty words and with an undercurrent of dramatic plot line.

Morgana eyed him cautiously as he toyed with the paperweight on his desk. He was not looking at her. He was looking downward as he sat in his huge leather chair, so smug, so aware of her attraction to him and so defiant in his stance against her proposal. He swiveled his chair around and faced the picture window behind his desk. "Well?" he asked, as if it had been he who had asked the question.

"You can't expect me to do that, Jordan," Morgana replied, knowing she would lose in the end. She could smell his rich, musky odor clear across the desk. It mingled with her own anxiety to make the air between them thick with promise, yet rampant with threats.

With a deep sigh, Jordan rose laboriously and hooked his thumbs in his back pockets, still looking out that damned window. What did he see out there? she wondered. It was dark except for the city lights. Perhaps his answers were out there.

"I'm not letting you leave until you give me your answer, Morgana." His words pierced the heavy silence like darts and they found their way through her armor, cutting her resolve like so many flaws in the proposal she had so carefully created and bravely guarded. She must not let him win this time.

"Jordan, you can't ask me to drop it now, not after all the work. . . ." Suddenly he turned and his steel gray eyes burrowed into the core of her being. Whatever she had planned to say next was lost forever and she was falling, falling into the abyss of his powerful presence. Morgana felt tears well in her eyes and realized she was losing ground. In a last act of defiance she rose to her feet, placed her hands on Jordan's desk, and began her final plea. "Jordan. This has nothing to do with us. It's for the good of the firm. How can you—"

Jordan stopped her speech by rising from his chair. As casually as if they had been in her bedroom, he came around from behind his desk and roughly grabbed hold of her face. He held it tenderly in his palms as he searched her face for clues to her deception. He brought her mouth close to his, but he did not kiss her.

"Don't you think it's about time you quit pretending," he said, in that too cool voice she'd learned to hate. She made a move to pull away at that point, but he had her in his grip. His hands held her physically, his manly aroma was playing havoc with her senses, and his masculine arrogance held her emotions in a state of upheaval.

How dare he accuse me of lying, she thought, yet as angry as she felt, her heart wasn't in it. She was drowning in the pool of his eyes and wondering if he would kiss her now after all this.

His grip loosened and Jordan brought Morgana's face closer yet to his own. He teased her by not continuing, by taunting her with his eyes as they darted back and forth from her hair to her lips to her eyes. She could smell his breath, a slightly minty scent like fresh herbs from his garden. She could smell his body, rich and aromatic from his long day's work in the oil fields. But what bothered Morgana the most was the feel of him. To have that muscular body ever so close to her own, waiting for her to make the move that would seal their fate once and for all, was agony.

Morgana could stand it no longer. She pushed her face out of Jordan's hands and up into his. She kissed him hard and wildly, passionate to the point of pain. Her mouth was pressed against his teeth, but she did not stop. She would not stop. Jordan put his arms around her and held her tightly against his body. His chest muscles pressed against her breasts, smashing them, giving them the sensual treat he'd been teasing her with since the affair between them had started.

Then, as suddenly as it had begun, it was over. Jordan pushed her back and held her at arms' length. Morgana's legs were weak and they nearly buckled under her as she held her breath in anticipation of what he would say to her next.

"I don't know whether to believe you or not, Morgana. You're an enigma to me."

Hey, this is fun! I think I've found a new career, folks. You can have all my video blurbs and sex articles and I'll try my hand at romance novels. Although these scenes are definitely erotic, we're sliding back from the hardcore adjectives and the cum shots into the world of the never-never, where hardness meets triangle and where people fall in love before they fall into bed.

By the way, I forgot to mention a few little things. The hero almost always has gray eyes and has breath that smells of mint. I don't know why; it's a convention. The heroine's clothing is always described in detail, and she often has a self-esteem problem. She thinks she's not that attractive, she trips and stammers a good deal and she's always surprised when a man finds her sexy and worth pursuing. It probably makes her easier to identify with for the reader and also, it gives her something to work out before the end of the story. She often achieves self-confidence by her acknowledgment and acceptance of Mr. Right's love. I guess if somebody attractive loves you, that means you are also attractive. The conflicts are never major ones and there are no alcoholics, drug addicts, deaths or child abuses involving the major characters in these books. Even the problems they do have, have an upbeat tone to them. If you can manage all that, this may be your next stop.

Your narrative is often subjective. You will almost always be telling the story from the heroine's point of view—nothing can happen unless she's there to witness it—but more than that, you may choose to insert her impression of the scene, as I did with ". . . looking out that damned window."

Whether you want to write gothic, teen, regency, historical, category or Christian romance novels, you'll have to familiarize yourself with the various publishing houses and their lines. Any bookstore manager will steer you to the right shelf with no problem. Skip the library, though; they don't carry the steamier models. Those books on how to write a romance will give you some short cuts too and don't forget to send for the tip sheets.

One more handy hint. Many of the articles I read during my research contained suggestions about how to get in the mood to write a sex scene. Wearing a sexy nightgown was a popular idea, as was using scented candles, moving your typewriter to the table in front of the fireplace and perhaps pouring a glass of expensive champagne and slowly sipping it. Well, who am I to judge. Whatever works, right? But for heaven's sakes, don't quote me when your twelve-year-old wants to know what you're doing in your nightgown at three in the afternoon, or your husband gets ideas about the delivery boy. Or, for that matter, when the delivery boy gets ideas!

Good luck with your career as a romance writer. A combination romance/erotica artist ought to make for some interesting stories in both areas. Your erotica will become more loving and your romances more sensuous.

Poetry

What about poetry? I've had erotic poetry published, but only when I had a contract to do the whole magazine; in other words, when I was the editor-in-chief. I could hardly reject myself, now could I? Rarely will you see erotic poetry in a sex magazine. An exception is a relatively new publication, *Yellow Silk*. Lily Pond, the publisher, wishes she didn't get quite so much and would like to see some good, solid erotic fiction submissions. However, since she offers about the only poetry market in this business, she'll probably get it all. You may find erotic poetry in a literary journal or in a novel. I love D. M. Thomas' book, *The White Hotel*, which has some beautiful erotic poetry in it. It's filled with the kinds of images you could use in your work. If I could write like that, I would include a sample of erotic poetry in this book. But alas, I cannot.

So you're on your own. Use plenty of sensual adjectives and image-provoking descriptions and pay attention to your reader. If you're writing to your lover, speak through your poems.

Most of the poetry pamphlets floating around are not very enthusiastic about erotica just now, probably because they are inundated with the wrong kind. Editors are bored with the popular self-centered, woe-is-me type and say it's not universal enough. Not every piece about sex is sexy. But then, you know that or you wouldn't be reading this book.

If you're bound and determined to fight the tide against erotic poetry, there is a book on how to write it called *Pearls of Love*, available from The Electric Press, 3455 E. Lemona Avenue, Fresno, CA 93703. The author has included love letters with blanks so you may insert your lover's name and avoid the hassle of writing the letters all by yourself.

Fiction is not the only type of writing you will be able to sell to adult and newsstand men's magazines. In the next chapter, you'll learn about other print possibilities.

CHAPTER 2

THE MARKETPLACE FOR EROTIC NONFICTION

Articles

Articles in porno magazines are not always true. Sorry if I'm shattering your illusions. If you want to write serious nonfiction articles about sex and are willing to do all the research, get releases from everyone you interview, and provide photographs, more power to you. You are probably above this stuff and should go legit. However, if you want to write an article that is fictional and you have not gone through all those authenticated, documented channels, in most cases, this is OK too. Most editors do not expect an article entitled, "Six Girls Tell Why They Fuck Strangers" to be factual.

Most magazines which use fiction also take articles. *Forum, High Society, Firsthand, Pillow Talk* and all the video magazines will buy articles, if they're relevant to the focus of the magazine. Do your homework and make sure you understand the magazine before you waste time and postage.

Your articles will often contain or be composed entirely of case histories. These bring your point to life for the reader. Case histories are really fun to write because you can use your friends' input and even your own experiences, altering them along the way to make them more fun and/or fantastic.

These case histories, by the way, do not have to be as chock full of buzz words as so-called fictional erotica. Articles are expected to be more serious and conservative, at least in terms of the writer's voice. As for your subjects, they can talk as rank as they please.

Here is an example of the format: After a brief introduction to the situation (using the title I just mentioned), we introduce our characters. Remember, your intro will sound as if you are dead serious in your approach, intent on getting the truth out of these little rascals, and your interviewees will talk in dialogue, each one with a slightly different speech pattern, but all of them lusty and bursting with sexy images.

Linda B., a twenty-four-year-old waitress, says that she gets her best lays from strangers. On-going affairs bore her. "It's just that guys who've never had you get more turned-on," says the pretty brunette. "I mean, like they will do anything to get into your pants. I dig it when a new guy eats my pussy. He'll stay down there much longer than somebody who knows he's gonna get screwed no matter if he does it good or not. And it's always an adventure to see a new cock for the first time!"

Here is an example of an article published in *Lipstick* magazine. It is relatively straight and a variation of this theme could just as easily have appeared in a mainstream magazine, except that the writer, Leeanne Hayes, hadn't been accepted in those circles yet and got tired of not selling her work.

How to Get Laid
BY LEEANNE HAYES

It's worse than Russian roulette. How can you guys even predict scoring? The ones that look like they will, won't. The ones that look like they won't, will. The ones you wish you'd never met, offer to blow you when you haven't even asked. The aggressive ones scare the hell out of you by backing you into closets at parties and groping you while the guests look on in amusement.

Cocktail waitresses can give you a million ideas on what

doesn't work, bartenders can give you a million ideas on what does.

What's a man to do? It doesn't appear in Amy Vanderbilt and even if it did, her advice probably wouldn't work either. The athletic club is no counseling center; you might as well go to Planned Parenthood. Christ, fellow jocks who probably haven't had a piece in months, expounding on secret trysts that never occurred. No guy is going to tell you HE ever failed. All you men get is unrealistic hype—hints that don't make it. Hence, My Personal Guide For How to Get Laid.

Tip 1. Know What Makes Them Weak. They all have a soft spot, somewhere, hidden behind that iron feminist demeanor. Women are always on the defensive so you won't reject them first. They feel you will no longer be interested if they act like they like you. Doesn't everyone always want what they can't have? They were taught to play "hard to get" from the time they were tots and cultivated the habit from watching you pursue girls who were indifferent to you. All women have a sentimental streak. But what works for one will not necessarily work for another.

Tip 2. Act Nonchalant. This will cause them to think you date regularly and have sampled many different women, which will cause them to try harder to please you. Everyone wants to be respected. No one wants to be exploited. You can always exploit them later.

Tip 3. Never Act Desperate. Don't appear at the door with a giant hard-on, get down on your knees claiming you only have one month to live or that you have prostate trouble and if you don't have intercourse, the urologist said your life will be in danger. Women are wise to this. They have heard every imaginable excuse. If you're going to bullshit them, you'd better be extremely creative.

Tip 4. Don't Try Anything (at First). An excellent way to work your way into her pants is to go out with her a couple of times and don't try anything at all, even a goodnight kiss on the cheek. Every woman expects to be approached. They are hopeful and eager for it, even if they are going to reject you. Not trying is a sure winner. It drives them crazy. They'll call their girlfriends and their analysts and marvel in utter disbelief, "He didn't even try."

How humiliating to have a man like you for your mind in this day of raw sexuality, where Gay Talese and Hugh Hefner are the most admired people of junior high school students. Women want to be desirable as well as intellectually stimulating. They want to be coveted like a *Playboy* centerfold but you lay a hand on them before they're ready and VA VA VOOM!!! They want to be lusted after, even if they hate you. Rejection bothers everyone, no matter what people say.

Tip 5. Be Natural. I know it's hard to be natural in California but try. Don't drive up in a rented Bill Blass Continental, complete with a Pierre Cardin shirt and tie, Gucci shoes, Bijan scarf. Be unique but be yourself. Boring is better than bullshit.

It seems that nowadays everything has a signature: jeans, purses, even condoms. Don't go overboard on appearance. Don't arrange items on the back seat of your car so you appear interesting, i.e. professional journals, intellectual books, athletic equipment, expensive cologne, etc. It looks like you hired a personality decorator. If Woody Allen tried to be George Hamilton, it would never work.

Tip 6. Chemistry. A lot can be said about chemistry. You know the feeling. Once in a while chemistry will occur (she could even be ugly, but she sews her own clothes and has a quick wit). It doesn't matter where you take her, what you say, how you dress or dance, you shall overcome. Women know after five minutes if they are going to sleep with you, either that night or in the future.

Predicting what a woman will do or how she will react is like trying to predict the weather, but it doesn't hurt to be ready, just in case (you know, clean sheets, maybe a bottle of champagne). Sometimes, during the course of an evening, they change their minds. I have known so many women who said, "I'd never sleep with him in a million years!" But as the evening wears on, they begin to weaken. Your charm and attractiveness come through and they decide to have sex with you after all. These sudden decisions can occur at any time (during the first course of a meal, at intermission, riding in the car).

Tip 7. The Kamikaze Approach. Don't come on like a vocal, financial and intellectual hurricane. You know what I mean: In the first five minutes you boast how you became a millionaire, traveled the world, own houses in every country, got bored with jets, are sick of yachts, country clubs, polo, hotels and Club Med. A woman can tell if a man has money; it shows even if he never speaks.

Don't ask them before the first cocktail if they'd like to go to San Francisco for the weekend. Firstly, if they say yes, you have nothing to work for. How impressionable she must be; this girl is definitely looking for a Sugar Daddy or a fast whirlwind weekend. You don't want freeloaders. Secondly, if she says yes in the first five minutes, how is she to know you're not Richard Speck? Too impulsive.

Sex and lust should occur because of overwhelming tenderness, that crazy feeling that possesses you, not because, "I bought you dinner so you owe it to me" or "Well, we're both here, what the hell."

Tip 8. Sport Fucking. If you are like a little boy in a candy store and must sample everyone, do so with decorum and hygiene. But sooner or later, this will become an exhausting, abominable way of life. You won't be able to remember what story you told to whom, or who you took to certain restaurants. You'll say things like, "We sure had an elegant meal at Ma Maison" to your Tuesday night companion. She will know perfectly well it was some other cupcake who was the recipient of that wonderful meal. This will really piss her off if you've been taking her to Denny's.

The thing that offends me about sport fucking is that it's like having a second cup of coffee, as routine and commonplace as brushing your teeth. Sex should be special, always. If you need sex that much, jack off (you don't want the title of one-minute-wonder, anyway), or buy yourself an inflatable doll to practice with, or hire a prostitute. There is nothing wrong with zipless fucks, but I assume guys want "semi-meaningful" relationships, as well as sexually satisfying ones.

Don't be the sexual Bruce Jenner on your block. Sooner or later you will get tired of the juggling, scheduling scene.

Tip 9. (Don't Be) "The Professor of Desire & a Budding Dr. Masters." Even if you are a George Hamilton, don't verbalize about how you were interviewed for the Kinsey report because of your talent, how you study human sexuality, edited such books as *The Joy of Sex, The Sensuous Man,* and quarterlies like *Human Sexuality.* Don't admit you were asked to pose for *Playgirl.* It never hurts to keep a low profile. Good lovers need not boast. And big talkers don't necessarily make good lovers. All that hype can damage your psyche.

Tip 10. Never Call Them Cunts. Speak about all past, present and future women with great admiration, affection, concern, and fondness, but not at great length. They will figure you have a wonderful relationship with your mother (even if you don't, lie) and love women in general. This means respect: Respect means action.

Tip 11. Sympathy. Another way to get them really cranked up is that old line "I was hurt so deeply, I'll *never* fall in love again." Immediately they want to rehabilitate you, cook your dinner, clean up your house, work in your garden, spoil you. "I'll show him it *can* be different" they're thinking, wanting to smother your pain away with their breasts, stroking your face, deviously working on a new campaign to abolish your hurt.

Tip 12. Macho Is Out! Don't brag about how you can't wait for hunting season to begin and that you race dragsters on the weekends. Personally, I find men who are sensitive to animals (especially cats) appealing. (I have three of them.) Goldfish don't make it. Birds maybe.

Tip 13. Cheapness. Randy Newman can sing about "Short People" but nothing is more offensive to women than cheap men. God help the guy who brings a sack lunch and takes his date to the drive-in. Never mention the high cost of living before you give your order to the waiter. Never admit to not making your child support or alimony payments. Bra-burning feminists could become violent, visualizing your children praying for subsidized school lunches.

Tip 14. "Fools Rush In." You remember that old song. Don't push. Be patient. Women are used to being "expected" to put out. They are on the defensive. One false move and they'll duke you. Be coy and they'll probably rape you. Then you'd better have the goods to deliver.

Most women I know prefer genuine, even unattractive men to handsome bimbos. A relationship is like a tennis game—you want to play with someone who hits better than you do, or at least as well. Likewise, most women want a man who is as smart as or smarter than they are. No one wants to go around with an uninformed, social klutz. You wouldn't. On the other hand, some women I know prefer weak men so they can push them around and dominate them.

Tip 15. "Your Castle" shouldn't be overdone. It shouldn't look like Sexual Revolution Headquarters. No monogrammed wine bottles, beepers. Don't have the answering service call you repeatedly to make you appear popular. No penicillin bottles in plain sight. Your shampoo should not be Kwell.

Tip 16. Your Profession. Don't play the part; don't come over with a stethoscope draped around your neck or a slide rule in your hip pocket. Never take her to your office so she can see you've "made it." This process produces the reverse; by showing them, you are trying to reassure yourself. Besides, it's so pompous.

Tip 17. Welfare Fucks. These are the girls you owe it to but can't seem to get it up for and dread having to do so. . . .

We all have people to whom we owe fucking. People that have been overly generous, helpful and kind because they genuinely wanted to help you. People who went out of their way to assist you when the chips were down and asked nothing in return. (See, asking nothing in return makes you want to reward them out of guilt.) But beware . . . you don't screw your friends; this can't help but change the comfortable relationship you share now. And inevitably, the reason for this close, fond friendship is the *absence of sex.* Always wondering makes it more fun. *Never do anything unless it feels right.*

Tip 18. Those Angry Libbers. Feminists can be so trying. Everything you say can and will be used against you. Everything you say is wrong, sexist. Don't tell them they look nice or they'll accuse you of using them for sex symbols. Be ambivalent. Tell them you think Bella Abzug is beautiful, you make less money than they do for the same job, and you love to make coffee in the morning and deliver it to co-workers.

Tip 19. Too Close for Comfort. You know who they are, the people you've known for some time and have always been attracted to; business associates, people you've been curious about. A note of caution—be careful. What happens if something serious develops? This could be difficult to explain to your steady. Perhaps the *Too Close for Comforts* are the unions that should take place, but think twice. If you hate each other someday, you might really be sorry you fulfilled your lustful desire.

In closing: What can I say? Some of us will do anything after an elegant meal and a bottle of wine. The more we drink, the mellower we get. The more money a man spends, the more we extend our affections.

Remember, excitement comes in many forms. We're nervous too. We would put out to all of you except there is a rumor going around that nice girls don't and if she does, she won't be respected.

But who wants to be respected? You can't get an orgasm from respect. We want to fuck as much as you do, but it's up to *you* to convince each of us that you're a great lover and worth fucking.

Video Box Cover Copy

Box cover blurbs are never done on spec. You have to find a free-lance art director who is making up video boxes and ask him to farm some work out to you. The going rate begins at $7.50 apiece, which is not bad pay when you get at least twelve at a time and sometimes up to one hundred of them, and each one is usually only four lines long.

Your job is to describe the contents of the video box in 258 characters precisely. You learn quickly how to exchange five-letter words for four-letter ones so you can fit exactly within the parameters.

Because the material is going to appear on the outside of the box, inside a video store where Mickey Mouse cartoons will also be sold, you must keep the adjectives soft and the nouns vague. This factor, plus the little input you'll get from your employer, is severely limiting to your Muse.

For instance, you might get one chrome (a color slide) of a blonde girl with her truck-driver boyfriend, and a note that says: ass-fucking. With that mountain of information to go on, you must let your reader know what he's buying (or renting) without letting his kid brother know.

If the couple in the chrome are sitting in the kitchen, you can expand your information. For example: *John came into the kitchen for breakfast but Mary had a better idea*. Notice how soft this copy is. Your reader has already guessed what Mary's better idea was and his kid brother hasn't got a clue.

Now for a big problem. Ass-fucking has its own following, and it's a big one. It has plenty of return clientele looking for those buzz words which disguise his fetish. The main one is *back door*. There's also *Greek style, the other place* and *both places*. Use your imagination, but don't get too creative or no one will know what you mean. Your blurb might wind up looking something like this:

> Big John was hungry for breakfast but his buxom wife had a better idea. She climbed up onto the kitchen table and showed him something he'd been hungry for for a long time, the back door.

I know. All right. It's silly. When you have a job writing fifty-two of these suckers, the only way to get through it is to keep thinking about the money. The first one will take you a half an hour. Soon you'll be able to do fifty-two in two hours with time to spare. At $195 an hour, you can afford to be silly.

One way for a small video company to rake in easy money is to buy old "loops" and string them together to make a feature. A loop is a short, plotless porno movie. Sometimes the producer will provide a narrator who takes you through what are supposedly her friends' erotic adventures. She will make a voice-over. If the original loops were silent, other actors and actresses will come in the studio to make the "ooooh" and "ahhhh" sounds. (Listening to this from down the hall can be a riot!) Anyway, the final product is supposed to appear to be one unit.

Your job is to make it sound like one unit with your box cover copy. See if you can count the loops in the following sample. This job pays slightly more per blurb, about $25 to $65, and takes even less time to do than a pile of shorter ones.

By the way, note the running time on this tape. In fact, always note the running time when you're renting or buying an X-rated videotape. This practice will keep you from paying more than you should have to for what you're getting.

Joys of Erotica
Volume 4

This girl really knows how to greet a man after he comes home from a hard day's work. She wears just the right panties and that's about all. Chuck can barely keep his wits about him until he strips her down to the raw flesh and gives her something he's been saving up all day. She languishes in the liquid and laps it up. After that Tom gets a big treat when he meets a breast erotic. She can't wait to pull out her huge knockers and give him a look, or a taste, whatever he wants. He admires their fullness and beauty and makes love to them tenderly and soon finds himself with an uncomfortable bulge in his jeans. But never mind. This girl knows how to handle all such situations and where to put the little monster when he gets ready to come. Then Rennée Summers, who is staying at Michael Morrison's place, gets so bored she has to find something to do. Herschel Savage turns out to be her latest toy. When Michael comes home, all he wants is a piece of the action.

APPROXIMATE RUNNING TIME 30 MINUTES

Each line of videos will use about the same amount of copy on all of their boxes, to create continuity. The more they have to sell, the longer the copy will be. As video companies get into higher budget productions, which use longer scripts, more locations, and top stars, they will want to see the money they have spent reflected in your sales pitch.

Here's a box cover for one of my videoplays. I wrote the box copy as part of the package. But I have written box blurbs for other scriptwriters' material, since not all fiction writers can also write ad copy. Copy is not merely a synopsis of the tale inside the box, it is a hook to seduce the buyer. It is designed to make him curious, in this case, about this particular establishment and how the heroine solves her dilemma.

The Best Little Whorehouse
In San Francisco

Fanny Mae (amply played by CANDY SAMPLES) has it made in the shade. She's got the best staff of girls and the best whorehouse in San Francisco, and her trade is the *creme-de-la-creme.*

The problem is not that the mayor wants to close the place down. Hell, he wants to open up franchises. And, it's not her boyfriend, Sheriff Ned Swinger (HERSCHEL SAVAGE) wanting her to quit the business. He's making too much profit on what she's learning from the clientele.

The problem is that Fanny's number one girl, Lisa La Rue (AMBER LYNN), is pregnant, and she wants to get married and settle down. But with whom? Which client is willing and able? Most of them are already married.

And who could ever take her place on the job? Lisa was the best at B&D, at S&M, and at T&A. She was so popular that even when she didn't have anything left in her, the men still paid extra to have her in the room while they turned to neophytes for their pleasures.

The solution is obvious. Fanny Mae and Lisa simply put the other girls through a special training course so that they'll all become number one at the best little whorehouse in San Francisco!

Box blurbs can be indirectly responsible for your getting larger jobs from the same client. I wrote video box blurbs for Joint Video Productions, as well as several other video production houses, for a year before I actually did a script for them. When I was recommended to the client as a scriptwriter, he already knew my name as someone who had produced some excellent work for him in box cover copy. And, coming from still another direction, his director at that time knew me from my magazine work. Diversity is the nature of this business, unlike other fields where screenwriters don't stoop to television and playwrights won't touch commercial ad copy. So dig in wherever you get your first opportunity and then get ready to grow in whatever direction opportunity takes you.

Paperback Cover Copy

There's a really easy job that brings in a bit of pocket money on a regular basis: paperback blurbs. Remember those erotic novels I mentioned? Since adult publishing houses re-cover, or put new covers on, books they have already published, someone has to write the new cover blurbs. (Now and then they hear from an irate reader who purchased the very same novel under a different title, supposedly written by a different author, with a different blurb on the cover. He is pacified with a couple of free books.)

Your job is to create new cover copy making this little erotic novel even more exciting than it was the first time around. You skim the book, write a short paragraph on it without giving away its plot line, and send it off into the reading public again under its new banner. Publishing houses own thousands of these little novels and you can tell by reading them just how long they've been circulating. The heroine may be wearing a miniskirt and platform heels and the man sporting a new crewcut. But heck, a buck's a buck, right?

If the book is about incest, you must imply this without spelling it out. The sophisticated reader will catch your drift because he knows what clues to look for. Such as, "I lusted for her, even though she was much older than I was, and her bedroom was just down the hall." Get it? He's talking about his mom!

This job pays $10 to $15 per book and you usually get a set of 12 books at a time. After some practice, you should be able to turn out all twelve an hour. Don't worry about getting involved in the novels. They're not exactly Steinbeck, and even though there are rumors that some of our most eminent literary celebrities once wrote porn for a living, I don't think I've run across their work as yet in these kinds of books. I keep hoping.

Here is an example of a paperback blurb, complete with the teaser line: "She had to find the secret to satisfaction," which appeared on the front cover. If you read this very closely, you will see how the characters are related.

Secret Lust

Chuck and Tom were always fighting over Tom's drunkenness and Vera was caught in the middle. Not only that, but she could no longer find satisfaction with Tom and she was beginning to get nervous and restless. Soon Chuck started looking good to her and though she fought her inner desires, her lust won out. Tom must never know, and neither must Tina, Vera's daughter. But how could they keep this wondrous thing a secret?

Advertising Copy

After you've been in the business a while, clients will come looking for you to write advertising copy for their products, usually mail-order close-out magazines, videotapes, or sexual paraphernalia. Close-out magazines are the ones that didn't sell out the first time around or are re-covers (old magazines with new covers).

As you know, there are big-time ad agencies which specialize in print ad copy, but it isn't likely that your client will be going to one of them. He wants his ads down and dirty and in by last Tuesday. You won't have a great deal of time or inclination to get overly creative.

Magazine ads are usually for "fetish" magazines, where one line will cater to men who are into top-heavy girls and another to those who are into lesbian sets. There will often be a volume discount. Although the magazine originally sold for $6, the customer can now get three for $15. You can learn how to write these ads by copying the ones you see in the newsstand and adult bookstore publications, but you can't make money doing it until someone hires you.

Your copy will include a sales paragraph of about four sentences that no one will ever read, a headline, a small blurb for each magazine and a coupon asking for the order. The copy will describe the selection of models and their attributes, closing with a line stating what makes these magazines unique. When I wrote these ads, the publisher loaned me copies of the magazines so I could see what they were about. But after a few months in the business, all breast books will look alike, as will all black girl books, and so on. If a favorite model is featured, play that up. If there are over a hundred photos in the book, use that. Try to make each one special.

More and more ads for videotapes are taking over advertising space in magazines. The profit margin is tremendous, as it costs very little to produce and print one of these little home movies and they sell for up to $70. There are volume discounts on videos too, for the collector who can't get enough.

When the client has more than six tapes in his line, a synopsis of each story is composed and half- and full-page ads begin to appear in magazines. Many of these ads are trade-offs in one form or another, so your client doesn't have to pay for the space. That gives him more money to spend on the ad, but don't count on him spending it on you. Don't count on advertising copy being as easy to write as fiction, either. It isn't.

As with all ad copy, you're selling the sizzle, not the steak. In your case, you've got one of the most sizzling subjects going: SEX. The products themselves, videotapes for example, are not always great. If you saw one of the many low-budget productions, you'd really have to wonder why any person in his right mind would send away $69 and more for one of them. The range in quality is vast, depending on the production budget more than any other factor. Videos are being made for as little as $8,000 and shot in one day, all the way up to $200,000 for a fourteen-day shoot. The average range is between $25,000 and $60,000, but even here you won't find consistent quality. There are many variables, from the ability of the director all the way down to the acting talent and the script.

Assuming you get stuck with the lower-line stuff, you won't have much of a story to talk about in your ad, because they come plotless, for the most part, your stars are not as well known as the usual movie stars and you probably won't even get to view the tape anyway. So what else have you got to sell?

Basically, your end product is orgasm. Somehow, in fairly straight copy, you have to imply that your customer is going to have multiple orgasms from any tape in your line. For only $69, plus postage and handling, he's set for life with the girls of his wet dreams. Make him into a connoisseur of erotic video because he is choosing your client's product line.

The advertising layout will nearly always use reproductions of the boxes and the copy will talk about whatever is pictured on the box covers. You will most likely work directly with the packager or distributor on these campaigns and he won't be easy to please. These jobs are hard to come by and often slide right by the writer onto the drafting table of the paste-up artist, who steals his ad copy from the video box cover and ad-libs a headline. But once you're in tight with a production company, you're in until someone outbids you. If you get hooked up with a fairly large outfit, you could be doing four to eight campaigns per month.

If you think you could do a good job of writing print ads for videotapes, check out a few of them and match their style, then better it. Call on the advertiser and see if you can steal some business from him. Chances are he'll give you a crack at it because he can always use more sales.

Ads for feature-length films—those which are actually shown in adult theaters—or first-run videotapes, are generally part of a whole advertising campaign, with posters, brochures, and camera-ready art for newspapers and magazines. These campaigns are done very close to home, as the packagers are intent on getting the greatest market share possible. Often, the chief source of copy is the script and the accompanying synopsis is provided by the script-writer. Therefore, there's no work for a hired ad writer. Some scriptwriters also provide ad lines, such as "K. C. Valentine as you've never seen her before," or "This girl is really bad."

If the packager has no synopsis and no script, he sometimes sends the tape itself along to the writer or art director. Many full-page video ads have very little copy at all, just the title of the story and credits. The picture is what sells it. Flyers or brochures that are mailed out to theaters, buyers and others, will often be a one-page number with a reprint of the ad on the front and some ordering information on the back. Copywriters are not necessary for these jobs.

With all the stiff competition out there in the new video market, packagers and producers are searching madly for the secret of how to get people to pay attention to their latest tape. Video stores rely on magazine reviews, a top-ten list of best sellers circulated once a week, and only as a last resort, what personally appeals to them in an ad, the story angle, the stars, the fetish or even the box cover itself. Most of the advertising money goes into the box cover design and production.

One producer told me that he was in the business of selling superlative video boxes, with a free videotape included inside each one. He meant that he is willing to spend good money on getting the best package design, knowing that in this one case at least, people do buy the book by its cover. After all, what else can the customer see when he opens a brochure or visits a video store? Once he's opened the box, it's too late for him to change his mind.

There will be no sample ads in this book, but you can find them in most adult newsstand publications. You'll see that they are big on visuals and slight on copy, though what copy there is will be hot.

Public Relations Material

Public relations, or P.R., copywriting jobs are usually easy to get and your end product is easy to place. Magazines are always looking for articles on porn stars, videos, movies, awards shows, anything that makes good, photographical copy for their publications. Especially if you can double as a photographer, P.R. is an excellent way to make money. Although the private phone numbers of adult film actors and actresses are hard to get, once you get hold of one, chances are you'll get a story. The stars want as much publicity as possible. They know their days are numbered in this business and the more they can get their names in front of their audience, the more jobs they'll get.

It is common knowledge in the business that eighty percent of adult film actresses are in and out of porn in less than two years. Many do so intentionally. They are in for the quick buck, to get money to go back to college or start a new life, and they have what it takes to remember their goal and stick with it. Others can't hack it and drop out. Acting in porno is a challenge to even the most well-balanced, emotionally stable of them. Still others burn out quickly or fall through the bottom of the porn world. Some work very hard for a year or so, quit and do something else for a couple of years, then come back to the field when they're older and wiser and know a bit more about playing the game.

Even those actresses with the fortitude and intelligence to keep working, and keep their dignity as well, may still have trouble getting leading roles after they reach their mid-thirties, since the current trend is toward younger girls. There are notable exceptions to that, such as Kay Parker, who didn't do her first film until she was over thirty, and Gloria Leonard, who began acting at thirty-five.

Actors fall off in less than two years, although there are about ten male super-stars who seem to show up in just about any feature or video you pick up. Men are good until slightly past forty, when they begin to have trouble getting up for their work, shall we say. It's difficult enough to perform prolonged sex in the privacy of one's own home with one's own lover. Imagine what it must be like to do it with a girl you met an hour ago, perhaps a girl you don't even like, in front of two cameramen, a sound crew and a host of other strangers. Not to mention doing it under blaring lights, in an unfamiliar environment, and having just done it three hours before.

All this volatility contributes to actresses's desires to get their names plastered around in video or men's magazines, or anywhere. Male stars are also accessible, although some are difficult to interview. On the whole, stars know it is to their benefit to get exposure in the print media, because as their popularity increases, so will their job opportunities. They may also be in the enviable position to command a larger slice of the next production and a shot at the better parts.

A friend of mine called up Kitten Natividad, a stripper and adult film actress, and said he wanted to do a whole magazine just about her. She jumped at the chance because she knew she could use the finished product at the nightclub where she performs. She now sells the flashy, full-color publication to her fans.

Publishers want the stories because that's what sells their magazines and legitimizes their otherwise girlie-book look. But you don't even have to limit yourself to the adult market to sell these stories. Interviews with and articles about X-rated film stars Seka, Kay Parker, Kitten, Harry Reems and John Holmes, and adult magazine publishers Al Goldstein and Gloria Leonard, have appeared in such classy literary slicks as *Harper's, Vanity Fair* and *Newsweek*, as well as in most major newspapers. If you've got a clear shot at Harry or Seka, go for it. Get Seka to grant you a private interview, a tour through her beautiful house, an insider's peek at her secret personal life, and you could probably sell this article almost anywhere.

If you're good at placing news items, you might even find work as a freelance publicist for these stars. Think of all the interesting people you'd meet!

Collateral

Other sales materials include all the promotional brochures, posters and catalogues which are given away at trade shows, exhibitions and sales meetings, and mailed out to people by way of huge mailing lists. This material is known in the advertising business as collateral or support material.

You may have gotten yourself on one of the adult mailing lists by ordering some totally unrelated product, and are already familiar with adult sales brochures. The content can make for interesting reading on a dull, rainy night.

If you haven't seen any yet, you can arm yourself with a load of these in several easy ways. Order at least one product from any adult distributor of sex toys, magazines or videos, or attend the next Consumer's Electronics Show, or send for them directly. You'll get more than you'll ever need.

The Consumer's Electronics Show is held at least twice a year, usually in Las Vegas and Chicago, and includes all kinds of electronics displays, of which X-rated videotapes are only one segment. The adult video section is usually cordoned off and clearly marked to avoid admitting minors, as well as accidental penetration by the shy and uninformed or people without convention badges. When I visited the latest CES, I saw badges in the X-rated section from more than a few stray conventioneers. They probably told their wives they had to attend the data software exhibit and then stole away to the fun zone. Why pass up a chance to get your favortie porn star's autograph and see her in the flesh, no less? I also couldn't help but notice the tell-tale plastic carryalls sported by conservative businessmen, chock full of videotapes. Special promotional copies of X-rated tapes are often sold wholesale to vendors in the hope they will order more.

If one of these conventions passes through your town, stop in and take a walk through these star-studded booths. As long as you're over twenty-one, no one will stop you from going in, whether or not you're a distributor looking for a product. The brochures and flyers are free for the taking.

While you're there, you might as well ask if there is any work. All the big shots will be there at one time or another during the convention. Ask for the person in charge of the creative end—he or she will have any number of titles, from art director to pro-ducer. If the person you need to see is not there, ask when they will return, then keep trying. Leave your card. Take their card. Ask for rates. (They may not be willing to pay enough to make the work worthwhile.) Then give them a call after the convention is over for an interview. They'll be more receptive to you on their home ground, when they're more relaxed.

At the last CES, I asked five distributors if they were looking for writers and three of them said yes. Some companies are willing to try out new talent even when they're loaded with writers, espe-cially if they can get it cheap.

Reviews

Nearly every sex magazine uses movie reviews. There are also sev-eral dozen new video magazines which are devoted almost entirely to video reviews. *Adult Video, Adam Film World, X-Rated Movie Handbook, Video X, Cinema X* and *Adult Video News* are just a few. Look in these magazines for examples of the format. Many magazines have staff writers do reviews, but that doesn't mean they won't pick up some extra ones from you if you're any good. The poor editor who has to sit through 100 new tapes a month would probably jump at the chance for a breather. If you are in the position where you get to preview the latest videos and features available, you can probably sell reviews. After you break into print with a few, you may be able to get distributors to send you tapes in exchange for some P.R. If you get a regular position as reviewer for a certain magazine, you can name-drop and get free tapes that way.

Magazines are released to the stands three full months after they're put together, so you should be ahead of the game to make it count in terms of new feature reviews. On the other hand, films and videos are available for sale or rent for years afterward, so don't worry too much.

Seems like a soft job, doesn't it? Just sitting back in your living room looking at erotic movies with little or no story line and writing a paragraph about how it worked or didn't work? Read a few reviews and see if you still think it's easy. You have to supply the punch that wasn't in the film.

Your review will be stacked. If it's a theater feature, you want people to go and see it so the client will continue to advertise in your employer's magazine. If it's a home video, the same rule applies. Notice as bad as these reviews may appear, the redeeming qualities of each production overwhelm the negatives. This situation is especially true in the lower-level publications and less so with the major-leaguers, which are less dependent on the income from small advertisers.

If the story has no plot, it might have the most beautiful girls in home video entertainment. If the girls aren't pretty, maybe they're experts at sex. If neither is true, then maybe it's the set or the costuming that caught your erotic eye. I remember one review where the writer could only find one outstanding feature: The girl had a hole in her leotard and was entered through it. Must have been a pretty bad show. If nothing is great, surely you can find the orgy scene arousing. Find a hook, look for the gimmick the producer installed just for you, then play it up and your work is guaranteed.

This chapter is not as much about writing erotica as it is about picking up some other work in the same market. Advertising, interviews, P.R. and reviewing can help supplement your income while you're struggling with the fictional end. Very few writers of this material will come from outside the business, so the work is yours for the taking. If you get one of these assignments, you can easily get more.

CHAPTER 3

Writing for Special Markets

Aiming toward your reader is as essential in erotic writing as it is in any other field of writing. You would not be likely to send an article on the joy of crocheting to *Golf* magazine. Neither would you submit an essay on the ideal girl to a gay men's magazine.

After you've written a few stories, you may discover fetishes you never knew you had, or at least proclivities toward certain areas of sexuality. One writer friend of mine prefers to write for spanking magazines but not because he likes to get whacked on the bottom himself. He finds them the easiest to write for because they give him a platform for his story line. Spanking stories have a built-in theme.

Another friend really enjoys writing stories about S&M. Though she's experienced very few such episodes herself, she can easily imagine herself in those situations because she likes dominant/passive sex. My leanings are toward big bust and lesbian stories. My very favorite theme is sex between people who are in love with each other—writing everyday type, ordinary, heterosexual love scenes, with lots of kissing, caressing and talking to one another.

Fetish Markets

You too will find your niche and you will surprise yourself with how much fun it is to write about sex. Just to be sure you have considered every possibility, here are the categories of fiction and articles you may be able to have published:

Breasts   The adult store carries about one-third of its softcore stock in bust magazines featuring oversized breasts. You don't have to write an entire story about breasts, but words on the subject will be sprinkled generously throughout the piece. "Confessions of a Breast Erotic" and "Keli's Bath" (pages 35 and 39) are examples.

Adult store titles: *Big Boobs, Melons & Mounds, Heavy Hangers*

Ass   Photographs in ass books, when softcore, show the woman bending over a good deal, with her rear end toward the camera. They are targeted toward the man who likes to approach his lover from that angle. Your stories will concentrate on bottoms. Long fiction or articles for these magazines will usually be about ass fucking, or will include at least one episode of anal sex. An example of this type of story follows.

Adult store titles: *Ass Parade, Bottom, Chubby Cheeks*

Legs   Long-legged girls, or girls with lots of leg shots on their proof sheets, often wind up in leg magazines. They're shown dancing, doing gymnastics or just putting on nylons. Leg magazines are often the softest of adult magazines and their fans are the oldest and most devoted. Leg magazines were among the first girlie magazines on the scene. "Valene" (page 43) is an example of this fetish, and of the lingerie fetish.

Adult store titles are: *Legs & Lingerie, Tip Top, Long & Lovely, Leggs*

Lingerie   Lingerie magazines feature underwear and nightwear. Girls will be shown in the prettiest Frederick's fashions, usually wearing stockings, a garter-belt and high-heeled shoes with their shortie nightgown. Your copy will elaborate on the softness and silkiness of the various fabrics and how sexy the girl feels wearing them.

Some adult store examples: *Legs & Lingerie, Silky, Silk, Satin and Lace*

Young Girl   Photos of the youngest girls in the business are in young girl magazines, although all of the girls will be over eighteen. They may be dressed youthfully, with bobby socks, Mary Jane Shoes or worn-out tennis shoes, and have their hair tied up in pigtails with satin ribbon. The sets may have teddy bears and dolls strategically placed around the bed. The girls are usually flat-chested and have often shaved down below for the photo session. Your copy will indicate that the girls are virgins or at least not very experienced, and can be about anything beyond that. Below I've included a sample of this type of story.

Some adult store titles are: *Pet Pussy, Baby Doll, Naked Nymphs*

Black or Ethnic   Books about ethnic women are very popular. There are magazines which feature blacks, latinas, or orientals. The copy is about females, not races, so it will read pretty much the same as ever. Occasionally, you might want to throw in a laudatory phrase such as, "Nobody knows what passion's about like a black woman," or "Latinas are the hottest women alive."

Some adult store titles are: *Black Mama, Black Satin Dolls, Oriental Lust, Latin Lovers, Black & Lusty*

Lesbian   Most lesbian publications are not for lesbians at all, but for men who like to watch two girls in action with each other. This description particularly applies to the adult store variety. There are some notable exceptions, which I will go into later. This market appeals to the reader who wants to see touching and fondling of breasts, etc., but has no interest in watching another man do it (particularly if he's well hung!). Your stories can be about anything you want as long as two females wind up making it together. You can include men in long fiction and articles and not disrupt anything. Do try, however, to learn the subtle differences between sex where only women are involved and the heterosexual kind. Most lesbians do not have "cock fantasies," and some do not even like insertion. If you are lucky enough to become associated with a publication that is trying to reach the true lesbian reader, more power to you. That end of the adult business is wide open. Lesbians have been complaining for years that there is nothing for them on the stands. Two examples in this book of lesbian stories are: "A Lesbian Love Story" and "Stood Up" (pages 44 and 49).

Adult store titles: *Lesbian Lovers, Roommates, Sappho, Girls Loving Girls, Hers & Hers*

Fat Girl Magazines featuring fat women do very well in the adult stores but there are still relatively few of them around. It may surprise you to know that the accompanying copy is not about the joys of sex with fat women at all, but about food. If you enjoy eating, you'll write this material well. I have read some fan letters for these magazines, and the readers want to hear how much the girl weighs, what kinds of foods she gorges herself on, and why she enjoys overeating. They do not want to know anything about her sex life. I wrote a fat girl calendar that could double as a cookbook since each of my models presented her own recipe for chicken and dumplin's, cheese lasagna or chocolate mousse. It sold extremely well, but I haven't heard yet if any of our fans tried out the recipes.

Adult store magazines: *Chubby Cheeks, Big Mama, Big Boobs*

Pregnant Some men get turned on by seeing a woman heavy with child. These magazines generally do not destroy the maternal image with perverted attacks on the female's distorted form. Instead, they celebrate it. They put the mother-to-be on a pedestal of virtue. According to some readers' letters they wish the girls got in a family way without any contact with a man. The photographs are soft. The girls tend to wear soft white or pink lingerie and in most cases, be in demure poses, at least in the softcore variety, which sells best. There is a new line of hardcore pregnant magazines where the woman is being made love to by her gynecologist or her husband or both of them. I'm not sure these books will find their audience, but if nothing else, perhaps they'll serve to educate those men out there who can't find anything wonderful about making love with a pregnant woman. Some sexologists use these magazines as teaching aids for their clients.

There are no recurring titles for these publications, but you can spot them by the cover photo.

Pretty Girl Magazines featuring pretty models are fun to write for because the girls are gorgeous and sexy and it's easy to dream up adventures for them. Sometimes you'll be required to make up statistics such as measurements, age, birthplace and so on. Over the years, some of these models have acquired quite illustrious and varied biographies which they had nothing to do with creating, a mystique that their writers are entirely responsible for.

Again, most of these magazines are specials and titles will be a girl's name or *Beach Blondes* or something similar.

Spanking   Spanking magazines have gone out of style, but they are coming back. The photo sets show girls who are bent over with red marks on their bottoms (made with lipstick, not strap), and a pained expression on their faces. Or, there will be a spanker present. Stories will be about spanking, often connected with sex. A typical story is about a girl who was spanked as a child and learned to enjoy it, then craved spanking by an adult male. One title still in print sometimes is *Crack!*

Milk   Milk magazines show pregnant or recently pregnant women squirting milk from their breasts. Supposedly, since most women cannot ejaculate quite as visibly as men can, squirting milk is the closest facsimile. The milk following is a devoted one and wants to hear about how the girl's breasts ache to be expressed.
Titles are *Milk Maids, Milking Mama, Milky*.

Leather and Latex   Some readers like to see a girl all dolled up in leather or latex bodywear, the kind you see in sex shops. She wears spike-heeled boots, a spiked leather collar and a mean expression on her kisser. Her hair is often black and pulled back tight against her skull. She's the Dominatrix and she's out for your ass! Your copy will tell how this leather version of a wonder woman likes to seduce men the hard way, against their puny will. This might be fun to write in a kinky sort of way. This fetish very possibly had its beginning in the rubber apron fetish and even rubber baby pants. But at last count, there were no magazines available for sale which cater to the specialized audience of rubber, and readers may have switched to latex and leather. These magazines are usually one-shots and the titles constantly change.

S&M   S&M stands for sado-masochism, but this year's material isn't nearly as horrifying as some in the past. Publishers have toned down a bit because enough women have complained that this particular kind of porno magazine may have a negative effect on the male's image of and conduct toward females. Contrary to what you might expect, in the current market the female is not the victim in most S&M material. She plays the sadist role, not the masochist. The stories revolve around a dominant female and her poor slave of a lover. I've never seen an S&M magazine that actually shows the sex act, only the prelude of faked whipping and teasing and punching a spiked heel into the flesh of the lady's victim.

Publishers are slowing down production on these magazines and there are no recurring titles.

Bondage or B&D   B&D stands for bondage and discipline. These magazines all but disappeared in the seventies but are back in the mainstream in the eighties. The pictorials have very little to do with sex. The women are clothed and tied with rope, leather or tape. Editors claim this is good-natured, nonviolent, nonexplicit play. Copy will be about the last time you or one of your friends was tied up or tied somebody up. They print fiction in the form of readers' letters.

Popular titles are: *Bondage Life* and *Bondage Parade*

TV   No, TV has nothing at all to do with your television set. It stands for transvestites. This heading includes material for transsexuals as well. A "transvestite" is a person who likes to cross-dress, or wear the clothing of the opposite sex. For adult publications, this person is always a male. A "transsexual" has already made some physiological changes and has deliberately become a hermaphrodite. He will have breasts, a penis, and an extremely feminine physique and face. Photographs of both of these types will be in the same TV magazines. Your copy will be about how the boy loves being a girl. He thinks of himself as a female and so should you. You will write *she* instead of *he*. A third variety of TV is the transsexual who has gone all the way over and had his penis surgically removed and a vagina built in its place. These new females have trouble getting work in the adult business after their sex change and only show up occasionally in before-and-after sets. One exception is Shannon, who now plays female roles in X-rated videos.

Titles: *TV Tricks, TV International*

Miscellaneous Adult Store Material   There are many one-shots on the stands that sometimes work, sometimes don't. Long-haired girls, blondes, girls who wear short-shorts and so on. If you have an idea for a fetish that hasn't been exploited yet, write to the publisher of this type of magazine and query them with your idea. They may build an entire magazine around it.

Newsstand   Up until now, I've been telling you about publications you'd probably have to go into an adult bookstore to buy. The regular, nationwide variety is probably more familiar to you. *Playboy, Penthouse, Oui, High Society, Hustler* and a few others not only lead in sales, but also in submissions. They are hard to break into, except if you want your letter to the editor published. You might prefer to try a lower echelon first, to get your confidence up. *Gent, Cheri, Buf* and others have fewer submissions from which to choose yours.

What is in a newsstand adult-oriented magazine? Each magazine has a centerfold single girl set of photographs and often several other sets of single girl photos. Now and then, an issue will be brave enough to include an excited male or another girl in the layout. Copy that goes with the sets is written in-house, which means you can't do it unless you work there. Articles and fiction, however, are often purchased from freelancers. Read several issues to get an idea of their running themes. *Hustler* fiction has to have a plot line to support the erotica. *Playgirl* fiction often isn't even about sex. Remember that the higher up on the circulation scale your choice of publication is, the harder it will be to get in. There are many other magazines you've never heard of on your local newsstand and they all use freelancers, if approached in the right way. Query them, send them something, phone them if you can. They are usually willing to buy even second-rights (previously published) articles and fiction.

Some newsstand men's magazines are also fetish-oriented, like *Juggs*, for example, and *Gent*, both big-bust magazines. Others may not cater to one particular fetish. Only a quick reading of the magazine will give you this information.

Among the appendixes, you will find a listing of major newsstand men's magazines, with information on how to submit to them.

Bikers   On the other end of the market is a line of men's magazines that doesn't fit neatly into any of my categories: the motorcycle magazine. Some titles are: *Easy Rider, Iron Horse,*

Supercycle, In the Wind and *Outlaw Biker*. These use erotica, as long as the macho theme is clearly evident. The main story is a biker's adventure in a hostile environment. His momentary distraction with the female element and/or a sexual adventure is only just that: momentary. But make that moment a whopper!

In the several stories I read there were female hitchhikers who dropped their cut-offs for a ride on a Harley; a winsome, tattooed nymph, who stopped to wash off the bike dust in a nearby pond, knowing she was being observed by a leather-vested peeping tom; a barmaid who loved her customers to bits; and an ol' lady, all of twenty-six, who supported her ol' man by slinging hash in a diner.

Another convention is the biker's brotherhood with his fellows. It's almost as if his relationship with the other members of his gang is more important than scoring chicks.

They talk about girls, about doing it with girls, about having girls do it to them, but the girls aren't the main characters in their stories, unless it's a photo set devoted to one of them, as with the water nymph. There are cops and gang members with names like Animal, Fuzzy and Monk. Women work at jobs like cashier and waitress, while guys just ride, fight, booze and rap.

The language is tough too. My favorite opening is for a story called "Oh, Officer," by a dude named "Tunes," in a recent issue of *In the Wind*:

> The ghosts mc wound along curvy Main Street in a serpentine line of chromed steel intent on murder. They were coming to kill. . . .

Gets you right into the story, doesn't it? There is a whole jargon connected with biker stories and you better get it right or nobody's going to read your stuff. If you could do it though, this is an excellent market since there's seldom enough room in an easyrider's saddlebag for a portable Selectric.

You may have noticed I have entirely skipped over a very important, and very broad area of the adult market: the gay magazines. For your edification on that subject, read on. Meanwhile, here are two stories illustrating how to write for a fetish publication. The first is for an ass-oriented magazine, the second was published in *Naked Nymphs*, a magazine devoted to younger models.

Robyn's Nest

The best thing about me is my asshole. I know that sounds weird, but let me explain.

I've always been very sensitive there, you see, and when I've masturbated myself, my pussy and stuff, I always moved my fingers around that part too. And before long, it was really erotic for me to put my fingers inside of it while I was manipulating my pussy lips. Then I noticed it was getting all puckered and puffy and I got into showing it off to my boyfriends, and that turned them on and one thing led to another until I started getting balled there.

So now you know why my asshole looks like a little rosebud and why guys like to suck on it and fuck it.

But sometimes, that's all guys wanna do and that's no good because I just love to get balled. One thing I really get off on is when a guy's got my legs up over his arms (I'm on the bottom) and he's ramming his cock into me and every time he comes forward, his balls slam up against my cunt. But, you see, they also hit my asshole! So it's like getting a double-fuck!

And don't think I didn't think of that! I just can't get two guys who want to try it. But if I could, I would put myself on top of one guy, with his cock inside me and have the other guy on his knees behind me, balling the hell out of my asshole.

Or wait a minute, now that I think about it, what I'd really like is to have a cock to suck on while I was getting fucked. But that would take three men . . .

I guess when you're onto something good, it's hard to get enough. I mean, if one man is terrific, just think what two or three would be like!

Come to think of it, wouldn't it be fun to have a cock between my breasts too?

Sophie

My mom and dad said: "Before you get a man, get a degree!" But I'm only in my last year for my bachelor's (degree, that is) and I still have two years before I get my master's, and then if I get a doctorate, I'll be in college forever. That's a long time to wait for your first man.

Plus, I'm taking Life Science this term which means we study anatomy. One more color illustration of the glans penis and I'm going whacko!

In my freshman year, I was taking physiology books home to jack off to, but then I met Stuart, who was doing the same thing. We decided to get off to each other instead.

So ever since then, this is what we've been doing: We go up to his room at the dorm, or mine at my parents' house, supposedly to study for some contrived mid-term. Then we turn the radio on (my mom knows I never study without it), lock the door, and strip down naked.

Stuart sits across from me in a chair and brings out that gorgeous prick of his, and I sit on the bed, spreading my legs so he can get a good view of my pussy.

I keep my eyes on that growing cock just as long as I can keep them open, and he watches my cunt fill up with juices and swell up, ripe and red.

Sometimes he sits a little closer, because the closer that throbbing prick is to my face, the bigger it looks and the more excited I get.

We keep talking to each other, you know, telling each other where we are. Like Stuart will say: "I think I can hold it about one minute." So I'll say, "No, wait, hold on," and then I'll start working myself faster to catch up.

So I'm watching Stuart's hand holding onto his cock and sliding very slowly up and down the shaft. I can see the head glistening and ready to pop. My own clit is getting tingly and every move I make sends shivers through my cunt.

When I know I'm ready, I say "Stuart, I'm coming, here I come." And just then I see white drops spurt out from his cock. He's coming too. What a sight!

My pussy's clamping down on my fingers, Stuart is moaning in whispers so my parents won't hear, and then it's over. And we giggle about the mess we've made. Someday my mother is going to have to hire the rug cleaner to get after those white and yellow spots all over my green shag.

New Trends

And now for something completely different. There is, as I've told you, a movement toward erotica and away from pornography. The writers aimed in this direction are looking for new ways to attract "normal" people with "normal" sex drives, who are sick of exploitation and degradation. Writers became publishers when they found nowhere to publish their work and this movement led to the latest trend in sex magazines.

It seems to be a life and death struggle for these small publications to stay alive, since many disappear soon after they surface. Without national distribution and a major publishing house backing them financially and otherwise, it's hard to understand how they make any headway at all. Distributors are reluctant to carry a magazine with a small print run and little or no advertising or subscriptions. With no distributor, they can't get on the newsstand. No newsstand sales means mail order only, which means advertising money must be spent. And how do you solicit ads with no public awareness of your product?

A few magazines I wanted to include in this book have already gone out of business. There are others still around for which I can no longer find ads. (Ads for obscure sex magazines often appear in the classified sections of mainstream magazines, such as *Ms.*) One magazine that's still around is *Yellow Silk*.

Yellow Silk is one of the first sex magazines with female-oriented erotica in it. Between the covers, you'll find some excellent, off-beat fiction, poetry (lots and lots of poetry), satire and letters. These letters are real letters, not the kind that are composed.

Lily Pond, the publisher, describes her editorial content as anything which fits under her motto, which is: "All Persuasions: no brutality." Ms. Pond asks that writers try for literary work with shades of erotic imagery, rather than the hardcore approach.

Subscribe to *Yellow Silk* or send for a sample copy (at $3), by writing to: *Yellow Silk*, P.O. Box 6374, Albany, CA 94706. Your sample issue will have all the information you need.

Another small press publication is *Eidos*, which publishes articles and fiction. A sample copy may be obtained by sending $3 to: Ms. Brenda Tatelbaum, Publisher, Brush Hill Press, Inc., Post Office Box 96, Boston, MA 02137.

I recently acquired a copy of an anthology called *Erotic Fiction Quarterly*. Though this first edition looks more like a literary journal than a slick porno book (and that's by design), the quality of the material contained astounded me. Some of it is really first-rate fiction, which happens to deal with sexual themes. Some of the stories have no plot, which may be missed at first reading. Some ask more questions about the characters than they answer. But the imagery is sensual and provocative and the scenes created are unforgettable. If you have a story to sell that doesn't fit into the mainstream, try this publication.

EFQ buys fiction manuscripts with sexual themes with no restriction on length, content, style or explicitness. But they expressly request that they not be sent "standard pornography or men's magazine–type stories, contrived or formula plots or gimmicks, broad satire or parody or poetry."

You can buy a copy by sending $10.95 to the following address, or request specifications for your manuscript by sending an SASE to: *EFQ* Publications, Post Office Box 4958, San Francisco, CA 94101

The Gay Male Market

Gay males have made the most dramatic moves toward alternative publications and now have publishing houses thriving in all areas of the country. Books—self-help, how-to, adventure and fiction—and of course magazines proliferate. Still, with all this growth, you may have difficulty finding such material in your home town. Chances are, you'll have to send away for it.

One way to become apprised of this market is to subscribe to a newsletter or get hold of a publisher's list. I picked one up at the American Booksellers Convention, a great place to look for publishing information. *The Carrier Pigeon* can be ordered from Alyson Publications, at 40 Plympton Street, Boston, MA 02118. In it you will find a listing of the latest publications of this press and many others, plus backlisted books available through this distributor.

At the American Booksellers Convention, I talked to one of the editors at Alyson Publications about their novels. He said he'd rather not give specifications to prospective writers, as he likes variety in his list. Short novels are sometimes very softcore and have few sex scenes. Others are hardcore from the first line. Some are murder mysteries or gay gothic novels. And some are clearly "coming out" novels and autobiographical pieces. Among these books are anthologies in which gay writers publish their short stories.

If you are interested in this market, send for their booklist and read the book descriptions. See where you fit in. Buy a few of the ones that appeal to you and then write one of your own. Submit your short stories to Alyson for consideration too. I can't vouch for the pay, but breaking into print is just as important.

Alyson also carries feminist titles which are hard to find elsewhere, political works, and female-oriented erotica, including lesbian.

There are many lines of short fiction books, on the order of the hardcore paperbacks I told you about in Chapter 1. Unlike those, however, which are reprints of volumes a decade or so old, gay male novels are still an open market for writers. Manuscripts run 160 pages and are teeming with hot, male on male sex. No holds barred. Every fantasy and perversion is explored. Pay runs from $400 to $750, with most publishers paying $500 for all rights.

For information about the magazine market, try writing to The Gay and Lesbian Press Association (GLPA) at Post Office Box 7809, Van Nuys, CA 91409. Or look for magazines on your newsstand.

Newsstand gay men's magazines include such titles as: *Firsthand, Stallion, Honcho, In Touch, Mandate, Blueboy* and *Playguy*. But don't be surprised if your home-town newsstand doesn't have them. They're fairly hardcore.

Newsstand gay male magazines play by different rules than adult store ones. Just as our hetero magazines have to grace their pages with "legitimate" copy to make them socially relevant, so do these.

The gay male magazine is one of the fastest-rising areas of erotic material. You can find these magazines in every major city and the gay men are constantly looking for new material. Your stories will involve gay encounters and include ass fucking, rimming, blow jobs and lots of oral sex and/or mutual masturbation. If you don't know anything about being a gay male and you don't have a close friend who is one, but you still want to write gay fiction, there are ways to get this information. Buy a few magazines and rent some videotapes and see if you're still up for it.

You will have to write convincingly. Gay publications are not interested in reading any material from "the outside." Don't write from the straight point of view. On the other hand, if you are straight and you've always wondered what sex between two men would be like, you can sell stuff on this fantasy. It isn't that gays are prejudiced against straight men; they like straight men very much—straights represent forbidden fruit. It's that gays, like all of us, don't want to be made fun of, used or put down. They want to celebrate the joys of gay sex. This market is hungry for new writers.

The newsstand variety of gay male magazines will not be likely to have photos of hardcore sex (intercourse) in it, but the newsstand pulp (newspaper) might. Newsstand publications are loaded with fiction and first-person confession-type stories. The stories are often about an older man with a young, hunky trick, or about the steambath/workout gym scene. There seems to be a proliferation of shoe-fetish stories and those involving punishment or beatings. Some very popular gay newsstand magazines specialize in leather, bindings, latex and body suits and attracts the gay male reader who is into S&M and bondage.

Two titles of adult store gay male magazines are *Skin* and *Stroke*. J. B. Morris, editor-in-chief at Magcorp, one of the largest publishers of gay material, gave me a spec sheet for gay erotic fiction. The following is taken from his guidelines:

All stories must have more of a plot than boy meets boy, boys have sex, and boy does/doesn't leave boy. Some other element of dramatic tension, some other question must be resolved in the course of the story.

First person is usually better, so that there is a pronoun difference between the two men. No first person with non-gay or "bi" characters. Describe both guys well. If the characters are under eighteen, then they must be within a year or two of each other and the story must be in the first person from one of their views, perhaps as a reminiscence. No adults with anyone under eighteen. No prostitution of an under-age guy. No scatalogical sex. No death of a character while involved in sex. No description of permanent disfigurement in the sex scene. Stay away from blood.

Manuscripts may range from 10 to 20 pages. We pay $10 per page, 24 to 26 lines per page, double-spaced, 60 character lines. We buy all rights. Payment is rendered 30 days after acceptance.

This is the kind of guideline sheet you may get if you send to a magazine for specifications. Magcorp's gay male, adult publications are pretty standard, and a story you write aimed at one of their books could be sold elsewhere.

However, pay attention to the subject matter of each magazine. Specific magazines have specific themes. Here are the requirements for *Stroke*:

Will deal with topics such as incest, bondage, humiliation, discipline—in general, the more absurd and bizarre aspects of male-male sexuality, yet it also demands an excellent writing style and command of the language.

Gay male sex publications get into some extreme hardcore areas, where hetero sex mags fear to tread. Take a look at several of these magazines before you try to write for them. It's not as easy as it may appear to be. And there are vastly different types of gay magazines for men.

Skin and *Stroke* magazines are examples of borderline adult store material. They're trying to look like "real" magazines by virtue of their content. Inside you'll find articles, ads, a publisher's statement, a table of contents and letters to the editor. They are a good deal like the newsstand men's magazine and the only reason they're held back in the adult stores is that they insist on showing full erections, and occasionally, two men together.

The graphic sexual content will give them away as hardcore sex publications. Inside, you'll find photographs of young men with erections, sometimes masturbating to climax. They are extremely explicit. In fact, you ladies who are looking for more exciting visual stimulation than *Playgirl* offers in its center-fold may want to check out a few of these slick productions.

The more typical adult store fare is the picture book. Because of their high cover price (they start at $6 and some sell for more than $75), they don't carry ads, or even articles and fiction. They are color photo albums with occasional copy blurbs. They're printed on high-quality, heavy weight paper and the photography is excellent. Whereas the "borderline" adult magazines occasionally travel across the counter onto the newsstand, sometimes sealed in cellophane, the "picture" books do not.

Generally speaking, these magazines will be one of two basic types: One type will have three to five men alone (often in the wilderness, or sitting on a motorcycle) in varying stages of undress, winding up in a close-up jack-off scene. If there's any copy at all, it will be brief and will talk about what a hunk the guy in the photo is, his luscious round buns and of course, his steel-hard rod. The other type will have photo sets involving two or more men having sex together, usually a collection of photos taken at a video shoot. The story line will follow the video screenplay script and is often about the pool maintenance man and the horny tenant, the paperboy and his older trick, or two boys working out in the gym. This is a case when men become boys in the same manner in which women became girls. Even when there's a script to follow, the copy generally consists of short paragraphs with brief descriptions of the action and maybe some dialogue. The main emphasis is on the photos, which fill the page with close-ups of sexual action.

By the way, some gay male adult magazine stories are written by women, since women are also attracted to hunks like these. If any of you ladies happen to have a gift for hard locker-room language, and can easily imagine what it's like to sit on top of one of these larger-than-life hard-ons, go for it.

J. B. Morris has submitted the following story as an example of hot, gay male erotica. He told me to warn you that there is no typical story for the gay male; they vary from dominant/submissive, gang-bang, bondage and S&M, all the way back to the basic love story. The following is only to educate you on the gay male point of view and what he considers erotic.

"Full Service Pump" was written by Sean Ridings and first published in *Skin* magazine, vol. 5, no. 2.

Full Service Pump
BY SEAN RIDINGS

It was last summer, and I had just turned eighteen and was on the graveyard shift of my uncle's all-night gas station on a lonely stretch of Interstate 70 in the middle of Kansas.

It was 2:30 in the morning and I hadn't had a customer in over thirty minutes. My uncle runs a self-service station, but at least I get to talk to the customers when they come in to pay; it helps keep me awake.

I was just starting to nod off when I heard the unmistakable roar of a motorcycle pulling up to one of the pumps. My head snapped up, and I saw a big, muscular dude with windblown blond hair dismount the bike. But instead of going up to one of the pumps, he just sat side-saddle and looked toward me, his expression one of total unconcern. My first thought was that the dude had to be illiterate, for the SELF-SERVE sign sat right on top of the pump in front of him. I figured if I stayed put, he'd eventually get the message and draw his own gas.

After a couple of minutes, though, that obviously wasn't going to happen. He just sat there, looking at me with that bland expression, his legs crossed in front of him with his ass on the seat of his Harley.

I'd had plenty of time to study him, and what I saw made me slightly uncomfortable. Not in a frightened sort of way; it was more sexual. His shorts were cut-off jeans, terribly faded and ragged, and they were incredibly short. He wore only a vest on his upper body, no shirt or jacket, and his muscles were obvious. I could see from my vantage point, roughly seventy-five feet away, that he was a body-builder.

There was a slight stirring in my pants as I decided I'd better see what the dude wanted, or tell him this was a self-serve station. As I got closer, I saw that he had an incredible bulge in his crotch. He retained his indifferent attitude as I neared him. Finally he broke the silence.

"Hello, Skinny."

That pretty much sums up my looks. I'm handsome (and somewhat vain), but there's no denying I'm skinny. That's about the only way to describe six-foot-four and a hundred-and-fifty pounds.

I nodded as I made my own assessment of him. Roughly six-two, maybe two-fifteen or two-twenty. No fat, just muscle. Beautiful pectoral muscles with erect nipples on an almost hairless chest turned totally brown from the sun; large thighs, also muscular. A huge basket in his skimpy shorts. Hair blond with streaks of brown—thick, windblown, and long. One-word description: Hunk. Make that two words: Beautiful Hunk.

"This is a self-serve station," I said casually. "You can help yourself, sir."

For the first time his expression changed. He let out a short, harsh, barking laugh. A one-syllable laugh. It made me uneasy.

"I need some help," he said in his low sexy voice, and as he said the word "help" I thought he gave an ever-so-slight arch of his mid-section. When I didn't respond, he made it more obvious (he must have thought I was pretty dense). He gave his bulge a rough squeeze and said, "You can fill 'er up while I go to the john. When you're finished, if I'm not back, you might want to check on me."

I knew exactly what he was driving at, and while I was turned on, I couldn't leave the station unattended. I told him so.

"Shut the place down for awhile," he suggested. "Turn out the lights and no one will stop. Simple, Skinny."

I protested. "I can't shut the place down! If my uncle finds out, he'll fire my ass!"

The hunk sighed. He unsnapped his jean-shorts, and the huge beast inside caused the zipper to descend on its own. I gasped; I mean really, audibly gasped. A semi-hard cock, the biggest I'd ever seen (or fantasized about), bounded out. It was long and it was fat, and it was uncut. And it wasn't fully erect yet.

"Shut the place down," he said again.

"Yeah," I managed to whisper. "Yeah, okay."

He smiled and ambled casually toward the john. There was pure sex in every step he took, and he didn't bother to zip up his pants. I couldn't take my eyes off him. As he got to the restroom door, he stopped; he removed his shorts, and then walked bare-assed into the john. I almost fainted at the sight of that beautiful ass, the white outline of skimpy trunks contrasting sharply with his dark brown body.

It took me several tries before I got the pump nozzle into the bike's tank. The gas had never come out so slowly before, and I cursed it time and again before the tank was filled. I fumbled with the cap and finally managed to get it back on, then I almost ran into the station, fearful that another customer would pull in before I could shut down the lights. The lights went out, and then I almost turned an ankle as I hustled to the john.

I shut the door behind me and locked it, just in case. When I looked up, there he was with that damnable smile, leaning against a wall, hips outthrust. His cock was fully hard now, and I swallowed (somewhat fearfully) as I beheld an incredibly thick, eleven-inch rod. I'd seen big dicks before (though never one this big), and most of them that had braggable length and width were so heavy that they seemed to droop. Not this one. It was a rock. The balls that hung below it looked like goose eggs.

He had removed the few pieces of clothing he had been wearing. The jean-shorts (no undershorts or jock), vest and black boots were tossed carelessly into a corner. He faced me totally nude, like an Adonis, and I needed no words to tell me what I should do.

Weak-kneed, I managed to stumble to him. I dropped carelessly to my knees, heedless of the crack as bone hit concrete floor. My mouth opened, and I could barely get his head inside. He placed his huge hands on the back of my head, and his fingers ran roughly through my dark locks as he rocked me back and forth on his huge fucker. I didn't even notice that slowly, very slowly, more and more of his giant cock was disappearing into me. The sides of my mouth felt like they were being ripped apart, but I soon had almost half of him in me. That was as far as I could go, and he sensed it and was satisfied.

He grunted and commanded, "Eat that big fucker, you cocksucker!"

As I continued, his big hands slid down the back of my

shirt, and with a savage motion he ripped it off me. He tore the shirttails out of my pants and tossed the ruined material to one side. I could feel his ample foreskin sliding back and forth in my mouth as he bent lower and grabbed the waistline of my pants. Realizing what was about to happen, I tried to shout, but that's difficult to do with five inches of throbbing cock in your mouth. He must have got the message, though, for he stopped. I then removed my pants the civilized way. I might by able to make up a believable lie about the condition of my shirt, but never my pants! I kept sucking him without missing a beat.

"Oh, yeah, Baby, you give good head!" he hissed.

At least I had graduated from "Cocksucker" to "Baby." I felt proud.

His chest was heaving uncontrollably, and I knew the sign. His hips pumped faster and harder, and I would have been ready for the eruption even if he hadn't said, "Let's see how much of my cum you can handle, Cocksucker!"

Cocksucker, again. Oh, well.

I'd love to lie and tell you that I handled it all. Or even most of it. No such luck; when he came, he came with a force I was not prepared for. His cum exploded in rapid-fire action, and before I could compensate it was running out the sides of my mouth and down my chin, so much of it that you wouldn't have known his dick was in my mouth. He laughed, and I realized it must have been a joke to him; he knew the force of his orgasms and had to know what was going to happen; he was enjoying my failure.

Finally he pulled his still-hard rod from my mouth, and with it spilled out the load of cream that I had not yet been able to swallow but which was still in my mouth. I knew I had swallowed a huge load of cum, yet a spectator would have sworn I hadn't gotten a drop; there was enough on my face and down my chest to have made up two normal loads.

In my naiveté, I assumed our session was completed. As I reached for my pants, he snapped, "What the fuck do you think you're doing?"

My eyes opened wide and I stammered, "I . . . aren't we finished?"

Looking down at his rigid monster, he asked sarcastically, "Does this look finished to you?"

It certainly didn't. He bent over, leaning against the outside partition of one of the stalls, and ordered, "Rim me."

Now wait a minute, I thought. But I only thought it. No use making the dude angry. I'd been rimmed by an older buddy once, but I'd never done it to anyone myself. To be on the receiving end was a hell of a turn-on. I wasn't so sure, though, how much of a turn-on it would be from the giver's point of view.

He was getting impatient, wiggling that hot ass in my face. "Come on, man, eat it out!"

Not wishing to risk bodily injury, I complied. My skinny fingers grabbed either side of his cheeks and spread them. I admit the sight of his asshole made my own dick point toward the ceiling. I'd have given anything to have fucked it, but I knew if I tried I'd be lying in several pieces on the floor. And I had a sneaking and very uncomfortable suspicion that before we were finished, it was *my* ass that was going to get fucked.

Deciding it was no time to be tentative, I dove right in. My tongue planted itself firmly on his hole, and he sighed ecstatically at the contact.

"Lick it, Baby!" he gasped. "Lick it all over!"

Well, at least I was "Baby" again.

My tongue was still wet from his cum, not to mention my own saliva, and I went to work on his beautiful asshole as if I'd been doing it all my life. I have to admit it wasn't at all unpleasant. The musky odor was more of a turn-on than the opposite, and I reached between his hard-muscled legs and began squeezing his magnificent balls. Then I clutched his cock and began stroking its incredible length.

"Just make a fist around it!" he ordered, and I did. He began to thrust his hips, so that he was, in effect, fucking my gripping hand. I was really turned on. His asshole was completely saturated with my spit, my now-eager tongue having rimmed him completely. On one of his back-thrusts, as my fist slid towards his cockhead, I felt the slipperiness of pre-cum.

Without warning, he snapped, "Bend over!"

Oh, shit. Here it comes.

I knew it was going to come and I dreaded it. But before it did, I got the surprise of my life as his giant hands spread my cheeks, and his own tongue dug savagely into my own asshole. I practically yelled, "ohhh, FUCK!" and he gave me the most beautiful, the most thorough, the most eager rimming of my life—and I've had several since then.

It lasted about ten minutes. Then his fingers replaced his tongue, and they began to penetrate and to stretch my hole. It hurt like hell; I have never experienced such pain from a finger-fuck before, but I knew he was preparing me for something much bigger, much thicker. He dug into me very roughly, and although I gasped and grunted I never cried out in any tone that could be interpreted as pain. He seemed impressed, for he said, "You're a tough little fucker, you know that?"

As the fingers of his left hand stretched me from behind, the fingers of his right grasped my dick and began to pump. I was pleasantly surprised again, for I didn't imagine him to be the kind who would play with cock—somebody else's, I mean. He had barely paid any attention to my dick before this, yet he commented, "Nice cock, Kid. About seven-and-a-half?"

He hit it right on the nose, and by so doing let me know that he had enough experience with other cocks to judge their length accurately.

His hand was rough on my rod, but I like it that way. Soon my own chest began the tell-tale heaving, and he recognized the sign. Roughly he spun me around, wrapped his lips around my dickhead, and I shot a hefty load into his mouth. I was in too much of a state of shock to comment as he turned me backside up again. He spread my cheeks and then spit my entire load of sperm against my asshole. He rubbed it in with his tongue, then stood and planted his rod firmly against my ass.

This time I couldn't control myself. I let out a scream of agony as his massive head penetrated. He stopped abruptly, and rubbed my sides as he said, "Easy, Kid; you can take it, Baby, you're a real tough fucker."

As the pain slowly subsided (comparatively), he inched more of it into me. I'm convinced I would have been ripped apart had he not prepared me with those savage fingers. As it was, it hurt like fucking hell, but I could take it. His hands caressed my buns as he pushed forward, and soon all of him was in me.

"Oh, Baby, what a fuckin' nice ass!" he hissed.

He ground his hips roughly, then began to pump. His thrusts were savage, and his stomach made a loud slap with the culmination of each forward slam. He fucked for about five minutes, then shot another load almost as violent as the first. I felt the first part of it; the last part I saw as he ripped himself out of my hole and let me watch as the jism splattered on my ass.

We both stood weak-kneed, exhausted. He reached down and tugged gingerly at my black cockhair, saying, "Baby, that was some kind of fuck. You got a fuckin' hot ass that just won't quit."

I smiled. "And you got a dick that won't quit, either."

I was amazed that it was still almost fully erect. "It's always at least half-hard," he told me. "I can't get enough."

As he pulled on his shorts, he said, "You work every night?"

My heart started beating rapidly. "Midnight to seven," I said.

"I'm headed for Denver," he told me, "but I'll be coming back in about a week." He paused. "I'll stop back in here. And I'm going to save it for you," he said, squeezing his crotch.

I smiled. "From what I've seen, that'll be awfully hard to do."

"Awfully *hard* is a good way to put it," he said with a smile, "but you can count on it. Keep that ass hot, okay?"

"It always is," I said, and he walked out the door. I stayed in the john, listening as his bike started up, and I heard him screech out of the station lot. It suddenly dawned on me that my blond Adonis hadn't paid for his gas. I laughed. Who the fuck cared? I'd have to pay for it, but a buck and a half was a small price to pay for the service he gave me.

And when he returned a week later, it was even better. . . .

The Gay Female Market

Just like their hetero brothers, the gay male books, magazines and videos are way ahead of the gay female's. In quantity, anyway. One distributor of lesbian material is Down There Press. Joani Blank, the publisher and president of the company, also owns a vibrator and sex-toy store called Good Vibrations in San Francisco, and owns and operates a mail-order business for sexy gadgets as well as for feminist, lesbian and heterosexual books. You can obtain her booklist and mail-order catalog by writing to Good Vibrations, 3942 22nd Street, San Francisco, CA 94110.

In addition to women's publications, Joani has gay male books and books for kids about sex. If you're having trouble locating *Pleasures, Male Sexuality, The G Spot* or any other sex titles, you can order them from Joani.

Joani Blank is always looking for writers for her erotica anthologies and wants to include heterosexual and lesbian stories in the same volume. Write to her at the above address when you have something.

New books on this market are often published by small presses like Down There and although you may get royalties on a book or payment on a story, you can't expect much. These books don't make a great deal of money because the market is so new and untried. Don't expect to get rich, just published. Ask for free copies of the finished product which you can use to impress future publishers of your work. When I found a publisher for *How to Write Erotica*, it didn't hurt at all to mention I had a story in *Pleasures: Women Write Erotica*. So even though I didn't make a monetary killing with that short story, it helped me up the ladder.

On Our Backs is the only true-blue, by and for lesbians magazine with a fair-sized circulation that publishes fiction. There are at least four other lesbian magazines, and numerous newsletters and lesbian lifestyle quarterlies, but these are less well known and harder to locate. These gay small press magazines have the same difficulty as hetero ones. Without national distributors, newsstand exposure and proper advertising, staying in business is a constant month-to-month challenge. You can buy a sample copy of this magazine by sending $4 (this includes postage) to: On Our Backs,

P.O. Box 421916, San Francisco, CA 94142. They use fiction, articles, poetry, cartoons, graphics and photography.

I've been writing lesbian stories for five years and I got an education from this magazine. The first thing I learned was just as gay men often refer to their effeminate mates as "she," lesbians sometimes call their butch girlfriends "he." And, although some lesbians are against penetration of any kind, others have what they call "cock fantasies." This latter type enjoy dildos and insertable vibrators and go for stories which include this fetish.

At the American Booksellers Convention, I met Susie Bright, a staff member of *On Our Backs*. She's a delightful young woman who is ecstatic over the way things are going for lesbians. Of course, she lives in San Francisco, which is the lesbian capital of the world. I doubt she'd feel as optomistic if she lived in Ashland, Oregon, or Quakertown, Pennsylvania.

Susie doesn't want to give specifications for your fiction and articles. She'll leave it up to you to make those editorial and artistic decisions. Just make it hot and double-space it, include a SASE and hope for the best. Some of the fiction is terrific, but some is still floundering. You should be able to get work here and at least get tear sheets.

Susie sent me "A Piece of Time," a story by Jewelle Gomez, as an example of good lesbian fiction. You'll see that it is erotic for straights as well. This story was first published in the Summer 1984 issue of *On Our Backs* and represents the erotic, loving point of view of a lesbian. Lesbians are also capable of getting into violence, S&M and dominant/passive sexual situations in their fiction. Therefore, don't accept this as the last word on lesbian fiction. This type of story is by no means the only acceptable way to write.

Some lesbian fiction is not really fiction at all, but a kind of personal revelation of what sex is like between the author and her partner. No story, no dramatic plot, no character development, just sex. Other fiction follows fantasy into reality in much the same way as the gay male piece does, shown earlier in this chapter.

Because there are no strict boundaries, you can follow your own daydreams and come up with something original and stimulating without worrying about where plot points have to occur or how to fill up ten pages. My guess is that a good story would have an excellent chance of being printed in this magazine.

A Piece of Time
BY JEWELLE GOMEZ

Ella kneeled down to reach behind the toilet. Her pink cotton skirt pulled tight around her brown thighs. Her skin already glistened with sweat from the morning sun and her labor. She moved quickly through the hotel rooms sanitizing tropical mildew and banishing sand.

Each morning our eyes met in the mirror just as she wiped down the tiles and I raised my arms in a last wake-up stretch. I always imagined that her gaze flickered over my body, enjoying my broad, brown shoulders or catching a glance of my plum brown nipples as the African cloth I wrapped myself in dropped away to the floor. For a moment I imagined the pristine hardness of the bathroom tiles against my back and her damp skin pressed against mine.

"OK, it's finished here." Ella said as she folded the cleaning rag and hung it under the sink. She turned around and as always seemed surprised that I was still watching her. Her eyes were light brown and didn't quite hide their smile; her hair was dark and pulled back, tied in a ribbon. It hung lightly on her neck the way that straightened hair does. My own hair was in short, tight braids that brushed my shoulders; a colored bead hung at the end of each braid. It was a trendy affectation I'd indulged in for my vacation. I smiled. She smiled back. On a trip filled with so much music, laughter and smiles, hers was the one that my eyes looked for each morning. She gathered the towels from the floor and in the same motion opened the hotel room door.

"Goodbye."

"See ya." I said, feeling about twelve years old instead of thirty.

She shut the door softly behind her and I listened to the clicking of her silver bangle bracelets as she walked around the verandah toward the stairs. My room was the last one on the second level facing the beach. Her bangles brushed the painted wood railing as she went through the tiny courtyard and into the front office.

I stepped into my bathing suit. I planned to swim for hours and lie in the sun reading and sipping margueritas until I could do nothing but sleep and maybe dream of Ella.

One day turned into another. Each was closer to my return to work and the city. I did not miss the city nor did I dread returning. But here it was as if time stood still. I could prolong any pleasure until I had my fill. The luxury of it was something from a childhood fantasy. The island was a tiny neighborhood gone to sea. The music of the language, the fresh smells and deep colors all enveloped me. I clung to the bosom of this place until everything else disappeared.

In the morning, too early for her to begin work in the rooms, Ella passed below in the courtyard carrying a bag of laundry. She deposited the bundle in a bin and then returned. I called down to her, my voice whispering in the cool, private morning air. She looked up and I raised my cup of tea in invitation. As she turned in from the beach end of the courtyard I prepared another cup. We stood together at the door, she more out than in. We talked about the fishing and the rainstorm of two days ago and how we'd each spent Christmas.

Soon she said, "I better be getting to my rooms."

"I'm going to swim this morning," I said.

"Then I'll be coming in now, alright? I'll do the linen," she said, and began to strip the bed.

I went into the bathroom and turned on the shower.

When I stepped out of the shower, the bed was fresh and the covers were molded firmly around the corners. The sand was swept from the floor tiles back outside and our tea cups were put away. I knelt to rinse the tub.

"No, I can do that. I'll do it, please."

She came toward me, a look of alarm on her face. I laughed. She reached for the cleaning rag in my hand as I bent over the suds, then she laughed too. As I kneeled on the edge of the tub, my towel came unwrapped and fell in. We both tried to retrieve it from the draining tub. My feet slid on the wet tile and I sat down on the floor with a thud.

"Are you hurt?" she asked, holding my towel in one hand, reaching out to me with the other. She looked into my eyes. Her hand was soft and firm on my shoulder as she knelt down. I watched the line of muscles in her forearm, then traced the soft inside with my hand. She exhaled slowly. I felt her warm breath as she bent closer to me. I pulled her down and pressed my mouth to hers. My tongue, pushing between her teeth, was as fierce as my hand on her skin was gentle.

Her arms encircled my shoulders. We lay back on the tile, her body atop mine. Then she removed her cotton T-shirt. Her brown breasts were nestled insistently against me. I raised my leg between hers. The moistness that matted the hair there dampened my leg. Her body moved in a brisk and demanding rhythm.

I wondered quickly if the door was locked. Then I was sure it was. I heard Ella call my name for the first time. I stopped her mouth with my lips. Her hips were searching, pushing toward their goal. Ella's mouth on mine was sweet and full with hungers of its own. Her right hand held the back of my neck and her left found its way between my thighs, brushing the hair and flesh softly at first, then playing over the outer edges. She found my clit and began moving back and forth. I gasped and opened my legs wider. Her middle finger slipped past the soft outer lips and entered me so gently that at first I didn't feel it. Then she pushed inside and I felt the dams burst. I opened my mouth and tried to swallow my scream of pleasure. Ella's tongue filled me and sucked up my joy. We lay still for a moment, our breathing and the seagulls the only sounds. Then she pulled herself up.

"Miss . . . ," she started.

I cut her off again, this time my fingers to her lips. "I think it's OK if you stop calling me Miss."

"Carolyn," she said softly, then covered my mouth with hers again. We kissed for moments that wrapped around us, making time have no meaning. Then she rose.

"It gets late, you know," she said with a giggle. Then she

pulled away, her determination not yielding to my need. "I have work to do."

"I know," I said. "Will you come back later, today or tonight?"

"Not tonight. I see my boyfriend on Wednesdays. I better go. I'll see you later."

And she was out the door. I lay still on the tile floor and listened to her bangles as she ran down the stairs. Later, on the beach, my skin still tingled and the sun pushed my temperature higher. I stretched out on a deck chair with my eyes closed. I felt her mouth, her hands and the sun on me and I came again.

Ella arrived each morning. I only had five left. She tapped lightly, then entered. I looked up from the small table where I'd prepared tea. She sat and we sipped slowly, then slipped into bed. We made love, sometimes gently, other times with a roughness resembling the waves that crashed against the sea wall below.

We talked of her boyfriend, who was married and saw her only once or twice a week. She worked two jobs, saving money to buy land, maybe on this island or her home island. We were the same age and although I seemed to already have the material things she wanted, it was me who felt rootless and undirected.

We talked of our families, hers so dependent on her help, mine so estranged from me; of growing up, the path that led us to the same but different place. She loved this island. I did too. She could stay. I could not.

On the third night of the five, I said, "You could visit me, come to the city for a vacation or—"

"And what I'm goin' to do there?"

I was angry but not sure at whom: at her for refusing to drop everything and take a chance; at myself for not accepting the ocean that existed between us or just at the blindness of the circumstance.

I felt narrow and self-indulgent in my desire for her. I was an ugly, black American, everything I'd always despised. Yet I wanted her; somehow, somewhere, it was right that we should be together.

On my last night, after packing, I sat up with a bottle of wine listening to the waves beneath my window and the tourist voices from the courtyard. Ella tapped at my door as I was thinking of going to bed. When I opened it she came inside quickly and thrust an envelope and a small gift-wrapped box into my hand.

"Can't stay, you know. He waiting down there. I'll be back in the morning." Then she ran out and down the stairs before I could respond.

Early in the morning she entered with her key. I was awake, but lying still. She was out of her clothes and beside me in a second. Our lovemaking began abruptly but built slowly. We touched each other's bodies, imprinting memories on our fingertips.

"I don't want to leave you." I whispered.

"You not leaving me. My heart go with you, just I must stay here."

"Maybe you'll write to me," I ventured. "Maybe you'll come back too."

"Don't make promises now, girl. We make love."

Her hands on me and inside of me pushed the city away. My mouth eagerly drew in the flavors of her body. Under my touch she made the sounds of ocean waves, rhythmic and wild. We slept for only a few moments before it was time for her to dress and go on with her chores.

"I'll come back to ride with you to the airport?" she said with a small question mark at the end.

"Yes," I said, pleased.

In the airport she talked lightly as we sat: stories of her mother and sisters; questions about mine. We never mentioned the city or tomorrow morning.

When she kissed my cheek she whispered, "sister-love" in my ear, so softly I wasn't sure I'd heard it until I looked into her eyes. I held her close for only a minute, wanting more, knowing this would have to be enough for the moment. I boarded the plane and time began to move again.

PART TWO

HOW TO WRITE PRINT EROTICA

CHAPTER 4

THE BASIC FORMULA

Above and beyond the normal story breakdown—introduction, jeopardy, climax, resolution—the erotic story has a basic pattern which, loosely followed, will provide the reader with the stimulation he or she seeks from reading it. (That's about as clean as I can put this.)

Plot

Depending upon which publication you are aiming your story for, a secondary plot line will either dominate the sexual action or be permitted to weave in and out of the action. Take for example, "Parisian Lay-over" (below). The heroine, Julie, is an executive, traveling in Paris, but that is not essential to the sexual plot of the story. The key element is her current dilemma, that this excursion has put her into the position of being stranded without a sex partner. Her jeopardy is that she's moral but horny.

Most erotic stories are about a character who wants to have sex. The harder it is for the protagonist to get laid, the more tension is created. In Julie's case, she needs only to let her guard down a little and not be afraid to get to know a stranger.

Then she is presented with the language barrier, which is easily avoided through speaking the language of love. Her next feat is to get past the hotel authorities with her gigolo. Once she gets the young man into her hotel room, this part of the drama is over with. Here the sexual drama takes over. The reader has been sufficiently teased with the foreplay in the downstairs bar. Now he is ready for some details.

Parisian Lay-over
BY DARIEN LYNX

"If I don't get laid pretty soon, I'm going to cum in my pants," I said. We were walking down the Champs-Elysées, struggling with some packages. Our work in Paris was just about finished and Peggy, my secretary, and I had gone on a shopping spree to celebrate our last day in the romantic city.

"You're just too particular," she said. "Just because you're bright and beautiful, you insist that all your lovers be the same. Some of the best fucks look like common, ordinary men with their clothes on."

Peggy was always so logical, but she didn't understand. She couldn't afford to be particular, she was always horny. Since we landed here ten days ago, she'd had sex at least seven times, twice with other women. Why she did that, I'll never comprehend. What can you do with a woman?

"Why do you make it with chicks anyway?" I asked her.

"Don't knock it, Julie, till you've tried it." Peggy whistled for a cab and we climbed in.

"Hilton, please," I told the cabbie.

"Why don't you use your French?" asked Peggy.

"Quit trying to reform me," I snapped. I was instantly sorry. "I'm sorry, Peggy. It's just that I'm so horny . . . I'm a nervous wreck."

"So what else is new? Why don't you do something about it instead of biting your friends' heads off?"

"What am I supposed to do, flag down the first good-looking guy I see and rape him?" I was thinking it was too bad there weren't any whorehouses for women. Then I could buy what I wanted. I sat back in the cab and let out a long sigh. Being the European Rep for anamorphic lenses was not as romantic and adventurous as I had thought it would be when I applied for the job. It's just a lot of country-hopping, skipped meals, and jet lag. I was totally exhausted.

"Yes," said Peggy.

She pulled me out of my daydream. "What?"

"I said, yes, pick up the first dude you see and take him to our room. What have you got to lose?"

I laughed. "Oh, sure."

"Hey," she said suddenly, "let me off at the café over here, I want to try my luck."

The taxi pulled over. "Peggy, you're incorrigible!"

"Come on, mom, it's my last day to make it with a Frenchman." Peggy piled her share of the packages into my lap and climbed out of the cab. I continued on to our hotel. At least I would have a few hours of privacy before she got back; maybe an evening too if her quarry had his own apartment.

I decided I would sleep through my last day in Paris.

As I pulled all my bundles together to get out of the cab, I found myself almost in tears. I don't know what it was exactly, the loneliness, frustration maybe, but suddenly I couldn't face going up to my room alone and wasting this last precious day. I knew I would regret it when I got back to the states.

At the front desk, I sent the shopping bags up to my room. Taking a deep breath and reassuring myself with a pass at the lobby mirror, I headed for the bar. A scotch would cool my nerves, and perhaps provide the fortitude necessary to pick up a guy, or the drug to put me to sleep.

My eyes had trouble adjusting to the dim light. As I felt my way toward the bar, I almost sat in a man's lap. I apologized profusely, but he just grinned. Remembering Peggy's advice, I tried to look pleasingly attracted, but the more my eyes adjusted, the more ugly this poor stranger became, until I was embarrassed to have looked at him at all.

I took my scotch to a booth and tried to discourage his advances with my nonchalance. I assumed my "waiting for somebody" pose and glanced casually toward the entrance.

There in the doorway, silhouetted against the bright light of the lobby, stood a tall, shapely, young man. I could see him very clearly, but he couldn't see me in the dark. I could see that he had curly black hair, broad shoulders, youthful narrow hips and a bulge between his skinny legs. His bare arms and skimpy shirt accented the fine muscular structure. I was beginning to wonder just how young he was. Was I becoming a lecherous old woman at thirty-one?

My heart began to pound and I could feel my pussy lips swelling. One would think I were in a sexual embrace, the way I was getting so hot, so fast.

I couldn't take my eyes off him. When his eyes focused, he fixed them on me.

He began walking straight toward me and I knew I should look away, but I couldn't. The closer he came, the more details I could make out in his face. Fine cheek and jaw line, baby-soft skin, huge brown/black eyes with long lashes. When he smiled, he showed perfect white teeth.

He was leaning over my table, telling me something in French.

"I-I-I'm sorry," I stuttered. "I don't speak French . . . very well." The truth was that I'd forgotten all my French the moment he stepped into the bar.

"Ah," he said, in a deep but boyish voice. *"Americaine."*

"Yes," I smiled agreeably. Thank God he spoke English.

"I sorry, *mademoiselle,*" he said as he slid into my booth. "I speak no English." Then he pointed to himself and said: "René."

I told him my name was Julie.

"Ah, Julie," he exclaimed, as if he'd fallen in love with my name. "Julie," he repeated, and then he put his hand on mine, which was at present trembling on the wet glass of scotch. He stroked my hand, then my arm, smiled, and said something very soft and very sexy, in French.

I looked into his eyes and they were becoming even blacker. I meant to take a deep breath to clear the tension from my lungs, but it ended up as a quivering sigh.

He kissed my hand; I didn't pull away. His other hand was under the table, now stroking my thigh. He had found the slit in my skirt. His hand went higher each trip up my leg. I hoped that he wouldn't climb all the way to my panties and find that they were soaked through.

Then I wished that he would. My pussy was opening and closing on its own, reaching for something to pet it, enter it.

And then he did. He found the wet panties and he shoved

them aside with one finger and entered my cunt with another. It felt so wonderful I wanted to lie down on the bar room floor and let him fuck me right there.

René started murmuring in French again. Whatever he was saying, he seemed to be expressing a certain delight with his find under my skirt. He seemed to be swearing with a smile.

He kissed my neck. The kiss sent heat waves up my throat to my ears. My forehead even began to perspire. I was shuddering now with passion and desire and I wanted René so badly, I probably could have come without him.

He pulled his hand out of my crotch and licked his fingers. The sweet smell of pussy filled our booth. Then he slid his hand into my blouse and held my bare breast. The nipple was erect long before he got there.

He began to swear again, in a sweet affectionate manner, his lips pursed the way only the French can do. Sometimes his teeth were clenched and his eyelids lowered. He took my hand, which was wet and freezing from the tight hold it had on my scotch glass, and placed it over the crotch of his pants.

I thought I would faint with desire. I felt the huge erection through his cotton jeans and I could feel my own, throbbing and hot.

To hell with propriety, I wanted the guy. I wanted to fuck the hell out of him. I wanted to suck that gorgeous prick until it exploded in my mouth. I hadn't so much as seen a man's penis in weeks. Just to look at it would have been a pure pleasure, but to suck it, ah, that would be heaven.

I paid my bill and turned back to René. I smiled and made a universal gesture with my finger. "Come here," I said. "Follow me."

He did. As I crossed the lobby, I couldn't keep a smirk from crossing my lips. I was about to get laid.

Several of the hotel officials watched me cross. It isn't done in European hotels. They don't like women taking men to their rooms. But from the look on my face, they knew it would've been hopeless to try and stop me. I needed this fuck too badly now.

René was a little less sure of himself. He sort of crouched as he walked. But maybe that was in an effort to hide his obvious hard-on.

In the elevator, I gave him a huge, wet kiss, and he gave it back. Only the French know how to french-kiss. His tongue was as big as some guy's cocks, and he breathed into my lungs and took my breath away.

I let us into my room and René looked around a bit. He was interested in everything, as if he'd never been inside a hotel suite before. I let him play with the electronic drapes, turn the TV off and on and pretend to dial on the telephone, while I disrobed.

When he saw that I was undressing, he came to help, kissing each bit of exposed flesh as it emerged from the silk and wool of my outfit.

René kissed my neck, my shoulders, under my arms, my breasts, and then sucked a little on the nipples. He pulled my blouse down, kissing my chest as he went, then fell to his knees to unbuckle my belt.

All this time, he was speaking to me softly in French. I think anything a Frenchman could say would sound sexy. I love the way they move their lips around the words.

As he opened my skirt and slid it off my hips, he kissed each indentation and protrusion. The skirt slipped over the mound of hair at my pussy and René grinned, uttering some more of those foreign words. My pussy hairs are blonde and very soft and there are very few of them. The mound which they decorate is round and fleshy. René seemed to like what he saw. He nibbled on the soft short hairs and licked the insides of my thighs until I could no longer stand upright.

I thought I would collapse on the floor in a heap, but René caught me and moved me to the bed. There he finished undressing me and kneeled at the edge of the bed and ate me until I climaxed three times. I started coming as soon as he put his mouth on me and each orgasm was more powerful than the last.

Suddenly, he stood up and tore off his shirt, actually popping the buttons. (Americans could learn something from these romantic Frenchmen.) His chest was hairless and tanned. His nipples were large and pouting, they needed suckling.

He unzipped his pants and stepped out of them. His cock

sprang out of his shorts like a rebel, too large for its designated space.

He was about to continue sucking my pussy when we heard the door open. He looked at me in alarm but I assured him it was all right. It was Peggy, home early, but I could get rid of her, or so I thought.

When Peggy came into the bedroom and got an eyeful of my naked body, which she'd never seen in all the years we'd worked together, and this big, beautiful hunk standing above me with his cock bobbing about in front of him like a stray puppy, it was too much for her.

She sank into the bedroom chair. "Oh, my God."

I was shy about this. "Could you...um...wait in the living room, or maybe the lobby?" I asked feebly.

"Are you kidding?" she exclaimed, and began to take off her own clothes.

René smiled. He shook his head and scratched it, looking at me and then at Peggy. He laughed. "*Vous Americaines! Oooo la la!*"

It was a little unsettling, this whole scene. But just a little, since I was so aroused at that point, I was up for almost anything.

Peggy pulled off her clothes almost as fast as René had. She had beautiful, huge round breasts that stuck straight out like a teenager's. As they fell out of her bra, I found myself wanting to put my hands around them. When she sat on the bed, I did just that.

I sucked on one and Peggy got turned on right away. I had always wondered what a nipple tasted like, felt like, in your mouth. It was small, smooth and soft when I started, but then grew hard and bumpy. I was getting aroused again and René knew it. He pushed his still erect cock into my vagina in one smooth motion. I was so wet, it was no effort, but because it had been so long since I'd fucked a guy as big as René, it was also tight.

As he fucked me, he put his fingers into Peggy's cunt and I continued sucking on her massive breasts. But then she pulled away from both of us and began kissing us down where the fucking was going on. She licked my clit and his penis at the same time. René was moaning. He had his eyes closed.

I felt another orgasm coming and I clamped down on both of them with a groan. As I began to climax, Peggy took my clit into her mouth and René rammed his prick in as far up me as it would go. This prolonged my orgasm so long, I thought I would die right then and there.

But Peggy wasn't finished with me. She pushed René's still bulging cock out of the way and began to eat me, even better than he had. Then she put her hands on my boobs, fingering the nipples. René was not at a loss for what to do next, he merely inserted himself into Peggy's behind. She couldn't see what he was doing but I could. He would slip it into her cunt and thrust five or six times, then slide it into her asshole once or twice. Peggy was having convulsions on my clit and I was coming yet another time.*

René reached under Peggy and grabbed her huge dangling tits. She moaned. The vibration of her voice against my pussy made me want to come again. I'd lost count by now.

I think Peggy and I both wanted that gorgeous cock to come inside of us, but René had other ideas. I guess he couldn't figure out how to split his prize two ways. He pushed Peggy onto the bed beside me, but she didn't let go of my tit. We were lying side by side on the bed. René crawled up between our legs, putting one knee in my crotch and one in Peggy's. His body rose above us, the huge cock bobbing up and down, dripping the milky forerunners of his cum.

He grabbed hold of his cock at the base and the rest of his giant prick seemed to swell and turn blue from pressure. I think he might have been trying to stop from coming too soon, but the expression on his face told us both that it wouldn't be long now, no matter what he did about it.

I doubled up and reached for him with my mouth. I sucked on the head of his prick and licked the tip of it inside my hot mouth. Then Peggy did the same thing. We took turns. Our

*See page 188.

cunts were still pressed against his knees and Peggy seemed to get an orgasm just from that.

She shouted, "Oh, my Lord!" and fell back onto the bed in a tremor of ecstasy. She grabbed her pussy and held onto it as she thrashed around on the bed. I shoved my fingers in underneath hers and inside her cunt to keep her going as long as possible. It's very exciting to watch another girl come. Sucking René's cock and fingering Peggy was driving me wild.

René pushed my head off his cock and I rolled back to see what he was up to. He was about to come. I nudged Peggy to open her eyes so she wouldn't miss the best part.

René was frowning or wincing. Anyhow, he had this pained expression on his face. His purple cock was bulging out of his hand like a separate animal. Then it happened.

Like a volcano spitting hot lava, René's cock exploded white cum. It shot out from him all the way to the headboard, but some of the drops landed on Peggy and me and we smoothed it over our bodies. René kept coming and coming, as if he couldn't control himself. It was raining cum.

We kept René in our room all night long and were dead tired on our way to the airport the next morning. In town, we dropped him off and gave him 80 francs. That wasn't much in American currency, but from the look on his face, it meant a good deal to him.

He kissed us each goodbye and gave us some advice in French, which we're trying to remember until we can get someone to translate it.

"Do you think this is close to what men feel when they've laid a whore?" asked Peggy.

"God, if it is, maybe we should go into the male whorehouse business."

She laughed at that and then retreated into her own thoughts for the rest of the drive. Maybe she was thinking what I was thinking. If all the studs in our whorehouse were like René, it could be a woman's paradise.

In female-oriented erotica, many of the details are sensual. Descriptions are heavily laden with adjectives designed to evoke tastes and smells as well as simple action and character. Male readers tend to hurry toward the finish line. In male-oriented erotica, more action verbs are supplied with brief hints about the physical attributes of the characters. These distinctions apply to the market, not the author. Anyone can write either. When one is writing to a male audience only, the work tends to be hardcore. Female-oriented erotica is not for females only, but for anyone who appreciates a softer touch, a more seductive approach and fewer graphic details. Some writers call hardcore sex stories pornography and softer stories, erotica, but with the current blurring of terminology, and the requirement that the reader must make this purely subjective determination, we shall use male- and female-oriented. We shall discuss more about the differences between the two throughout this book.

Character

Your characters should be introduced to the reader as briefly as possible. The female need not always be voluptuous, with 42-D breasts and golden hair, nor must the male always be a macho super-stud. In fact, it is often better if you give the reader a person with whom he or she can more easily identify, such as in the classic story of the shy, studious type who is seduced by an aggressive female. "Car Wash Cookie," at the end of this section, exemplifies this recurring theme.

Almost anyone can identify with being sexually frustrated. When your body aches for physical contact and it is unavailable to you, you become distracted, irritable and maybe even lonely. In "Parisian Lay-over," Julie let us see her vulnerability by admitting to this need. Then she expresses her moral character by explaining why she can't do what her friend and co-worker is able to do in order to satisfy this need. By the time the handsome young man appears in the doorway of the bar, we are on her side and we want her to get what she needs. This situation is all you require to hook your reader. Nobody has to have a gun in his hand, nobody has to get hurt.

Once you've established your main character and his or her dilemma, you can move into the tension of how the sex is going to happen. You may include as many variations of the sex act as you have room for, or if you are writing for a fetish magazine you may concentrate on that area. "Parisian Lay-over" was printed in a magazine called *AC/DC,* and that's the main reason her secretary had to get in on the act. *AC/DC* is for the threesome fetishist.

Serena: Car Wash Cookie

I work at a car wash. I used to be a secretary but I hated working with all those frumpy women. Gray ladies, I called them, because they always wore dreary colors and had gray hair and looked forward to their lousy 45-minute lunch hour and crummy two-week vacation as if it really made it worth it to waste your life away in a windowless, air-conditioned insurance office.

They made up for their boredom with gossip, and their favorite subject was me because I was the only single girl there. Finally, one of them got me fired. She told my boss that I'd been dating one of the salesmen. Which was true, but that's beside the point.

My boss had been after my ass since I took that job, so he was not only teed off, he was jealous as hell.

So he fired me. And this time, when I went to the unemployment office, I said forget it to those girly jobs. I want a man's job. Men know how to treat a girl.

Well, the only thing they had was this car wash job. It wasn't exactly what I'd had in mind, but as soon as I started working there, I knew it was perfect for me.

First of all, I work only with men. My boss is a man, the counter person is a guy, and all the other grease monkeys and car washers are guys. Really neat guys too. We even have our token intellectual.

We kid around a lot, play water games, tell dirty jokes. It's a helluva lot more fun than working in a stupid office with a bunch of prim prissies.

One of the things I've learned to do is wear nothing at all under my overalls. They give you these blue overalls, see, with a zipper in front. It really feels sexy to go naked underneath. It's like keeping a secret.

Sometimes, just to remind the guys that I'm not really one

of them, I'll zip the front down real fast and flash them my tits.

It drives them wild.

One of the guys, Gene, is not really a professional car washer, not that any of us are, but at night he goes to medical school.

You can tell Gene's got a little more class than the rest of us, and not only because he wears glasses. I think it's kind of neat the way he's working his way through college and all. He says he likes this work because it's "mindless." He can think about his studies while he's scrubbing down the cars. I had a real case for Gene for a long time.

Then one day he seemed really down. So during our break, I sat down to talk to him. He said he'd been up all night studying for a chemistry exam and then flunked it anyway.

He took off his glasses and rubbed his eyes and said, "What I need is a good lay." That really got to me, but then he apologized "I'm sorry," he said, "I shouldn't be talking like that."

I leaned over so that my low-cut uniform exposed part of my breasts. I don't know why I did that. Maybe it was a present for him. Maybe I wanted to turn him on. Or maybe I just didn't know what I was doing.

But anyway, he noticed and his eyes got real big as he looked down my shirt. Then he looked up at me as if to apologize again, but I stopped him.

"Are you doing anything after work today?" I asked.

"No, exams are over."

"Want to stop by my place?" I couldn't believe how brazen I was, picking up a guy at work.

Anyway, Gene drove me home. We came up to my place and I couldn't wait to get into his pants. I don't know what came over me. I'm usually quite shy about sex, especially the first time with a new guy. But I just went crazy.

All the way home, I'd been thinking about it. The harsh, starched uniform was scratching my erect nipples and the crotch was riding up my wet cunt.

At my place, I was careful to roll up my uniform when I took it off, so that he wouldn't notice how wet it was. I would have been so embarrassed.

So there I was, naked as a jaybird, and there he was, still dressed. But I could tell he was aroused by the lump in his pants.

He said, "I . . . don't usually do this sort of thing. I mean, I haven't been with a girl . . . in a long time." Then he laughed nervously.

Suddenly I felt even more naked and insecure. I sat down and made an effort to cover myself with my hands.

"I'm sorry," said Gene. "I've just been studying awfully hard and I haven't even thought about sex for such a long time."

"You have done it before?" I asked, now really ashamed of my forwardness.

"Sure," he said, a little too quickly. Then there was a long silence. "Actually," he began, "I haven't."

Holy crickets! I'd picked up a virgin. "How old are you?" (Please don't let him be a minor.)

"I'm twenty-two." Gene didn't look at me when he said this. He looked down at his hands. "I was in the army for a while. All there were in Nam were whores and other guys' girls. Then when I got back, I started college and got all caught up in my studies. When other guys talked about going out and getting laid, I just closed them out. I put all my energy into my work."

I reached over to my closet door to get a robe.

"No, please don't," he said, "I really like looking at you. You're very beautiful."

I liked that. It made me feel more at ease. It made me want Gene even more.

"So what do you want to do?" I asked him.

"Well, if you wouldn't mind, I mean, if you wouldn't think it would be a downer to have a virgin, I'd like to . . . you know . . ."

"You'd like to fuck?"

"Yes," he said, his face a little pink. "I would like that very much."

My first virgin.

He was sitting on the edge of my bed. I live in a single apartment and everything's in the same room.

I walked over to him and stood between his legs, very aware of that fact that I was naked and he was fully clothed. Somehow, it made the experience more sensuous.

My breasts were just above the top of his head and I smeared them into his hair. Hesitantly, he put his hands on my waist, then wrapped them tightly around my body.

He looked up at me and smiled. I lowered my heavy breasts so that they surrounded his face. Instinctively, he took one into his mouth.

He licked it, probed the tip of my nipple with his tongue and then began to suck it ever so gently.

That was nice for a while but then I grew restless. I wanted it harder, faster. So I pressed my tit closer into his face. He had to suck or smother, so he sucked. God, he sucked me so good!

Then I guided his hands over my body. I ran them up and down my sides hard, so that my skin turned red from the friction.

My pussy was getting so wet, but I waited on that. When it became unbearable I could think of several places I'd want to rub it against.

Then I took his hands and placed them on my huge tits, now hard from excitement. They overflowed his small hands. I pushed his palms around so that my boobs would be rolled and mashed.

By now, Gene was breathing hard and his cock had made a little stain on his overalls. But I wasn't ready yet. I wanted to put it off just a little longer.

I backed up from him slightly. He was looking up at my face for direction. I took his head in my hands and pointed his eyes toward my cunt. He'd wanted to look at me there all along, but he seemed to have felt shy about it. I could tell. But with my permission, my guidance, he looked to his heart's content. His breathing increased to almost panting and he pushed his face into my muff. It was the first action he'd instigated on his own and I was surprised, but elated that he'd begun to act like a man.

I spread my pussy lips so that he could see what I was all

about. He pulled back to get a good look. Then he used his fingers to explore further.

"This is where it's the most sensitive," I said, pulling back my foreskin and exposing my clit. "See this little nub? It's my clit. My starter. The center of my orgasm."

He put his gruff finger on it and I jumped.

"Wait a minute!" I could see I'd jumped too fast as he was already forming an apology, so I explained. "It's very sensitive there. You have to be gentle at first, then you can get rough."

"How?" he asked.

Here was my chance. With other guys, you have to take what they gave. I could instruct Gene from scratch on how to pleasure me.

"Lick it," I said. I felt like an amazon bitch as I towered above this novice instructing him on my desires.

His first lick nearly sent me through the roof. After all that fooling around, I was really turned on, and my clit was extremely sensitive to his touch.

He seemed to get off on my cum, because he wasn't just licking now. It looked more like gobbling. He licked all the crevices and sucked on my pussy lips and drew my clit into his mouth as if it were a two-inch penis.

I could have done that all night, but then I remembered that beautiful gift wetting his pants with sex juice.

I backed up and unzipped his overalls. God, he had a great chest, the chest of an intellectual, smooth and almost hairless.

His nipples were erect so I kissed them as I pulled the top of his uniform down. He had to stand up so that I could pull it down the rest of the way, and when he stood, I could see that our making-out had had an effect on him as well. His cock made a tent out of his boxer shorts. The wet cotton laid on the tip of his prick and showed every detail of the little hole at the end of it.

I couldn't move fast enough now. I ripped those overalls off his legs, almost knocking him over. The shoes came off inside the pants and the socks I just left on.

I laid him back onto the bed, and God, I wanted that cock so bad, anywhere, whatever opening was closest.

I pulled his cock out through the opening in his boxers and sat on him. His prick was a steel-hard rod and it touched the very top of me when I came down on it. I could feel every edge of it.

But before I even got used to that position, his hot juices shot through me. He came so hard and so much, he was yelling from the pain of it. I thought it would never stop. I could actually feel the hot liquid shooting into me, again and again. He kept writhing about, holding me onto his pelvis by my hips, yelling, "Oh, ooooh, oh, my God . . . "

After about two minutes, it was over. I got off of him and his cum flooded out of my cunt. There was so much of it, it was all over my legs, the bedspread, his legs. And his shorts were soaked through.

Still, I couldn't help but be a little disappointed. It all happened so fast!

"When was the last time you jacked off?" I asked.

He caught his breath before he answered. "Uh . . . junior high school, I think."

"You're kidding!"

He was still breathing hard. As I looked down his long, slender body, I noticed that his cock was still hard. It stood straight up, saluting the sauce that drenched it.

"I didn't want to masturbate," Gene said, "because I thought it would make me need it more."

I couldn't take my eyes off his cock. It was red and swollen and showed no signs of wilting.

"Masturbation is fun," I offered.

Gene laughed, "I don't know if I would remember how."

It was my turn to laugh. "It's like riding a bike, you never forget." I would be glad to give him lessons. I touched his prick lightly. He jumped.

"I'm sorry, does it hurt?"

"No," he said. "It's just . . . like your clit . . . sensitive."

I touched it again, stroked it, smoothed the cum around the shaft of it. Gene groaned softly, so I guessed it was OK to continue.

It looked so delicious with cum all over it like that. So I took a lick and then I sucked on him for a while. I still hadn't climaxed, he'd been too fast on the draw, but I was willing to forego that for future pleasures. But that beautiful prick, standing so tall, looking so spiffy dressed in shiny white cum. I wanted to fuck it.

Gene looked up at me as I sucked his cock. "Do you think we could do that again?" he asked. "It was so short. I can't remember what it felt like."

"At your service," I said, teasing. And I placed myself on top of him again. But he rolled me over onto my back. We were so close to the edge of the bed that I couldn't put my legs down, I had to brace them against the wall.

He lifted my hips from the bed and pulled them toward his cock. I pushed on the wall to back up from his firm grasp, and then let him pull me onto him again. He went inside me so deep, the walls of my cunt were grabbing for him hungrily.

I was beginning to get hot again. I felt it first in my cunt, which was sucking wildly, more than I had with my mouth. Flames seemed to shoot up through the inside of my body. My nipples became erect and my breasts grew hard and big. They get bigger when I'm excited, I don't know why. Then I could feel my neck flush and my ears turn red. God, I wanted to scream it felt so damned good.

I could have come right away, as he had, but something told me it would be even better if I could hold it just a little longer.

"You look so beautiful," said Gene, as he plunged into my cunt. "You look so fuckin' sexy. Your face is red, your tits are reaching up to me . . . " He bent down to suck on one, but he didn't stop the motion with his hips. He was fucking me and sucking me at once. I couldn't hold back any longer. I had to come.

My legs began to tremble and an involuntary action caused them to close in around Gene's hips. He couldn't move as well but it didn't matter, because the insides of my cunt were doing plenty of moving on their own. They began to palpitate, throb, slam together and suck the hell out of Gene's cock. It was as if they had a life of their own, grabbing and pulling on his prick, sucking all of his juices out. It just kept coming and coming, as if we were being welded together with cum for solder.

I came so long and so hard, I got dizzy, almost faint.

Finally, it began to subside. My legs offered one final shudder and split apart. My pussy released Gene's prick with a bubble of air, and I was so relaxed I could have fallen asleep. Gene laid down beside me, stroking my breasts gently.

"That was wonderful," I said. "God, you were terrific. I don't have to teach you anything."

He kissed me softly. "Aw, but I was so looking forward to the lessons."

I laughed.

"It was much more fun than chemistry. Couldn't we do it again please?"

"I hope that's a joke," I answered, but one look at his rising cock showed me it wasn't. "Give me ten minutes, OK, Hot Stuff?"

He said OK.

The Setting

The elements of scenery you will require are minimal. The only thing that is really important here is that you never lose your reader. The reader mustn't have to wonder if your characters are still on the bed or have moved to the veranda. Information comes first. Descriptive prose can be worked into the sexual act:

When John turned on the bedroom lamp, Melissa was standing by the window next to the bed, her slim body silhouetted by the moonlight. As she turned, he saw the outline of her full breasts and he ached to touch her. Slowly he crossed the room. When he reached her, he felt heat emanating from her body and she was breathing hard. He took her by the shoulders, turned her around, and laid her gently down onto the bed. She watched his hands as he unfastened his belt and lowered his pants. Even in the half-lit room, he could see that her red, pouting lips were trembling.

We've moved the characters from their original positions with-out dropping the ball sexually. There is no break in the arousal to provide an explanation of who is sitting where. Notice also that this entire paragraph talks about sex without actually using any graphic, four-letter words. This copy is the kind you might write for the outside of a videotape box or for a softcore fiction piece.

The Climax

As you build to a climax, you will not increase the speed of your action. On the contrary, you will slow way down. Your prose will become heavy with descriptive adjectives, designed to inspire your reader with strong, visual images to help his imagination along.

In real life, the best part of the sex act, the orgasm, is all too short. In erotica, this part of the scene is stretched out to last as long as possible. Magazine layouts do this with pictures. You'll find pages of "come shots" and only a few frames of introduction, or maybe none at all. On videotapes, come shots are prolonged with multiple angles, repeated sequences, slow-motion and with other devices viewers never see on the screen, such as white cream rinse used as a substitute for ejaculate. In your written fiction, however, you're going to have to prolong orgasm with words. I'll show you how after a brief note on point of view.

Point of View

If you are working from one character's point of view, which is often the easiest and best way to describe a scene, you can write about what this character sees, thinks and feels, but you cannot move into the minds of other characters at all. Say, for example, a couple in a story is in the park, lying naked on the grass. (This park is very isolated.)

They've been making out now for about five pages. John has already gone down on Mary and Mary is now lying between John's legs with his organ in her hand. We are working up to that elongated climax I told you about. During the last phases of an erotic piece, you will use those so-called "dirty" words. It is the only way to do it. Calling body parts by their biological names will sound like an anatomy lesson. One does not open her labia and insert his penis. One opens her pussy and inserts his cock. Get it? These handy nouns combined with a sprinkling of similarly sensual adjectives ought to get your reader on his way. (See the list of sensual words beginning on page 282 or the Glossary at the end of the book for help.)

OK, back to John and Mary. It's Mary's story, told from her point of view:

I looked at the stiff rod in my hand and thought about how long I'd wanted this man, and how I'd dreamed of this moment. Never in my fantasies did I imagine he would be built so perfectly for me, that he would be so easily aroused by my touch, so responsive to my love. Here in my hand was the proof of his desire for me. I didn't know whether to suck it or fuck it.

I placed my lips over the tip of his cock and ran my tongue down into his hole, as far as it would go. He tasted salty and sweet. Then I licked him from the top of his knob to the bottom of his cock. My hand cupped his balls, grown hot from the summer sun. He was beautiful. He had this fantastic hard-on and it was all for me.

But everything felt so tight. I knew he was very close to coming, and still I couldn't let go of him. I knew then I wanted to watch him come.

I wanted to watch him explode. I wanted to see his white cum spurt up into the air and know that I was the cause of it, that I had loved him so well, he couldn't hold back any longer. And yet, I wanted to keep it too. I wanted it inside of me like a gift, a treasure. So I got up from my place between his legs and I sat on top of his cock.

Slowly I came down onto it. It felt stiff and unbending inside my cunt. I was so hot inside and so wet. He slid into my pussy with no trouble and then my pussy muscles closed in around him as if to squeeze out his juices.

John moaned. "I can't stop it," he told me, "I have to—" And then it happened. I held very still so I could feel it happen. His cum squirted up to the top of me and its wet warmth filled my insides. He pushed my hips down in order to move his body deeper into mine and my clit rubbed his belly so that I was beginning to come too. I didn't want to come yet.

I wanted to concentrate on feeling him. But the sensations were soon overwhelming and everything felt so incredibly good, I lost control. When I began to feel my orgasm, my cunt muscles tightened around his cock so strongly that John grunted. By now I was beyond wanting to listen to him. I was all cunt. I wanted to give in to this magical, wonderful sensuality.

My legs began to tremble. An involuntary movement of my pelvis loosened the suction and John's warm juices flooded out of my cunt like hot lava. And that brought me over. "I'm coming," I screamed. "Oh, honey, I'm coming. . . ."

I didn't mean to carry it on quite so long, but you see how it's done. Assuming both John and Mary have been brought to the moment of needing to have an orgasm before we joined them, you can see how long they can last. Probably a good deal longer than most of us.

This story is told entirely from Mary's perspective, her point of view. Nothing is talked about that she doesn't see, hear or feel.

The Denouement

How you wrap up your story depends somewhat on the publication you're aiming for and on your own unique personal approach. I like to provide at least a couple of sentences to conclude my story, or maybe insert a "kicker" which takes the reader back to the source of the situation. In *"Keli's Bath"* (page 39), for example, the kicker is that the gas man has cometh, and though he's out of commission, the hot water works fine.

Sometimes you'll provide your editor with a wonderful closing paragraph and when you see your masterpiece in print, it won't be there, or worse, the editor will have added a different one. Whatever you choose to write, make it relevant. None of this, "and so they lived happily ever after" business. If you can't think of anything better to close up with, insert something earlier on purpose just so you can. Sarah's story, below, begins with two bluejays fighting over a scrap of food. When she's still trembling with the aftermath of her spine-tingling climax, she opens her eyes to see one of the jays cocking his head, eager for her intended picnic to begin.

Sarah

Love is the best aphrodisiac. There is no doubt about it. And Kelly and I are in love, although he doesn't know it yet. He still thinks it's lust. Our problem is finding a private place in which to express our love-lust. In the good old days, it used to be the teenagers who had to sneak around to make out, now it's the parents.

Kelly has one daughter still living at home and I have two sons. We're not to the stage yet where we can tell the kids we're going to "take a nap" and then slip off into the bedroom, but we're way beyond the hand-holding point. Every time I see the man, I want to ravish him and he tells me how he spends the days behind his desk fantasizing about me. Anyhow, we've devised a probably not-so-unique solution to our problem: We meet at lunch time and make love in the park.

I won't tell you exactly where, in case you might decide to follow our example, but it's in Los Angeles' Griffith Park, not far from the observatory. Kelly and I drive to a small picnic area, hike up past the lunch benches, and walk in under the trees on the side of the mountain. We can see the world, but the world can't see us. He brings the blankets and I bring the Kleenex. One of us stops off at the market for wine, cheese and fruit, and we have a picnic.

Usually, we don't eat lunch until afterwards. We're too hungry for each other. It sounds risqué, but it's really quite safe and romantic. Yesterday was particularly wonderful. . . .

I was wearing a full skirt and bikini panties which Kelly immediately removed. I took his pants off too, to be fair, and we draped one of the blankets over us while we sat on the other. I sat with my back against his chest watching some noisy bluejays fighting over a discarded apple core. I moved my hands over Kelly's, bringing his fingers to my lips and then up under my blouse to my breasts. He stroked them gently, coaxing my nipples into erection. He nibbled at the back of my neck like a love-struck tomcat and talked to me about how good I smelled. His right hand wandered down into my lap and further, scooping up some wetness from below and smoothing it over my clit. He had the perfect touch. Most men rub too hard or too rough. Kelly is an expert. He gently rubbed his wet finger over the tip of my hard pearl, causing my legs to tremble and my heart to pound. I'd been thinking about him all morning, as usual, and I was ready to get off before we began.

I breathed deeply of the warm summer air and closed my eyes. My clit felt as though it was vibrating and I wanted to swallow his fingers with my cunt. He said, "Yes, yes, come on, darlin' . . ." and other such things that make me come. He brought me over the top with his words. As soon as I re-covered, I turned around to face him and said, "OK, now it's your turn."

His long stiff cock bobbed in front of him, looking for a home. The tip was moist and shiny. "That's what happens to it at work when I'm thinking about you," he said. "I have to wear a handkerchief in my shorts in case it leaks." I laughed, wondering what his secretary noticed more, the bulge of his erection or the bulge of the handkerchief.

I kissed Kelly's marvelous face, then I bent down, and hold-ing his hard shaft in one hand and his balls in the other, I kissed and licked the tip of his cock. Kelly leaned back a little, shuddering each time I moved one of my hands. He was so ready.

Making sure the blanket covered my back, I climbed over Kelly's thighs and settled myself on top of him, *Kama Sutra* style. I allowed his cock to penetrate me slowly. It was so straight, it didn't want to bend with my inner curves. Finally, I sat down on it all the way. Kelly sat up, holding me, and moved in and out a little too fast. I kissed him and then asked him to relax and slow down. "Maybe I'll be able to," he said, "after we've done this fifty or so times, but it's still far too exciting."

I let him go, but when he came dangerously close to losing his load, I stopped him. I pushed him slowly down onto the ground where he reluctantly lay still, breathing hard and waiting to see what I wanted next. "Don't move at all," I told him, and then I started moving.

With my knees folded on either side of his waist, I lifted myself off his body without letting go of the tip of his cock, then let myself down again with slow, deliberate movements. When I saw he was beginning to relax a little, I moved faster. Then I sat down on his cock, with the whole thing deep inside of me and I rocked back and forth. Inside my body, he was pressing all the right places; outside, my clit was resting happily at the base of his shaft.

My cunt was hot now, on fire. Kelly was watching me with his gorgeous blue eyes, which were rapidly becoming black with lust. Kelly is the only man I know who keeps his eyes open while he makes love. I've tried to keep mine open, but I can't. As soon as I begin to get high on a kiss or an embrace, they close automatically. It's more intense that way for me. For Kelly, the pleasure is expanded by watching. He loves to watch me suck his cock and he loves to watch my face when I'm coming.

So now I watched him. This time I wanted to see what *he* looked like when he came, which was going to be pretty soon. I loved the way his mouth was working, moving into erotic shapes as he tried to express his ecstasy. "Keep moving," he said desperately, as if I would think of stopping.

Now it was there, in his voice, in those incredible sounds he makes when he's going to let go of everything. My body vibrated on top of him, his cock wedged inside of me, helpless against my gyrations. Kelly's eyes opened wide as if to ask, "What are you doing to me?" and then he came. His head whipped back and I could see every muscle in his neck straining and red. His back arched and his hard cock stabbed into me one last time to get the best of the orgasm, the last drop of it.

He had closed his eyes, I suddenly realized. There are times when even he must close his eyes. Then I wanted to close mine. I was watching Kelly's face, this man whom I've dared to love, but my body was calling me to its center, my hot center, now closing in on his cock like a vise and taking over my consciousness like a drug. I was coming. Kelly opened his eyes once again and watched me, holding onto my hips with his strong hands, fingers spread wide apart, digging into my flesh. My eyes were shut tight against the daylight, against the world. My hard breasts bounced with the rhythm of our love-making and all the while, Kelly was calling to me from a great distance, "Come, baby. You're beautiful. You look wonder-ful. Come to me, darlin'. Sweetheart, come."

And so I did. I came hard and full, and an all-over sensation of love, wonder and joy filled me with warmth. I stopped moving and slipped, exhausted, down into my lover's arms. He stroked my back and whispered to me softly and I opened my eyes to the beauty of the day. Sunlight filtered through tall pines while eucalyptus leaves swished in the wind. A bluejay cocked his head at me as if to ask if it was time for lunch yet.

Sometimes I am resentful that this park is the only place two grown people can have some privacy, a place of our own. Yet at other times, like yesterday, I think that this park, where nature abounds, is the most perfect place in the world to make love.

Another problem, which you will have no control over, occurs when an editor has to make cuts in order to fit stories into a pre-determined space. The editor will try to slash it from the end first, the easiest way. In adult magazine stories, especially, you can write in a few extra sentences at the end which won't be missed if they're hacked off. But it's almost impossible for you to plan for what an editor might do. Just don't feel depressed when you see your five-hundred-word piece reduced to two hundred. Nobody hates you. The other stories were not any better than yours. It's all a matter of space and subject. Usually.

Sarah's story underwent a considerable re-write before it was published in *Playgirl*. First of all, I had done a little experimenting with present tense, which this editor did not like at all, and sec-ondly, she wasn't crazy about my bluejays and wiped them out. Well, the first set, anyway. I wrote for *Playgirl* for more than a year and went through three erotica editors. The first and second ones always printed my stories almost exactly as they were writ-ten. The third and current editor has adjusted the format of the erotica stories to reflect her style. This example shows that it pays to study what is currently in print before you begin to write. Because I hadn't read the other stories, I was not aware of the editorial transition that had occured. If you're good, an editor will put up with having to rewrite your stories, for a while. If you're very good, and have made a name for yourself, the editor will phone you up with "suggestions" before hacking up your work. But if you're just a run-of-the-mill scribe, you'll lose your position. Why take chances? Do your homework and adhere to the publication's formula. Save your experimental writing for obscure literary journals.

The best way to learn about story structure is to read lots of stories. After a while, you'll catch on to the rhythm. It's pretty standard. Then, after you've written a few, you'll establish your own rhythm. Also, I've learned that editorial restrictions tend to set up my pace more than anything else. If I have five pages to create an entire drama, my scene is set by paragraph one, my characters are already interacting and the action begins before the first page is over. When I have to tell an entire story in four lines, as is the case with videotape blurbs, I begin with the core of the action, the reason for the story. For example, if the story is about two girls on a pool table, that's what the first sentence is about.

As with anything else, the more you practice, the better you will become. In the next chapter, I'll tell you more about how to tell a story, give you more examples, and you can practice writing a few. Start with whichever one is easiest for you and work up to the others.

CHAPTER 5

TELLING YOUR STORY

Knowing Your Reader

The first thing to consider when writing a story is your reader. Who is he or she and what do they want to read about? This analysis will help you determine the sex, profession and character of your hero and heroine.

In my stories, I like to make my characters ordinary people for the most part. Construction workers, office workers, secretaries, telephone repairpersons and so on. Most of my readers are familiar with these professions. Now and then I'll write about the rich because that's an area our fantasies turn to when we need a lift.

If you were to venture into the adult bookstores to check out the action, it might surprise you to see what the customers look like. They don't wear trenchcoats (unless you're on the east coast or it's snowing out). Many have three-piece designer suits, and carry attache cases—executives on the way home from work. Others look like guys you wouldn't think would have any trouble getting a date, ever. Some very famous people are collectors of erotica. I won't embarrass them by mentioning names, in case it's supposed to be a secret, but take my word that you cannot assume your customer is illiterate and sexually suppressed so it's a good policy never to write down to him.

Anyway, the story belongs to your main character, who can either be a surrogate for your reader, or the girl of his dreams, or the man of her fantasies. For example, I've written a story with a female protagonist and a love interest who is a football player. It doesn't matter that my reader is sixty-two and balding; he will identify with my thirty-year-old handsome hero. He will be listening to my seductive, enchanting voice as if I am speaking directly to him. This voice is why the most effective stories written in erotica are told from the first person point of view, or in the "I." Not all your stories will be written this way. Third-person narrative (*she* did this and *he* did that) is also quite commonly used. But if you want your story really hot, or if you're writing a letter to the editor or relating something you purportedly experienced, it must be told in the first person. There is an example of each in the following section. Next problem:

Tense

First person combined with simple past or present tense, proves to be a winning duo. Present tense should be used in moderation, as it may confuse the reader, who is much more accustomed to reading the simple past tense. But present tense can come off really hot if you're going with it. I'll show you the difference.

Past tense:

It was the first time I saw John without his uniform on. His chest was massive. I wanted to bury my face in his curly hairs and clasp hold of his balls with my hands. I could taste his sweet cock in my mouth already. I came closer to him, pushed my fingers through his chest hairs and kissed his neck. His erection prodded a place for itself between my legs.

Present tense:

This is the first time I've seen John without his uniform on. His chest is massive. I want to bury my face in his curly hairs and clasp hold of his balls with my hands. I can already taste his sweet cock in my mouth. I come closer to him, push my fingers through his chest hairs and I kiss his neck. His erection is prodding a place between my legs.

Maybe you can't measure the difference in intensity. It's quite subtle, but it is there.

You won't always want your story to be that intense. In a softer publication, or in a softer story, the intensity could interfere with your style. And, since readers are far more used to simple past, it is the safest route. Some writers have made the present tense their specialty and can be recognized by this trademark. Consider your style, your market, the publication you're aiming for, the particular story you're working on, and then choose.

Perhaps you want to back up a little from the drama and become the omniscient narrator, third person, simple past. This is the fly-on-the-wall approach. Let's take a look at that same scene in third-person narrative and check out the difference.

It was the first time Mary had seen John without his uniform on. She saw that his chest was massive and wanted to bury her face in his curly hairs and hold his balls in her hands. She could imagine the taste of his cock in her mouth. She came closer to him, pushed her fingers through his chest hairs and kissed his neck. John's erection prodded a place between Mary's legs.

So what do you think? Of the three, which one would you have chosen for your construction worker? Third-person narrative is quieter, more subdued. If this effect is the desired one, as in romance novels, there's no problem. But if you're reaching for an orgasm, the more intense, the better. Which means you may have to get your narrator off the wall and back down into the story.

Now remember that your reader 99.9 percent of the time is male, but that doesn't mean he doesn't want to read stories from the female point of view. On the contrary, he adores hearing from women. He can't get enough of it. He thinks he's getting a woman's feelings here, especially in the softcore magazines.

When a man buys a softcore adult store magazine, the ones with photographs of girls alone, it's not to read about superstuds and construction workers; it's to look at the pretty girls on the pages. When he gets bored with the photos or they've lost their effect, he may glance over to the accompanying copy. You will not be writing about men at all, but the girl in the photos. She can talk about men or tell a story about a man she knows, but she's the center of your story. Your reader wants to believe she is really talking to him. Give the girl a sparkling personality with your copy, and your reader will relate the copy to the pictures in the surrounding photo set. Most men do not read the indicia, which is the fine print posted in front of almost every issue of every adult, or newsstand men's magazine, which clearly states that the words written within the photo sets are "not meant to be understood as the actual personality of the models." Regardless, the readers insist on reading the copy beneath the photo and relating it to the girl in the picture. Why? Because it goes with the fantasy. He *wants* to believe it.

Therefore, if you write a short story about Tina who loves to fuck, and you tell it from Tina's point of view, your reader will follow you through Tina's adventures and find out why she loves to fuck, when she does it and with whom. Even if the reader *knows* it's fiction, he'll want to believe a woman wrote it, someone a lot like Tina.

Here is "Monica," yet another single-mother story, written for *Playgirl*, to give you an example of first-person, simple-past tense. This story is softcore erotica and was published without photographs. Following "Monica" is a hardcore, adult store tale called "Jennifer," which is told in first-person present and was originally published to illustrate a photo set. It is an exposé of what Jennifer thinks about when she's masturbating. This story is designed to be arousing to both male and female.

Monica

Here I am in my sexual prime, and I never get laid. My nineteen-year old daughter has more sex than I do. I've got this fixation on setting a good example, so I kiss my dates goodnight at the door, while she takes hers up to Lovers' Lookout. But last night I got a little reprieve from my self-imposed abstinence.

A man came to give me an estimate on our garage conversion. My son needs room to practice his drums, and my daughter wants a place to entertain, so we considered turning our garage into an extra room. The salesman, Jerry, was only twenty-eight years old, but he was strikingly handsome. I realized I would not be able to afford what he was offering, but I found myself gaining interest in him. He had the cutest dimples in the corners of his mouth and intense blue eyes. What really impressed me, though, was his dynamic personality. Whatever subject he found himself on, he knew all the technology, jargon and dollar figures. I offered him a drink as he rambled on about an apartment house he was in the process of purchasing, his ranch property in Ventura, the computer at his branch in San Diego and the cost of keeping a New York condo. As it turned out, he wasn't just a salesman for the construction company, but was part-owner and was just temporarily pitching in to solicit new clientele.

I held myself in check until the last minute. I walked him to his car, a Mercedes sports coupe the same color as his eyes. I started thinking about how I'd never see him again, and I suddenly got very brave and looked directly into his eyes. "I've been wanting to kiss you all night," he said, picking up my body language, and then our bodies pressed together. His kiss surprised me. He opened his mouth slightly and used his tongue expertly. It was as if we were connected in some intimate way. I staggered away from the car like a good mom and waved goodbye to my only hot sex prospect in months.

Thank heavens he was more daring. An hour later he phoned. "I can't work anymore tonight," he said. "I've canceled all my appointments. Will you come out and have a drink with me?"

I was ready in ten minutes. We went to a neighborhood bar called Malone's, but it was football night and the place was deserted. We talked and touched and teased until the bartender called last call, and we were forced to leave.

As we walked to his car, I kept thinking about how I didn't want to go home alone. But my sensible, logical mind quickly went over the negatives: the difference in our ages, the 200 miles between our houses, and the fact that we had just met. Yet I couldn't quiet the throbbing in my clit or the tingle in my nipples.

When we got to his car, he didn't turn on the ignition. He put his arm around me and pulled me toward him, and this time we really kissed. Only the floor shift kept us from a full-on fuck in the parking lot. He moved my hand down to his prick. It was young and strong and so hard. The fabric felt like gauze between my hand and the warmth of his cock. I kissed him again with my palm wrapped around his organ, my fingers tickling its head. Just then I opened my eyes and saw a bunch of guys coming out of the bar. I sat back and laughed. "I feel like a teenager!" I told him.

"In that case," Jerry said, "let's go the Lovers' Lookout." We drove to the top of the mountain, a place I hadn't been to for years. He parked facing the city view, pulled me toward him and began stroking my cheek.

He kissed me slowly and gently all over my face and neck. He was talking to me, but I couldn't hear him because I was so involved with my feelings. He slipped his hand under my sweater, into the cup of my bra, and caressed my right breast. "I want to eat you," he said, stroking my nipple. Now I was listening. "I want to lick your pussy for hours." He told me how beautiful my breasts were, but in coarser language than I was used to. I was embarrassed, and yet, it was fun being talked to like that.

"I can't wait to get inside you," he said, pulling me up onto his lap. "You're so soft all over." Age is the great flesh softener, I thought. Why was I so cynical? Why couldn't I just relax? I kept wondering if I was really going to have the nerve to do this thing, but Jerry took control of everything. Somehow he got my pants and boots off, and I scrunched into the passenger seat with my feet on the dashboard and my legs wrapped around his body. He was kneeling in front of me, with his fingers making me wet, smearing my juices around my pussy lips. He unbuckled his belt and dropped his pants, letting his glorious cock spring free. I grabbed for it. I just wanted to hold it in my hand. It was hot and the skin on the outside of it was loose. I wished I could bend down and lick it for a while, but there was no way in these cramped quarters. Jerry knew his car much better than I did, and managed all sorts of maneuvers from his place on the floor. He pulled a lever that lowered the back of my chair, and then he lifted my sweater, unhooked my bra, and cupped my breasts in his hands. Moonlight made them beautiful, even to me, and revealed how hard and red my nipples were. He took a deep breath of appreciation and bent down to lick each tip. I watched his smooth young face, his glistening tongue, the way his fingers pressed into my flesh, and my breasts became harder.

I reached down between his legs and took hold of his cock again, steering the tip of it toward my opening. I tickled myself with it, rubbing it up and down my slit and over my clitoris until I had to have him inside of me. He moved his hands down to my buttocks and pulled me toward him, just a little, so that my pussy was at the edge of the seat. And then he came into me. He shuddered.

"Easy," I murmured. "Slow and easy."

And slowly and easily, he began pushing his prick into my cunt, then drawing it out, then pushing it back in. "Oh, Monica. You feel so good. You feel so damned, fucking good. I don't know if I—" And then it happened, of course, as I'd known it would. He came. And as he did, he bucked up against me like a new colt, grunting and moaning and telling me how fantastic it felt. I could feel his hard rod in the roof of my cunt, all the way up to my cervix, and I watched his face contort and his chest muscles flex. He pulled me up onto him by my hips, and my head fell back between the bucket seats.

I was about to try and extricate myself when I realized he wasn't through. His cock didn't shrivel, and as soon as he recovered from his massive orgasm, he began moving into me again. This time it was I who was saying how good it felt. My body caught up with my desire, releasing me from my inhibitions, and now I wanted to come, too.

We were very wet and sloppy, and it took a while for me to arrive at a position where I could feel him, really feel him, as deep and as hard as I wanted. Yet once I did, I was on my way. Jerry managed to get my left breast against his face, and he took the nipple in his mouth and sucked me. This made my cunt muscles contract so that I could feel all of him; I could feel how deep he was and how much he filled me with his thick cock. My feet were on the steering wheel by now—any place for leverage—and his hands were all over me at once. All of my energy was concentrated on my cunt. I felt it get hot, then hotter, and suddenly I lost my ability to move. An orgasmic spasm took hold of me so strongly that it paralyzed me. Jerry knew exactly what was happening, and he thrust his cock forward, ever so deeply into my channel, again and again, faster and harder each time until it was my turn to scream out. I was even louder than Jerry had been.

I'll never be sorry I did this, even if I never see Jerry again. I got royally fucked by a cute young guy who thinks I'm sexy as hell. What could be better than that?

Jennifer

It doesn't matter how often my husband fucks me, I never get enough. I spend the afternoon daydreaming instead of straightening up like I'm supposed to. And with the day-dreaming comes the masturbation. I can't seem to get through one single day without getting myself off one way or another!

It may have something to do with the fact that I love to do housework in the nude, or nearly nude. I find it even sexier to waltz around in a negligée or some brief, lacy underwear.

Then when my nipples rub up against the fabric and begin to get hard, I get excited, and I know it won't be long before I'll be down on the floor, rubbing my clit to climax.

It's just that I'm so sensuous. Everything I touch reminds me of sex. My skin becomes aroused at the slightest hint of erotica. I brush my hand across my lips and I want to kiss something, suck something.

My pussy takes the slightest flirtation from my fingers as a come on and the muscles draw my fingers in, wanting all of them deep inside.

I love the feel of my hand on the inside of my thigh. I like to run my fingers up and down, ever so lightly, coming closer and closer to my soft pussy.

My pussy begins to get wet and swollen, but I don't touch it yet. I just keep stroking it, and pulling on my nipples a little. I lick my fingers and push my way between the outer lips. I make circles around the clit, but not on it—not yet.

Then when I know I'm really getting hot, when my pussy's throbbing and my nipples are erect, I sink down into the near-est available piece of furniture and I think about cock.

I envision a huge, throbbing cock, blue-veined and bulging.

Its purple head is straining to find pussy. The cock is getting harder and harder and bigger and redder until I know it's about to burst with cum.

Then I touch my clit. With one finger I push down on it. With my other hand, I reach up inside my cunt and pretend to be that huge cock I'm imagining. I fuck myself with my fingers and I jiggle my clit in rhythm.

I close my eyes and imagine that cock getting ready to come. It's looming above me, it's standing straight up!

Heat rises to my face and neck and I know I'm about to come. But I control the dream of the cock. I tell it when to come. It waits for me.

I watch its swollen purple head glisten and strain. A tiny drop of clear fluid can be seen at its hole.

My hard clit begins to throb and my pussy lips suck hard on my fingers and I know it's time. As the first spasm begins, I watch my imaginary cock spurt forth huge white gobs of cum. They fly over my head and I come with them. I can't see my own cum spurt out like that, but I can feel my fingers getting wetter and stickier and definitely hotter. And watching this huge cock come so hard like that gets me even higher with my own climax.

When my husband comes home and the house is still a mess, he just looks at me and says: "Jennifer, not again."

And so I sorta smile and he knows he can't stay mad at me. It isn't as if I've been unfaithful or something, and jacking off gets me real wet and horny for his beautiful cock.

So he just pushes me back into the same chair I've just come in, and he brings out his hard-on and I get excited all over again. He even strokes it a few times as he kneels over me, because he knows that turns me on. But this time, when that big cock head gets hard and purple, he knows where to put it. Inside me! Then I close my eyes and I begin to re-design that big cock which will spurt over my head. We all come together.

Active vs. Passive

Always show the action when you can, rather than telling about it. Make it happen for the reader by bringing him into the drama whenever possible. For example, which is more dramatic?

Mary walked to the door, opened it and told John he'd best leave now. He refused by shaking his head negatively and folding his arms in a gesture of defiance. She told him that in that case, she would have to go, and with that, she walked out, slamming the door behind her.

Or:

"You'd best leave," Mary said, as she opened the door for John. But he remained standing there, his arms folded in an obvious gesture of defiance. He shook his head no. "Well, then, it'll have to be me." The words came out in a whisper as Mary reluctantly left. As a last act of aggression, she let the door slam with a bang behind her.

You should not only show your reader each event as it happens, rather than catch him up on what he's missed, you should also give each action an attitude. You are telling the way it happened. Mary didn't just say the words, nor did she scream them out, she whispered them. The door did not click shut, it "slammed with a bang." All these clues help your reader "see" the picture you are drawing.

Write actively rather than passively. Don't allow something to just happen to your heroine, have her cause it to happen. Here is the same paragraph in passive and active.

Passive:

Mary's arm was touched by John's long, manly fingers and her lips were kissed. His love for her was shown by the gleam in his eyes.

Boring right? Let's try again:

Active:

John stroked Mary's arm with his long, manly fingers and kissed her sweet lips. She could tell he loved her by the gleam in his watery blue eyes.

I threw in a couple of adjectives just for the heck of it. But you get the point.

This rule applies to the whole story too, not just individual sentences. A writer in one of my classes read out loud a work in progress that made every woman in the class angry at him because he had made a victim out of his heroine. He hadn't meant to, it just happened. It could have been prevented by changing the sentence structure.

Briefly, the story went something like this:

My husband Tom told me I was unappealing and frigid. Then he left me. Since he left, I've been lonely and afraid to go outdoors. Then a woman came to my house one day and introduced herself as Ursula. She said she was going to kidnap me for my own good and would help me discover my inner lust. Remembering what Tom had said about me, I went with her.

Ursula led me into a white building, and then into a white room, where four female attendants in white robes came toward me and took off my clothes. They laid me down on the floor where they ravished my body. I began to feel that arousal Tom had talked about.

Ursula asked me if she could give me a bath. I said yes. She massaged my breasts and played with my nipples and stroked my hair. She put her fingers up inside of me and moved them in and out. Then she laid on top of me, like a man, and I liked it.

When Ursula had taught me how to have an orgasm, I knew I was at last a real woman. I waited a few more months, and sure enough, Tom came home. He said, "Did Ursula come?" I said yes. He asked, "And did you learn your lesson?" I said yes. Then he took me, and remembering all I had learned in the white room, I responded as he'd always wanted me too.

This is, of course, the *Reader's Digest* condensed version. The original story was not quite as cold or short. I wanted to give you just the essence of it so you could empathize with the audience's reaction.

The story itself is not bad. The problem is that all the minor characters control the heroine. She makes no choices of her own, has no emotions but what she's taught to feel, and is too weak to tell us, the readers, who she is and what she wants.

Bill Norton Sr., the screenwriter of early Burt Reynolds' movies and many others, once told me what a story is. "A story is when someone wants something and then gets it, or comes to terms with not getting it." Ask yourself: What does this heroine want? Does she want Tom back? Then why doesn't she say so? Why doesn't she try to get him back? The women in the class wanted to know why she would want him back.

Why does Tom come off as such a brute? I don't want to answer all these questions for you. I only want you to learn to ask them about your own stories. If this writer wanted to get back at his frigid wife, he did a good job of it. She comes off as a weak, lily-livered, stupid, nothing person. She is uninteresting, unexciting and yes, unappealing. But the writer, in the voice of Tom, comes off even worse.

The class responded by suggesting that to fix the story, the writer should have the girl make the choices. She should research this white institution, seek out Ursula, then tell Ursula what she wants to learn.

If it were my story, I'd have the heroine learn so much, she decides she doesn't want Tom anymore. Who knows? Maybe she even wants Ursula.

Another very important element missing from this story is the heroine's emotional and physical reactions to what is happening to her. Wouldn't she be a little afraid to leave the house with a stranger? I asked the writer how he would feel if one day a strange man, call him Eric, came to the door, and told him he was going to kidnap him and take a bath with him. The example was so ludicrous, the class broke into hysterics, and yet, isn't this premise exactly what the writer expected us to buy in his story?

The writer said, "Well, in this society, it's OK for girls to be with girls, but I would never be with a man." So I asked the class, half-filled with females, who among them would have gone with Ursula, this bizarre and mysterious stranger. No one volunteered.

You see, the story lacks a certain reality base. If the heroine had made a friend of Ursula and their love-making had come out of this friendship, it would have been more credible to the reader. That would be another way to fix it. If the writer had first identified with his heroine, become a part of her, this result never would have happened. You've got to be on your hero's side, even when he's wrong, or you'll never learn enough about him, never understand him well enough, to bring him to life before your reader.

Pacing

Erotica has a tendency to come in short paragraphs. Each new action gets its own stage. This structure makes it easier to read and it gives special emphasis to each element in the progression of arousal. Take your time and describe every sensual aspect in great detail. On the other hand, don't overwrite. You'll know when you've had enough if you read it aloud. You'll get an even more accurate appraisal if you read it to a friend. If your audience is smiling or reaching for your body parts, the story is probably working. If he or she is snoring, looking through *TV Guide* or asking whether or not you made your dental appointment, you, probably messed up.

Sentence structure is a vital aspect of pacing. If each sentence measures the same length, is constructed the same or begins with the same subject, it comes off sounding like a recitation from the yellow pages. Here is an example which does all three:

I walked into the room. I put down my purse. I looked straight at him. I asked him for a cigarette. I took it. I lit it myself. I kept the matches.

I've given you enough good examples already in this book for you to know how to correct this problem. Basically, you string the information together with conjunctions, dialogue, action and so on and take out all those I's:

I walked into the room and put my purse down on the

dresser. Looking straight at him, I asked for a cigarette. When he offered it to me, I lit it myself and kept the matches.

Can't you just see Lauren Bacall and Humphrey Bogart? Can't you just hear Mickey Spillane's voice?

Focusing

The short erotic story has no room for going off on tangents. You must stick with the main plot line or lose your reader. Skip over the part about the truck outside the building, or the heroine's concern over her dirty kitchen. The reader wants to get to the meat of the tale and linger there. A small diversion can be inserted to create tension, but don't get carried away.

On a smaller scale, paragraphs and sentences must also toe the line. Keep your writing smooth and connected. Each sentence must flow naturally into the next without any sudden shifts in the action and never in your point of view. For example:

> Mary reached out to touch the crinkly fur on his chest. She kissed his throat and nibbled his chin. Outside it was raining. She licked his earlobe.

Obvious, right? You'd be surprised how many manuscripts turn up with major blunders like this one. Leave the rain outside where it belongs. Or, if you must have rain, have your character react to it:

> Mary reached out to touch the crinkly fur on his chest. She kissed his throat and nibbled his chin. When she licked his earlobe, she realized it has begun to rain outside and he would be stranded here for the night—with her.

I'm stretching this a bit, reaching for a solution. The best answer is to put the rain someplace else in the story. It doesn't belong in this intimate scene, not the way it's presently written.

Another similar blunder is a shift in point of view. One minute we're seeing through her eyes, the next minute, his.

Mary looked at him and saw the man of her dreams. He was dark and handsome and ever so virile. He thought she was pretty too.

Uh uh. No time for that in a short story. If you really must let the reader know what the man is thinking, you're going to have to let it come through Mary: "She could tell he thought she was pretty." Or: "The way he was looking at her betrayed his lust."

Even in a novel, shifting the point of view can be a catastrophe if it is not done with care. Sometimes even when it's done correctly, it is disconcerting to the reader, because it's like starting all over again with a new book. Novelists who must follow two or more characters often give them each a chapter of their own, then alternate. This technique cuts down on the confusion. But the rule for short stories is to pick your hero and then stick with him all the way through.

Creating Emphasis

One more rule for your erotic fiction: Don't underline, CAPITALIZE, or use exclamation points!!! There are exceptions. Some publications use bold-face type to accentuate the passion words, but that's the editor's prerogative, not yours. Most newsstand publications use few italicized words and no underlining or exclamation points. Hardcore magazine are often printed in all caps with bold-faced type, which is more difficult to read, but nobody seems to mind. There is minimal copy, however, which may be how they get away with it.

Of course if you're quoting or using the title of a book or article, or using foreign words, you'll need to underline. Whatever you underline in your manuscript will appear in italics in your typeset copy, unless you specify bold type. An occasional exclamation point in dialogue can be forgiven.

Writing and Reading

A last note on writing: Write. Write and read. Read everything you can get your hands on and stay on your turf. If you're in the process of learning how to write a short story, read short stories. If you want to write for camping magazines, read camping magazines. It helps you get in the mood and comprehend the style. Sometimes if you're trying to write like Hemingway and you burrow your way through a Thomas Mann novel, your writing will take on some strange affectations. Certain writers are capable of affecting your mood as well, so read Peter De Vries and Woody Allen when you're writing a comedy, Hesse and Baba Ram Dass when you're aiming at the spiritual side of life, and Anaïs Nin when you're writing erotica.

Keep a journal or notebook and tell the truth to it. This act is harder than it sounds. Once you learn to tell yourself the truth, it will be easier to put it into your fiction. Making little notes about the weather, somebody's new dress, and how you felt when Susan lied to you will all help your writing. If you can't bring yourself to pull out your pad in public, at least do it before you go to sleep at night. Notes on what you've read will be helpful also.

Writers find the time to write. For every excuse you can come up with, I can better you from the list of famous writers who made it in the face of even greater obstacles. If you're not writing, you are not a writer.

I'm assuming that you are already familiar with the English language, grammar, punctuation and syntax, but all of us slip up now and then and it's always wise to have a few reference books on hand. There is a list in the back of this book of some I've found. You might have already selected your own favorites. A good one to brush up on annoying word problems and to get a brush-up course on the use of the semicolon, dash and so on is Corbett's *Little English Handbook*. A well-known staple is *Elements of Style* by Strunk and White. My editor recommends the *Chicago Manual of Style*.

One thing you must have is a dictionary. I have four. A little secretarial speller, such as Leslie's *20,000 Words,* is a time-saver. It doesn't do anything but spell, so words are easy to look up. If you need a definition, however, it's no help at all.

The small *Random House Dictionary* is more convenient than the conventional size. Then, for those connotations or definitions which are not listed in this smallish volume I use the regular size, *Webster's New World Dictionary*, College edition or Americana edition. Every writer has his or her own favorite. I've found little difference between the various popular brands. Only compulsive full-time writers, such as you're going to be, will need the big one, the seventy-five dollar job it takes two hands to carry. Mine is the *Random House Dictionary of the English Language,* unabridged. I'm always proud of myself when I have to go to the big book because it means I've expanded my vocabulary beyond the college level. (Or else I've picked up an obscure word.) The last shelf to be filled will hold your set of encyclopedias, *Bartlett's Familiar Quotations, The Quotable Woman, Synonyms and Antonyms* or a *Thesaurus,* and of course the indispensable *How to Write Erotica.*

CHAPTER 6

MAKING IT SEXY

Writing Seductively

Sex is not always sexy—in real life or in fiction. Just as comedy is not always funny and tragedy doesn't always make the audience cry. What makes comedy funny is craftsmanship. You've heard two people tell the same joke; one had you in stitches, the other one blew it entirely. Those same two people could turn you on or turn you off by relating the same sex scene. The difference is that one is usually expressing action in seductive terms, while the other is merely relating a graphic description.

For example, I might write: "Standing nude next to the man she loved, Elvira felt vulnerable. Then Aron placed his hand just beneath her left breast heating her bare skin. Her face flushed, yet she found her body shivering and her nipples became hard." The reader is introduced to the action in terms of his senses.

Moreover, the location of Aron's hand is not direct. It is encroaching upon the area of an erogenous zone, not quite touching it, yet close enough to cause a physical reaction in the woman. This technique is one way to create sexual tension and drama in an act where the ending is obvious and expected. We tease. We sensationalize. While all along we also happen to be telling the action of our story.

The easiest way to achieve a seductive approach is through the reader's senses, as many of them as we can stimulate. First give him a visual image: "Standing there nude. . . ." Then create an emotional underpinning through character and/or dialogue:

"Elvira felt vulnerable. . . ." Then bring it home to him through his senses of touch, smell and hearing.

Here is same scene as told by your uncreative friend: "She was naked. He grabbed her tit and she started shaking all over." I've said the same thing, related the same scene, but I've taken all the joy out of it, all the emotion and tentativeness. I've given the reader nothing to do but read. A reader cannot become involved in a story unless you provoke him to conjure up his own images and find a common base with the characters so that he can identify with and care about them.

Why do you think mysteries are so successful? They give the reader clues, so that he can take part in solving the crime. Love stories give readers clues as well. We are often let in on secrets our heroine isn't aware of yet so we can watch her edge toward conflicts.

Well-written, popular stories are designed to create a bond between the reader and the hero or heroine. In erotica, you know Elvira and Aron are going to get it on, but you don't know how. And you don't know what they're feeling about it or what their bodies are shaped like or how excited they are. The writer gives you the clues and the graphic details, but slowly, to tease you, to seduce you into joining in their pleasure.

Gradual arousal with sensual imagery is part of story telling and even joke telling. But nowhere is it more crucial to the success of your written material than in erotica. You don't have much left if your erotic story is not erotic.

This fact is just as important when you're working on a larger piece, a mystery novel, a romance or any kind of story where sex is involved. When there's love, there is kissing and hugging and you'd better know how to put them into words.

A friend of mind who is a $150,000-a-year advertising creative director and who developed some of the best and most well-known print and television ad campaigns around, wanted to write novels. He had published some short stories and was ready to make the big leap, or thought he was. Several years later, his eight novels had still not found publishers, though they abounded in convoluted James Bond–type plots, espionage, intrigue and drama. He told me a frequent complaint about his work was his lack of sex scenes, which he claimed were not necessary in spy novels. "Besides," he railed, "there are sex scenes!" He showed me one which went something like this:

> Kozmov knew they were onto him, but he would have to deal with this tomorrow. He was much too tired tonight. After a perfunctory shower, he padded over to the bed, made love to his wife three times and went to sleep.

My first question, as you might well imagine, was what did he mean by "three times?" She came three times? They went out for coffee in between? Three strokes of the old staff?

This problem is common with otherwise talented and prolific writers. Either the subject embarrasses them; they have a moral problem; they're afraid their mothers are going to read their work or, and this is the most common, they just don't know how to write about sex.

There is one more explanation, of course, and that is that the writer prefers not to take the story into the bedroom. That's all right too. But the talented writer will find a way to build up to the sex scene and flow out of it or fade away at just the right moment so that there's no doubt in the reader's mind what will happen next, and so that the reader feels satisfied regardless. When sex scenes were *verboten*, writers found many easily understood ways to imply the goings-on. If you want some good examples of this technique, check out some older romance novels or some forties movies.

Creating Sensual Images

Every field of writing, even technical writing, employs descriptions. Because people think in images, not words, they require pictures to store in their memory banks, to help them visualize what it is the writer is trying to say. Therefore, it's logical to assume that once you learn to write effective, image-producing erotica, you will be a better writer in any field. I'm not saying that readers are going to get turned on while perusing your *Technical Approach to Genetics*, but they will enjoy your writing more. It's just plain boring to read dry copy. You know that. You've read enough of it in your lifetime.

When I was an editor, I received submissions from all sorts of people: doctors, lawyers, teachers, even newspapermen. Most of them thought erotica would be easy to write and that it would make a good cocktail party story to have been published in a men's magazine. Most of them were lousy at it. Just because you can think up a good sex scene doesn't mean you can describe it in such a way that your reader can see what you see.

Even if you really experienced something sexual, you may have forgotten all the important elements of it. Also, there are certain "buzz" words in erotic literature which the reader subconsciously looks for. Most of these words and phrases are sensual rather than graphically sexual.

For example, a nationally syndicated newspaper columnist sent me the following copy:

> I had always wanted Jane. She worked in my office. Finally she asked me over to her house and when I got there she was naked. She offered me some fruit and cheese and she sat on the couch with me while I ate it. Then we went to bed.

Well? Are you hyperventilating yet? Can you hardly wait to see what will happen to this guy next? Or are you yawning? Imagine sitting through ten pages of this stuff. Or, better yet, imagine what it would sound like with a few erotic images thrown in:

> Jane was a voluptuous blonde who worked in my office. Every time she'd bend over the bottom drawer of the file cabinet, my pecker gave a little leap in my pants. She had the finest ass I'd ever seen, and when she leaned over my desk to bring me my mail, her bounteous breasts reached out to me like ripe fruit waiting to be sucked.
>
> Tuesday, she invited me over to her house and when I arrived, I found her naked. I blushed when I felt my cock straighten up. She took me by the hand, led me to the living room, and then brought in some fruit and offered me a tender peach, after taking the first juicy bite out of it herself. I ate the peach, but watched her pussy. As I sunk my teeth into the fruit and licked the juices off the fuzzy skin, I imagined what it would be like to be eating Jane.

Now if your hero can imagine what it would be like as well as explain it in delectable, sensual terms, so can your reader. It's true I made this copy longer, but that is what it needed. The writer had originally bounced from one so-called erotic scene to the next until he'd revealed ten such encounters without pausing to *enjoy* any of them. He thought just because lunch with Jane turned him on, it would be an automatic turn-on to his reader. Wrong!

Also, think quality, not quantity. Three sensuous, wild scenes in a story are worth ten quickies. Come to think of it, that's also true in real life, right?

Let's take a look at some of the changes I made. "I always wanted Jane. She worked in my office." These sentences don't tell the reader why he might want her too, if he also worked in your office. By adding a brief description of the girl and showing her in the act of overtly displaying her sexual nature, we have given the reader a few more reasons to want Jane for himself.

Next, the hero comes to the door, finds her naked and is offered fruit and cheese. But what was he feeling? What was happening to him while she was sitting there naked? These are the kinds of questions you should ask yourself when you're writing a story: What am I feeling? What am I seeing? How can I describe this particular sensation? How can I bring this story to life?

How did the hero feel about the peach, and how did the peach relate to the woman? I answered those questions for myself and then put them into the story, designing them to evoke mouth-watering images in my reader's mind.

Slow way down and allow yourself to feel the experience before you begin to write about it. Then use image-producing words and phrases in your description of the scene.

It's better to write one long sensual scene than to write five short "action" scenes which don't build to anything. Don't use all verbs and no adjectives, all climax and no foreplay. You are taking your reader from a cold customer to an ecstatic one, literally. This transition takes time and seduction, even if he's quick on the trigger.

There is another audience that you might want to consider when you're designing your erotic stories: the couple. He buys the book and reads it to her or vice versa, but they're using it to get high together. And, like a glass of fine burgundy, it must not go down quickly. It must be sipped slowly, in slow, loving, tender phrases.

Once I read one of my erotic stories to the man I was writing about. I wasn't trying to get off on it or get dramatic about it, but I read it slowly and sensually, because erotica, like poetry, was meant to be read slowly and sensually. How can you read, "She offered me some fruit" with that kind of sensuality? You *need* those buzz words. If you don't know enough of them, look on my list at the end of this book. If that doesn't help, underline those you see in the stories and novels you read. Every good novelist uses sensual descriptions. Every good poet is an expert at using them.

Using Buzz Words

I've been talking about buzz words. By now, you should have picked up on what they are. Some are hardcore, like *pussy* and *cock*. Others are ordinary words, like *hard, soft, tender, sensual, juicy, delicious, erect, rigid, stiff, suck, kiss, stroke* . . . you get the idea. I feel like Karl Malden: "Don't leave home without them." Buzz words are your ticket to sensual success.

I've included a purely arbitrary selection of sexy words at the end of this book. Use it when you get stuck, or when you find yourself using the same words over and over again. All writers repeat themselves and have favorite phrases, so don't feel bad if you have to resort to perusing this list. It may even inspire you toward a brand-new story.

Writing a sex story with no sex words is a little like describing how to fix a transmission without mentioning the tools or car parts. Heaven help the car owner with a manual like that.

There used to be a running gag about the old porn novels regarding adjective overuse. Sentences would run into overtime with such memorable phrases as:

> The gorgeous, busty blonde planted a wet, hot kiss on the detective's flat, hairy belly with her red, wide, sensuous lips as she dug her long, painted fingernails into the tanned flesh of his muscular thighs. His big, thick, throbbing cock and rock-hard balls told him it was time to sink into her dripping wet, open, but tight, cherry cunt.

One reason for the adjective abuse was a word quota the writer had to fill to get his paycheck. The other reason, more important to us, was that he was stalling. He was stretching out the action between her belly kiss and his probe home in order to get the most out of this sex scene. The writer is giving the reader time to catch up, as well as get a glimpse of the sexual relationship.

In the ad man's story we had no idea how Kozmov felt about his wife—if he lusted after her, or if he was merely performing his husbandly duties. Nor did we have a clue as to what she looks like, feels like, smells like, tastes like or behaves like. All we know is that she goes to bed before he does and that's not enough.

Buzz words, used far more sparingly than in that dreadful example above, can convey sensual information at the same time you are telling your story. You can't just stick them in any old place though. The best way to figure out how and where to use them is to get a firm picture in your mind of the scene you are describing.

Describing the Scene

Get a fix on the bed. Is it a brass bed or a colonial bed? Is it a mattress on the floor or a cabin bunk? Is there a bedspread and is it quilted or made from animal skins? What color is it? How hot is it in the room? Is it summer or winter outside? Whose bedroom is it?

The more you know about your characters and their environment, and their place in each other's lives, the better your story will come out, no matter how little of this information you wind up using. It's the old "tip of the iceberg" theory.

For this reason, writers often borrow characters from their real lives, to shortcut the imagination process. TV and film writers often use stereotypes, so that you can recognize the characters without lengthy set-ups. The crotchety old fuss-budget, the pot-bellied sheriff, the rich, bored matron, and so on, have become staples in sitcoms and action/adventure shows. You can use stereotypes as well, and even by name: "She was a perfect Daisy Mae with black hair." "He came at me like Rambo would." Right away, your audience is in touch with your characters.

You can shortcut room descriptions too, by saying things like "it looked like a New Orleans bordello," or "his room was like a prison cell." The reader doesn't need a lot of details. As long as you convince him you know what the room looks like, he'll trust you not to leave out anything that's crucial to the story.

If the only way you can visualize a scene is to use one you've been in, then do it. Use your own bedroom and you'll know what kind of bed, bedspread and room it is. Use your own girlfriend or boyfriend and you'll know what happens when that person gets excited. But do have a complete picture in your mind before you go on to determine the appropriate buzz words. *Ornate* would not describe the prison cell anymore than *spare* would describe the bordello. These are extreme examples of common flaws in erotic writing.

You don't want to distract or disorient your reader with a carelessly written phrase. And just as I showed you before, overdoing it with an abundance of even the right words can harm your story too.

Another reason to insert salient information early on is that once you get into the story, you don't want to throw your reader a curve that confuses him to the point where he loses his erection. It's hard to give you an example without telling an entire story, but I'll try.

He came to the door and started banging on it so loudly, I thought the neighbors would awaken, so I let him in. Then he threw me down on the bed. He was wearing his uniform and all his gear. I thought about screaming, but it might have disturbed my roommate. Then I wondered if I could make a dash for the window.

Already your reader is confused. I have a mental picture of this girl's room, but I haven't given you any clues, and the information I have given you is more confusing than it is defining. Who are her neighbors? How far away are they? Is her roommate asleep in the same room or down the hall? And what kind of uniform is he wearing? Is he a cop or a sailor? What time of day or night is it? If it's important, it had better be there.

Now think about the scene you've imagined by reading that paragraph and watch how it changes when I change the clues:

He came to my dorm room and started banging on the door so loudly, I thought the kids down the hall would awaken, so I let him in. Then he threw me down on the bed. Even in the dark, I could see he was wearing his football uniform and all his gear. I thought about screaming, but it might have disturbed my roommate, Sandy, who was asleep in the next room. Then I wondered if I could make a dash for the window.

I rest my case.

One more common problem with description: Don't give the reader a laundry list. Nothing could be more utterly boring. Example:

He banged on the door of my room. It was my dorm room. The beds were on either side of the window. The door was on one end. It was dark. And quiet. I let him in because I thought he'd wake up my roommate, who was asleep in the next room.

Not only is it boring, it's hard to read. Everything must be made to blend together as it did in the treatment above.

Use nonspecific adjectives with care as they often obscure the image from your reader's mind. Words such as *incredible, amazing, fantastic,* as well as the basic descriptive words such as *good, bad, big, small,* and so on, only work when combined with defining words:

I saw this incredible car. It was so big. And its upholstery was amazing.

All right now, quick! What did the car look like? What did I just say? Nothing, right? This car could have been anything from a souped-up '55 Chevy to a Lamborghini, and its interior could have been sheepskin or satin. Moral: Be precise.

Writers tend to use nonspecific adjectives when they don't know what they're describing. They're more interested in their story line than in the objects in the story. Better writers are overly specific. A reader can always skip over some of the adjectives and still come away with a very clear idea of the object described. He can really see it.

Let's take that amazing car out for a spin:

> Mr. Penny drove a 1932 Model-T Ford which he had recently repainted a bright sunflower yellow. He snuggled into the driver's seat to take his position behind the wheel. The black leather tuck and roll upholstery had been a gift from his son. This thought always caused Mr. Penny's eyes to well with tears, as his pride for his beloved son was as strong as his pride for the old car he called "Matilda."

Is there any doubt in your mind about that amazing car? You can almost smell the leather upholstery. It's much more fun to deliver these bits of description with emotion and story, and the result is a paragraph that is more interesting to read than a list of facts would be.

Practice your adjectives. Go back to some unsuccessful manuscript you have lying around in the closet and see how you can improve it by bringing it to life with sensual imagery. I'll bet you'll surprise yourself with your newly acquired virtuosity.

Choose the precise word and use it the way it was meant to be used. In your effort to be creative, you may lose your reader in confusion. Don't feel you have to expand your vocabulary by trying out new words in erotica. This is one case in which your reader will not be looking up polysyllabic, multileveled locutions with his other hand.

CHAPTER 7

FINDING YOUR MATERIAL

Turning Your Experiences into Erotica

Almost any situation can be erotic, with a little imagination and a sense of the absurd. You've met people who see sex in everything they come across. When you begin writing erotica on a regular basis, you're going to become a little like that kind of person. Another habit you may get into is memorizing good lines when you hear them, or even when you say them. It can be most disconcerting to a lover when he's just finished pouring his heart out to you if you get up and scribble notes for your next story.

I wish I could say I am always successful at separating my two selves, but I'm a writer almost all the time. There are moments, of course, when my overactive imagination helps my Muse along.

For example, one afternoon, I went over to visit my friend Mike. He was a college student, working his way through school as a maid and he had a job cleaning a rich man's condo that day. When I arrived, his cousin was also there and they had just gotten out of the sauna. Mike is a very attractive, sexy young man and his cousin looks a great deal like him. I remember very well standing just inside the entrance of the living room looking at these two Greek-god types, dressed only in small towels around their waists and imagining the possibilities. And I wasn't even writing erotica then.

This little bit of information became the basis for "The Valentine Affair." I added another character toward the end of the story to accommodate the photographs that went with the story. In this case, the story was created before the photos were chosen and laid out. The art director gave me a stack of left-overs from other magazines to go through in order to find suitable shots that matched up. The only ones I could find with two curly-haired cuties in them also contained two females.

"The Valentine Affair" was written for *AC/DC*. The original *AC/DC* had photos and stories of two guys and a girl, or two of each, with the guys having each other somewhere along the way. *AC/DC* was one of the predecessors of the gay male magazines. Once gay photo books were firmly established, the magazine tried to appeal to the hetero male who didn't want anything to do with two guys together. Therefore, *AC/DC* came to feature just girls who swing both ways. The stories are about a girl who has sex with a guy, or two guys, or a guy and a girl, or any number of each.

The Valentine Affair

As I put the last of the wallpaper samples back in the rack and prepared to close the shop, I found that I was very angry at myself. Another weekend was shot to hell. I hadn't met any eligible men, I hadn't even gone out with a girlfriend. I had spent this weekend as I had every other weekend, working.

Even when that handsome Dr. Yeager came in last week to have his kitchen remodeled, I didn't give him a hint of a flirt. All business, that's me.

But it's getting harder and harder to curl up with my *Interior Decorator* magazines and fabric swatches instead of a nice warm man. More and more lately, I've found myself fantasizing about them, big and strong and virile. I imagine their rough-skinned, hairy bodies enfolding me, rubbing a massive, wet cock against my thigh, whispering to me to soften me up for the action.

And then I grab hold of my huge breast and squeeze it, closing my eyes and trying to believe it's a man's hand, and that he's going to suck me. Sometimes I'm almost convinced. My nipples get hard and erect in hopeful expectation. My cunt fills with juices and my clitoris begins its throbbing dance. My vaginal lips begin to swell and sweat. Then I remember where I am. A customer enters the store or the phone rings and my throbbing pussy and I are back to work playing Ms. Interior Decorator and trying to forget that we'd like to have our own interior decorated with some giant, hard rod and some hot, wet cum.

But it was 5:00, Saturday afternoon. My store was closed. I only had one stop on the way home, not counting the grocery store.

As I put on my lipstick and brushed my hair, I realized I was making myself beautiful for the check-out clerk, who was probably an acne-ed nineteen and had never done it with any-one but his hand.

Another Saturday night at home. Fuck.

I'd like to.

I got in my Mercedes and decided to put the top down. It was a summer evening and the sun was still shining like hell. It was actually hot out. I loosened the collar of my blouse and let the wind whip through it as I drove.

The hot air blew through my blouse and caressed my over-sized breasts. My nipples were tingling and I tried to rub my arm against them as I drove. No sense in turning on my fellow drivers.

I had to stop by Dr. Yeager's condo at the Marina to see how the boys were doing. My delivery boy, Mike, had taken on the chore of putting up new wallpaper with his cousin who was just in from Puerto Rico. I'd let him take jobs like that before and he'd always done well, so when Dr. Yeager asked if we could install his new kitchen and not just design it, I jumped at the job. It meant more money for me and Mike needs the work.

He was going to college. I guess that's why I always thought of him as a kid, but he isn't really. He was almost as old as I was. In fact, to be perfectly honest with myself, I had looked at him in that other way more than once.

I would watch him unloading those heavy carpet rolls. His bare back, tanned from surfing, would glisten in the sun and all his magnificent muscles would take turns expanding and contracting across his back and arms.

He wore cut-offs, constantly. The only change in uniform

was when he wore a T-shirt in the store. He had curly black hair, big brown doe eyes and an easy laugh. I liked Mike a lot.

I pulled up in front of Dr. Yeager's place and then searched through the maze of apartments, looking for M-492. I was hoping the boys were almost done because I wanted to see how it had come out. The pattern for the wallpaper was a new one and I was eager to know how that color blue blended with the walnut cabinets.

When I let myself into M-492, Mike and his cousin were sitting in the living room, wearing nothing but . . . what do you call those? Those little towels that button at the side. I was a little embarrassed.

"What are you doing?" I asked.

"We just had a sauna and a Jacuzzi. It was so great. Want to try it?" Mike was grinning. He'd been smoking grass again, I could tell.

"Did you finish the kitchen?" I asked as I walked toward it.

"Hours ago," said Mike. He joined me in the kitchen. It looked great. "Why don't you relax?"

I turned around and looked at him. I was anything but relaxed, and worse, I couldn't think of a damn thing to say. I leaned back on the counter for support. Mike grabbed hold of my arm.

"I'm all right," I said, too quickly.

"Hey," he said as he stroked my cheek. "What's going on?"

I looked down toward the floor, probably from embarrassment. But looking down just made matters worse as I could see that there was a small tent rising from Mike's little towel. (I think they're called sarongs, those things.) I flushed.

Well, Mike didn't go to college for nothing. Two seconds didn't pass before he realized the state I was in, which was *second-phase horny*. He held my face with his right hand, my arm with his left and then he brushed his clean-shaven cheek against mine and blew in my ear.

All right, so it's corny, but sometimes corny things work too. I practically sank into the new floor. Then he moved his hand down further and took hold of my left breast. My nipple sprang up right through the bra and blouse. Suddenly, I was worried about Mike's cousin.

"Let's go in the bedroom," said Mike.

I found I wasn't *that* worried about Mike's cousin. We walked right past him on the way to the bedroom, and I wasn't even introduced.

"What's his name?" I asked as we floated through.

"Valentine."

"What?"

"We call him Val. He doesn't speak very much English at all, so we don't have to explain anything."

"That's good," I said, peering back over my shoulder. Valentine looked a lot like Mike, same curly mop of hair, same strong tanned body, same tent. What? I took another look. It was true. Valentine had a sympathetic hard-on as he watched us disappear into the bedroom.

He smiled at me. I smiled back and giggled to Mike.

Mike drew me toward the bed and then threw me back on it, violently. I was about to protest about his sudden aggressiveness when I looked up and realized why he'd done it just that way. There was a mirror over the bed. I could see myself lying there, my breast half out of my bra, my blouse partially unbuttoned, my face red.

I scooted back further so that I could see my whole body. It was wild! It was like watching a whole different woman, who happened to look like me.

When Mike crawled onto the bed, the pleasure was doubled. I saw his long, dark body wrap itself around mine. I couldn't stop looking at our reflections. Then I saw his long cock pop out of his towel. It laid itself across my white leg in stark contrast.

Mike was stroking me and undoing things as he worked his way up and down my body. I was uttering strange, guttural sounds, involuntarily, and bending into his every motion.

Now he had my blouse opened and my skirt up and was working his hand into my panties. And suddenly, I don't know why, maybe I was afraid, I sat up and I asked him to brush my hair.

I pulled my long, thick blonde hair out of its tight hairclip and let it fall.

"I'd love to," he said and he rose to get the hairbrush.

Mike turned me around and began to brush my hair. "Wait a minute," he said, "what am I doing? In Puerto Rico, Valentine is a hairdresser. He should be brushing your hair."

I pulled my blouse shut and straightened my skirt and Valentine was called in. Mike sat in front of me and Valentine sat behind me. Valentine was stroking my hair as if it were skin, and brushing it so carefully and sensitively. I felt like a princess.

Mike was talking to me softly and still running his hands across my cheek. Sometimes he would continue on down my neck to my breast, and once he reached in and grabbed it.

It was weird. I had Mike in front of me and his double in back of me and above me in the ceiling mirror I had a duplicate of all of us. It was as if I were being made love to by four men, and I was two women, one who rejected the love, one who wanted with all her heart and body to give into it.

The heat of my excitement filled my neck and face. My pussy was wet and so were my panties. My nipples were so hard, they stood like two mountains upon mountains and their now-dark color showed through the fabric of my clothing.

Mike began to stroke my leg. He pushed my skirt up and my panties down with one motion. Before I realized what was happening, I was being laid down by the two men. One of them was cupping my huge breast and sucking lightly on the nipple, the other one was licking my pussy. I didn't even know which one was which and it didn't even matter.

I nuzzled my face into Mike's hair (or was it Val's?) and looked up into the mirror to see all of us.

My skirt had been removed, my blouse and bra were open. My legs were spread apart and there was a curly haired man with his head between them. The other curly head was at my tit. I began to moan. I could feel someone's fingers entering me and it felt so good, but I wanted more, more.

Now there were hands on both my breasts and my nipples

were being squeezed and my tits being pumped and mashed. Val's fingers (I think) were coming into my cunt faster and harder now and I was close, so close to coming.

Suddenly, I opened my eyes and looked up into the mirror and saw another body. *It was a woman,* a heavy-set woman with big, brown breasts and a hairy crotch. I jumped.

"It's all right'" said Mike, and gently pushed me down again. The woman began to suck my other breast.

"But . . . ?" I began to ask, but Mike answered.

"She's Val's girl, don't worry. She loves making love to horny women."

By then I was too far gone anyway to have protested. I felt as though there were loving hands everywhere. Mike was now kissing my neck and licking my ear and nibbling there or something. One of his hands was caressing my hair, the other was squeezing my right breast. His leg was wrapped around mine and he was moving it so that it brushed against the inside of my thigh—a very erotic place for me.

Then there was Val, who seemed to never tire of eating pussy. He was licking and sucking alternately, and he was using his hands to stroke and tickle and squeeze my pussy. His thumbs were somewhere near my asshole, not in it, just close enough to give me shivers.

The woman, Val said her name was Carmen, was doing marvelous things to my left breast. She was kneading it or something, whatever it was, I was about to go through the glass ceiling. And it was a real trip to see all of us up there, doing all those things. It was like seeing yourself and your lovers in a porno movie and acting out the parts at the same time.

I knew I was about to come, and I knew it would be the biggest climax of my life. But I wanted cock, one of those cocks, either one, it didn't matter.

Mike knew it. He pulled himself up on his knees, but he shoved his huge long brown cock into my mouth. And my mouth was so hungry. I gobbled that thing and took it as deep as I could while Carmen still worked away at my breasts. She was coaxing me in Spanish. Then, just as I thought I was feeling the supreme ecstasy, Val put his matching prick into my cunt.

Wham! He rammed it up deep inside me. He hit me so hard I pulled off Mike's cock, but as soon as I saw what was happening to me, I grabbed hold of it again. I was sucking the life out of Mike's gorgeous cock and Val was pumping me so fast and so deep, I could have screamed.

I could feel Carmen's hands all over my body now, and her wet mouth too. I could feel her wet, hairy pussy pumping against my leg as well. She was straddling it. I wanted to look up at the mirror again but I couldn't tear myself away from what I was doing.

I started coming. My pussy was sucking hard on Val's cock and my mouth was sucking hard on Mike's. As I groaned with my mouth around Mike's rigid organ, he groaned too, and his cum filled and overflowed my mouth. Val shot his wad deep inside my cunt. I could feel his hot juices all the way at the top of me. Carmen was jacking herself off. I could hear her moaning. As she began her rise to orgasm Val put his mouth on her cunt and she screamed with pleasure.

I looked dreamily up at the tangled bodies above us, a study in brown on white. And I fell asleep. It was the best sleep I'd had since I bought my store. And I dreamed marvelous things. I woke up a few times and noticed it was getting dark, I noticed the boys were gone, Carmen was gone, but I felt so marvelous and the bed was so comfortable, I just couldn't force myself to leave.

But the last time I awakened, I was in for a shock, because I looked up to see Dr. Yeager staring down at me. I was so embarrassed that I jumped up and said something dumb, like: "Oh! Dr. Yeager!"

He put his hand on my shoulder and said, "Please, lie down. Relax. It's all right."

I began to apologize, but he interrupted me.

"The kitchen looks fantastic. You've done a wonderful job. You deserve the rest."

"Oh, but . . ."

"Shhh," he said. "I'd been wondering ever since I met you

how I would get you to bed. I even had you do over a kitchen that was all right the way it was, but you didn't get the hint."

I smiled. Now I was really embarrassed.

"And here, all I had to do was come home, and there you are!" He laughed softly. "You look really great in this bed. When I bought it, I thought of you."

"You're kidding!"

"No," he said. "And you haven't disappointed me at all. You look beautiful. How did you get so sexy?"

I didn't answer that one. I just scooted over to one side and asked. "Won't you join me, Dr. Yeager?"

He said yes, took off his clothes and slid in.

I should be so lucky, huh?

Well, back to the subject at hand, my friend Mike and his cousin Val inspired this tale and fit my assignment. You may be saying to yourself, well, that's obvious. Anybody could see the sexual potential in that situation. What about *my* life? Well, I don't know what your life is like, but I'm positive there is material in it. Because let's face it, sex is an underlying force everywhere, even when only one sex is present. It's a very strong part of our make-up and even if we refuse to acknowledge it, it continues to prevail.

Gloria Leonard, publisher of *High Society,* says that every person is a sex object. It is not a matter of choice. The choice comes in when you decide how to use your sexuality or how to allow it to use you.

What really happened in my case was that I went into the bedroom with my friend, Mike, not to do anything serious, just to talk. It still seemed awkward and I got embarrassed, and tried to leave. Then Mike called Val in to show me everything was OK and he asked Val to brush my hair while we talked. All very innocent.

So Val began to brush my hair, which was quite long at the time. He stood in back of me; I sat on the bed. Mike sat in front of me and was gently tracing the neckline of my blouse with his fingers as he spoke about beach volleyball. What he was talking about didn't matter. I was so aroused by this situation that my skin stayed flushed for hours afterward. But this was real life, not fiction, and I was a young and innocent coward. I left for home, leaving my tale forever unresolved until it came to life as "The Valentine Affair."

The jump from what really happened to what might have happened, or even, what you wish might have happened, is not as big a leap as you might think. It's all there, waiting for you to reveal it.

Assume you're a housewife with two kids. Sex objects include your husband, the mailman, the nursery school teacher, anyone who delivers anything to your house from Diaper Dan to United Parcel, the gas station attendant, the grocery store clerk, the shopper standing behind you in line, and so on. There are sexual possibilities in almost any interchange.

I once met a handsome, interesting single father at my son's nursery school. The man who came to repair my typewriter turned out to look like Fabian. Even that cute teenaged babysitter could enrich your fantasy life. (But watch out—this could be addicting!) It's always there if you're paying attention.

OK, so for the purposes of this exercise, let's decide on one situation. This time let's take it from a male point of view.

What really happened: You are very shy and not into parties. You're bored with dating and singles bars and yet want to be in love again. You miss that feeling. The only woman in the world who is halfway appealing to you works in your office and is married. She's very pretty, has a bubbly personality and she makes you laugh. You'll never make a move because she works for you and because she's married, but if she weren't married and you didn't have to work together, well, then you'd. . . .

What would you do? This fantasy is where your story begins.

You said, "if she weren't married," so for the purposes of your story, she's single. Is she still working for you? Let's say she works for the guy across the hall. Now you've said you're shy, so you can make her the aggressor, as in "Car Wash Cookie." Or, since this is fiction, you can make yourself bolder.

However, all you've got so far is the situation. You still need a story, something to bring the two of you together. Perhaps she's been assigned a special project and needs your help to get through it. Already wheels are turning and I'm imagining how that might occur.

Once you've established the setting, introduced yourself and the girl—let's call her Jennie—the next step is to create the catalyst which will bring you together: her special project. Then, you sketch the characters through dialogue and behavior as you work on this project together.

Let me provide you with a very brief example of how this story might come about:

> The woman who works across the hall from my office has been driving me crazy. She's so pretty, she should be in the movies. Her thick brown hair falls in huge waves over her shoulders and bounces when she walks. And she's always smiling, always cheerful.
>
> She never fails to say good morning to me, as if I matter, and when she brings coffee for her boss, she always asks if I'd like some too. I think I'm in love.
>
> Her name is Jennie, and I never dreamed I would ever get any closer to her—until last month, when she came to me with a problem.

Bingo. That's your set-up. Now you will go into detail by allowing the characters to speak for themselves.

> "You see, Mister Barnard," Jennie said to me as she leaned against the corner of my desk. "I sort of told Ted I knew how to program computers." She smiled shyly. "It wasn't exactly a lie, but I think the Krantz project is a little over my head. Do you think you could help me?"
>
> Her big brown, trusting eyes were irresistable. So was her perfume. "Let me have a look at it," I said, reaching for the folder in her hand. Then she came around to my side of the desk to read over my shoulder. The words on the page before me blurred as I felt her closeness. She must have realized the power she had over me.

Now your hero is established as one who is not confident around women and your heroine as one who is apparently oblivious to her power over men, or one who knows how to get the most from wielding this power.

Since this story is for a sex magazine, these two sweet people will have to come together somehow. You could have them work

over the Krantz project in Jennie's apartment or keep them after
hours one night to work at the office.

Let's say, you're through with Krantz. He's tucked safely into
the computer and the job is done. Thoughtfully, you brought some
vintage champagne to the office to celebrate. All the other workers
have gone home and you and Jennie are alone in the computer
room. Jennie, usually prudent, gets a little bit tipsy, allowing her to
loosen her grip on some of that suspected underlying passion.

I poured one more glass of champagne into Jennie's cup. She
giggled as she tried to hold the cup steady to catch the last
drop.

"Mister Barnard," she said, "I do believe you're trying to
get me drunk." Then she downed the cupful as if to challenge
me.

"Perhaps I ought to take you home now, Jennie." I didn't
want to end this wonderful evening, but I was getting nervous
around her. Tipsy, she was even more beautiful. Her eyes
sparkled and she leaned on me flirtatiously. It was difficult to
control my urge to grab her and drag her to the floor. Taking
her home would be the safe way.

Again you are emphasizing your hero's dilemma. Not only is he
painfully shy, he's downright scared of his own sexual appetite.
This fear is his jeopardy and it is Jennie's job to release him from
his self-imposed bindings so that he can complete the task set forth
at the beginning of his story.

It's always better, however, if the hero is allowed to make the
first move. So let's permit him a brief moment of courage. After
all, Jennie has probably implied to him in ways he chose not to
comprehend, and more than once, that she likes him. In fact, let's
have her do that now and see what Mr. Barnard does.

"Mr. Barnard," Jennie whispered, her hand on my lapel. "I
like you. You are a very, very nice man."

"Oh, Jennie," I sighed, taking her into my arms. She must
have felt me trembling as I held her close to me. She must have
known how much I wanted her. "Jennie, you are just great.
Just super."

Now, you may think this dialogue is pretty mild for a man who has stated, albeit privately to us, that he is in love with this girl, but remember, his problem is shyness. He is not one to express undying love or grand compliments, even to the woman of his dreams.

But now that they're hugging, we're halfway home, and we can start punching holes in his parachute. Let's see . . . how about we do it with a set of long fingernails. Men just love long red fingernails.

> Jennie set her cup down and opened the top three buttons of my shirt. Then she slipped her hands inside, running her long red fingernails through my chest hair.
>
> "Mmmm, Mister Barnard, you are so sexy," she said, just before she kissed my chest. And then she kissed my neck. I held onto her tightly, trying to memorize this moment, certain it would never get better than this.

Won't it? Not if old Barnard doesn't put the move on and do some kissing up on young Jennie. Why won't he do it? Same old problem. Let's give him a kick in the pants.

> Suddenly Jennie looked up into my face and lost her smile. I thought she was about to pull away, but instead, she said: "Kiss me . . . please."

If that doesn't do it, we'll have to can Barnard and get us a real man. Anyhow, that's your story. Now you wrap it up and let's give some other reader a shot.

What really happened: You're a construction worker and you look really good in your bright orange vest and hard hat. Thousands of women pass by your site each day, but one in particular strikes your fancy. Every weekday morning, precisely at 8:30, you hear her high heels clicking down the sidewalk and you go to the edge of your floor to catch a glimpse of her. She has shiny brown hair which bounces with the rhythm of her walk. One day she smiles at you. . . .

There is an important element to this kind of story. It involves sex with someone the hero does not yet know. Sex with strangers is something that is interesting to your reader, partly because it's mysterious and tempting and yet most of us never dare to do it. It's so risky! Another reason is many of your readers will not have an active sex life, so the potential for them might only be with strangers. Most importantly, almost all of your reader's fantasies involve strangers, women they see on the bus or in the store—women they never actually speak to, let alone date.

So you've got a good set-up for your story. Now all you have to do is follow it through the same way Mr. Barnard did. If you find this impossible, try switching the point of view and see if that works. You play Jennie and admit a fascination with bare-armed construction workers. Then project yourself into an adventure with one of them:

> I called up to the one in the orange vest and motioned for him to come down. He smiled broadly and was down beside me in a flash.
>
> "I made an extra sandwich," I told him, "hoping I could entice you into having lunch with me over at the park."

The park gets a lot of action in my stories. After all, what better place for two working strangers to go?

Anyhow, now that Jennie's made another conquest, let's take one other commonplace example of the kind of story could happen to anybody.

What really happened: You're a part-time waiter at Petroli's Pizza Place and a beautiful redhead sat at your station. She was with a girlfriend and they tried to get a bee out of their lunch and safely out of the window. You came to her aid and killed the bee, whereupon she denounced you as a menace to nature, paid her bill and left.

What could have happened: Upon noticing the women struggling to get the bee off to safety, you arrived on the scene with a paper cup and a postcard and trapped the bee, setting him free outside the cafe door. Whereupon, the redhead, undyingly grateful, gave you her phone number.

Or, she rescues the bee without your help and you are enamored of her gentle nature and you give her your phone number.

Or, as you both struggle to shoo the bee outdoors, causing hysteria among the other pizza patrons, you wind up in each other's arms and forget all about the bee.

What really really happened, as I recall, is that I was the one who freed the bee, with the help of a paper cup from the good-looking waiter, who was really a Czechoslovakian biology teacher here to learn English (which makes the whole thing more romantic, because there's more to it than what you see at first glance).

The deal is, you take what you've got and you embellish it as much as you can. Squeeze every drop of story potential out of every incident and you'll soon find stories in everything you do. You'll find your heroes and heroines in grocery stores and banks. Listening to your friends' tales of woe will give you even more ideas. Once you have discovered the germ of the idea, getting from what really happened, which may have been very little, to what could have happened, is a snap. And yes, I did get his phone number.

Avoiding Misinformation and Checking Your Facts

If you are a male writer and you're writing from a female point of view, try to get your facts straight first. There's nothing more aggravating than reading copy supposedly written by a woman that is full of erroneous information about a woman's body, her sexual needs and her fantasies.

Witness my own *faux pas* when, as a beginner in this extraordinary business, I wrote one giant blunder. As a novice, with no experience whatsoever in anal sex, I was told it was necessary to insert it into my story now and then, but not how exactly to do it. Another writer set me straight, but only after my blunder had been published in 5,000 issues of a magazine.

In the story "Parisian Lay-over" (see page 128), my hero alternated insertion between two of his lover's openings, anal and vaginal. Besides being unsanitary and kind of kinky, it's just plain unhealthful, and potentially painful. Even Marlon Brando knew that in *Last Tango in Paris*. Since then, I've made it a point not to write about anything I didn't know about, if not from personal experience, at least from books or trustworthy friends. The best way to educate yourself on a subject, anal sex, for example, next to doing it yourself, is to talk to someone who loves it. A regular practitioner can tell you far more than a scientist in his master's dissertation.

When I first started writing for adult publications, I read a few current issues to get the gist of it. I was appalled by the misinformation that was being circulated. This experience gave me a political motive for writing porn. I set out to update information and reach the misinformed swingers of the world with what I personally felt was a more equitable view of the heterosexual, bisexual and homosexual lifestyle.

I hated that porn pushers were humiliating women, turning them into objects of lust instead of human beings. It's OK to lust for a woman, as long as one remembers she's a live person just like a man is. If she wasn't, he might as well have sex with one of those inflatable dolls.

Just to give you a brief example: In every lesbian story I encountered, there was a voyeur, usually the husband of one of the wayward girls, and an unhappy ending for the lesbians. They died at the end of the story. Why? Because these stories have been reprinted over decades and in the days when they were first written, lesbianism was still considered evil and against nature. The lesbians had to be punished. Some of you may agree but surely you would not advocate doing away with all those who dabble in bisexuality.

I rewrote a magazine called *Sappho* and changed all the girls to total, full-on lesbians, not bisexuals who wanted to show off for their boyfriends. I didn't knock anybody off at the end of the story. I had them enjoying themselves. Now and then I'd let one of them choose this path because of the way she'd been treated by men.

So what happened to the magazine? Did the readers fall away because there was no peeping Tom watching the girls have sex? Did they send in letters of complaint? No way. Readership picked up. Why? Because the stories were more realistic. The girls' motives were clearer, and the intimacy of their one-on-one adventure made the story more enticing. The reader took the place of the absent voyeur.

While I'm on the track of misinformation: If you want to write erotica and you don't know much about sex, there are ways to find out. First of all, ask whomever you make love with. Then ask somebody else. That famous doctor who wrote a whole sex book by asking his wife and getting only her opinion on such crucial matters as how many orgasms a woman must have to feel satisfied and what constitutes an orgasm, made a big mistake. He should have messed around a little. Alas, his innocent wife did not know everything and was confused about many of the things she thought she knew. For years women were looking for firecrackers and rocket ships instead of physical sensations and feeling perverted because they liked to come more than once a day, and confused when they couldn't distinguish a vaginal orgasm from a clitoral one.

On the other hand, when D. H. Lawrence asked Frieda to tell him about feminine sexuality, she gave him such solid information, he was able to write convincing details not just about sex, but about how women think and feel, so that an uninformed reader might even suppose his novels had a female author. If you're not willing to get into the water yourself, find a good swimmer.

Next, ask your friends. You'd be amazed to discover how many of them will eagerly tell you the most intimate details of their sex lives. It's a subject which has been off limits for too long and people are dying to let some of their secrets out, either to brag or to question. Fantasies are also easily shared, once you tell your friend it's for research, not because you want to pry.

Next, there are research materials at your local library. *The Hite Report* is great for information on women and so is its male counterpart (see the reading list at the back of this book). Nancy Friday's *My Secret Garden* and *Men in Love* are excellent direct source material. A number of other fascinating and informative books are available in paperback at your local bookstore.

I particularly recommend *Men in Love,* because, assuming these contributors were describing their true fantasies, it proves that men can dream up and write about fantasies that are just as erotic for women as they are for men. In other words, real men are as interested in expressing love through sex as they are in getting off. This book will also give you ideas for your stories.

Any book that is written by a person telling his or her own life story has information in it you can use. An important book in my reference library is Studs Terkel's *Working*. Finding out how a real person feels about his or her job, life, family or future is helpful input for fiction writing.

Where Not to Get Material

Don't trust other sex magazines for accurate sex information. They are written to sensationalize and distort, especially female desires and abilities. When Ginger Lynn or Pepper Bond tells you she had her first orgasm at six while riding on a hobby horse, don't believe it. And don't turn around and write an article that pronounces all women warped who didn't share that experience.

All adult magazine articles, especially interviews with porn stars, are beefed up for publication to boost circulation (after the star herself, or himself, punched it up for the interview). They didn't do half the things they say they did, but they know that's what their fans want to hear.

How does the saying go? Believe half of what you read and none of what you hear. Basically, you should trust yourself. If you went to an orgy and found it boring and stupid, there were probably a lot of other people who thought so too. If you found it degrading and humiliating to women, others shared your view. That's the truth and you'd never sell this story. How do you tell the truth and still make it exciting enough to interest a publisher? That's half the job of being a writer.

You take the basic truth and then you stretch it to the limit. You find that one girl at the orgy who seemed to be enjoying herself and you write your story from her point of view. You can still slip in your own editorial opinion, as long as the main thrust is positive, educational, tantalizing and written with dramatic appeal.

If you're daring enough to go to the orgy yourself, you could produce a realistic first-person, eyewitness account of what it felt, smelled and tasted like. But if you're a typical reclusive, retiring writer, find someone else who went and ask them. My guess is you'll get more positive information from a man than you will from a woman, and more from a repeater than a first-timer.

Fiction is mythology. Reality is what people live through every day. If they want to read about reality, they read nonfiction, science magazines and history books.

They expect you, as a fiction writer, to take them away from all that. Whoever believed in Peter Rabbit, Moby Dick, James Bond, ET, Scarlett O'Hara or Princess Daisy? We all did. Fact and fiction intersect. You take something that's true, add something that could happen, make everything prettier and more exciting and you come out with fiction. The more factual material you insert into your story, the more believable your fiction will be.

One popular myth is that single people have a better sex life than married people do. I know it's a myth because I have many single friends and they're not getting half the action that married people think they are.

People think just because one is single, he or she has an insatiable sex drive, a constant swirl of dating activity, and attends orgies on a regular basis. Married people are especially guilty of overestimating what actually goes on out in the single world. Single people, especially females, tend to romanticize married life in much the same way. Conservatives think liberals are all sex maniacs. Mothers are notorious for over- or under-estimating their grown children's sexual activities. Some grown men see budding nymphomaniacs in girls who haven't even begun to think about sex. Some teenaged boys think all women over twenty-five are sex-starved. When in reality, we must admit it's all nonsense.

In reality, married people have a better opportunity to have more sex, more often than single people do. Most married people have the potential for a fuller, richer, more intense sex life than do most single people. They have the added element of intimacy which comes from years of being together and caring for each other and practicing the art of sexual expression together. No night on the town through a series of singles bars is going to be as ultimately satisfying as an evening spent in front of the TV with someone you love, and have loved, for years.

The difference is not between marriage and singlehood, but between those who love each other and those who have no one to love. Romance writers, pornographers and those who write articles with titles such as: *Which 10 Cities Are the Best for Catching a Man, How to Find a Man over Forty* and *Where Have All the Old-Fashioned Girls Gone?* are writing for the person who hasn't made a love-match yet or has and it went wrong, or has and wished it was better.

In other words, we're writing fiction for those who want to believe in it. Never mind the reality.

Every one of us has things we wish the world knew. Erotic fiction is as good a place as any to express yourself. I once wished men knew how irritating it is when they get off after two minutes and then roll over and go to sleep. Many, many of my stories talk about this problem in their own subtle way. I constantly have the man trying to hold back his load, working toward his lover's orgasm, caressing her, kissing her, talking to her, bringing her up and taking her over the height of love.

And where in the world did men get the idea a woman likes to be thrown on the ground and practically raped? No woman I know wants the flesh of her vagina torn up by an inconsiderate macho man who can't wait for her to get wet. Erotica has given me a podium for my attempt at correcting years of misinformation.

You may argue that you know such-and-such a woman who has a rape fantasy, and even I know some girls who like to be slapped on the behind before being taken in the doggie position. There are women who like to be physically abused and dominated, but these women, at least the ones I know, say that they want to be in on the game.

I have a male friend who began dating a girl who on the third sexual encounter asked him if he would please tie her down, arms and legs spread, in a big X. It took some convincing on her part, but he did it. This kind of girl needs a co-partner who loves to tie girls up. However, if a man tried to tie a girl up who wasn't into this routine, that would be obscene. That would be sexual brutality and not what erotica is about. Can you see the difference? If it's a game, it's OK. Forced sex is out. S&M can be written about and is, especially in gay male magazines, but for our purposes at least, give the girl some control of the situation and allow her to stop the action if it gets out of hand. The more popular hetero S & M pieces are female domination anyway, but if you must write about male domination, let your heroine have some choice in the matter too.

Tell the truth whenever possible. Spruce it up with a flourish of fiction. Tell about what sex is like between two consenting adults, physiologically, emotionally and sexually. Make your characters breathe, enjoy, and take part in the story with energy and passion. And have fun. Writing isn't always fun. But writing erotica should be lots of fun, or you're not doing it right.

CHAPTER 8

GETTING YOUR STORY
PUBLISHED

Deciding Where to Send Your Work

OK, let's say you've got a great idea for a story, but you don't
know where to sell it. First, take into account the elements of your
story. Is it a mystery? An adventure? A drama? Or just a sex story?
What would you like it to be? For the sake of example, let's say
you've got a straight sex story, ten pages in length, with no mystery to it. Your basic "Girl Meets Boy and Fucks Him Crazy."

One thing you are going to have to do eventually is take a trip
down to your local newsstand and check out the action. Of the
260 girlie magazines in print at last count, your stand should handle at least a dozen or so of them. You are almost sure to find
Playboy, Penthouse, Hustler and *Oui*. They're on the high end of
the genre—slick pages, high-quality color photography and well-
written articles.

On the next plateau, you'll find other semi-slicks with fewer
pages, second-rate photography and fewer articles of a less general—specifically sexual—nature. Your newsstand may carry
Cheri, Mayfair, Close Up, Gem, Buf, Pub and others. The cheap-
est publications are printed on stock that feels something like
newsprint, called pulp. The photos don't show up as well. The
topics for articles are hard to believe and the magazines sell on
almost pure sensationalism. The last type of girlie book or men's
magazine which you'll find on a regular newsstand, is the sex
newspaper, selling for 25¢ to $2.50. These have big blow-ups of

poor-quality black-and-white photos, some sex articles and lots of ads, for everything from massages to sex toys.

Which publications you'll find in your town will vary, depending upon where you live. Some states have laws protecting their citizens from certain types of sexuality in magazines and yet they'll take other stuff that's just as bad but in a different way. Sensationalized violence, for example, or illustrated water sports, scatalogical material in relation to sex acts, bondage, mutilation, exploitation of amputees' sexual needs and other such distortions that I don't need to press on you here. Some sexist officials will allow porn based on female exploitation, such as the infamous girl in a meat grinder shot of *Hustler* magazine, but will not permit issues of *Playgirl* when their centerfold happens to have a semierection. It's a pretty subjective selection at best and one for which I doubt there are any hardcore (so to speak) rules.

I could tell you to look for *High Society* and you wouldn't find it, but you'd have other magazines that I can't get in California. Many newsstand and adult store publications do not even cross state lines.

Look at what there is for you in your hometown, buy a few issues and take them home to study them. This may cause some embarrassing moments at home, but most people who are related to writers know we do weird things. Pick out one you like. Read their stories, articles, ads, everything. The ads will tell you a bit about their audience, especially those little classified ads in the back.

Zero in on one specific magazine and outline one of their stories. Study the rhythm of it. See if your story matches up. Check out the length, subject matter and type of characters.

If your story is that type that fits the magazine and the length is right, but, say, the hero should be a male instead of a female, see if you can make this change without hurting your story.

Count the words of their feature story and make yours the same. (You don't have to count every word—count one line, then lines per column, then columns, etc.) If their story is 2,500 words, that's ten typewritten pages, double spaced.

Query Letters and Cover Letters

Let's say you've written your story to the specifications of *Macho* magazine and it's every bit as good as the one in this month's issue. Now you're ready to send it off. You have two choices:

You may query the publisher to see if he's interested in seeing your story, or you can send it in cold, with a cover letter introducing yourself. There are no statistics on which approach works best. Some magazines insist on being queried first, such as *Forum, Screw* and *Oui*. Others, such as *Juggs, Gent, Gentleman's Companion* and *Leg Show,* prefer to see your complete manuscript.

Even when a magazine insists on queries, you can take a chance and mail in your story without asking first. Several of my students, who had never been published before, did it this way for this reason: They had no record of past sales, no tear sheets, no reputation. However, having attended my seminar, they did have some good material. Fearful that they would be immediately rejected on the basis of their query letter—which is unfortunately, probably exactly what would have happened—they took a chance and won.

Let's suppose you're not sure *Macho* magazine is looking for freelance writers, so you decide to query first. A simple "will you buy a freelance story" will do, if it's accompanied by a self-addressed, stamped envelope (SASE). If *Macho* magazine does not normally buy outside material but you're convinced that your story is perfect for them, a more serious query is in order. Let's say you've got a hot tear sheet and an even hotter idea. Here is what your query letter might say:

Mr. John D. Eros
Macho Magazine
123 Sizzle Street
New York, NY

November 6, 1986

Dear Mr. Eros,

Enclosed please find my published story, "Love in the Cannery."

I have read your magazine, *Macho,* with interest and I feel I can write for you. I have the perfect story in mind: A big, burly jock, just out of prison, comes into a small town for some action and meets this busty waitress. She wants to knock off her old man and sees him as the perfect dupe. I'll call you in a few days to talk about this.

Sincerely,
Susie Sunshine

And then call him! Believe me, an editor won't call you, unless you blow him away with your tear sheets. (By the way, forgive me if there really is a *Macho* magazine. If there isn't, there probably should be.)

The wrong kind of query letter goes on for pages and says nothing, or worse, relates the long history of the writer's undeserved rejection. Another no-no is condescending to, or worse insulting, your potential employer. Something on the line of: "Well, I guess I've sunk to the lowest level of literature to have to write to you for work." Unless you can prove that you are jesting, you'll never hear from this guy again. And humor doesn't always translate on paper, where the person can't see your impish grin.

A cover letter is pretty much the same thing, except that you will include your completed story in the package. Again, be brief and to the point.

Mr. John Eros
Sex Magazine
12 Erotic St.
New York, NY

November 6, 1986

Dear Mr. Eros,

I am a freelance writer of erotic fiction and I have a great story for *Sex* magazine. Please take a look at the enclosed and I'll call you next week.

Sincerely,
Jane Writer
Enclosed: SASE

Always enclose a self-addressed stamped envelope, one that is large enough to hold your manuscript. This practice doesn't mean you have a negative attitude and you know you're going to get your story back. It shows that you're a professional. And if the editor doesn't want to buy your story, he'll be more likely to return it instead of sending it to the circular file underneath his desk. He's not going to send it back if there's no SASE.

Preparing to Submit Your Manuscript

Here are a few odd tidbits of information every writer should know and every editor wishes every writer knew. It's true writers send in manuscripts with misspellings and typos which sometimes get published, as do some novels which were submitted hand-written on yellow pads. It's also true that someone wins the Irish Sweepstakes every year. But chances are it's not gonna be you.

If your messy manuscript is sitting on an editor's desk with a pile of neat, carefully written ones, yours will be sent to the end of the line without ceremony. You owe it to yourself to go that last mile and clean up your act before it leaves your hands:

1. Use 20 pound bond paper or quality photocopy.
2. Type on one side of the paper only.
3. Double space, use 1-1/2 inch margins.
4. Number the pages in the right top or right bottom corner, or top or bottom center, but be consistent.
5. Make sure your final draft is easily readable. Replace typewriter or printer ribbon when necessary.
6. Do not bind manuscript. Use a paper clip for a short piece, a box for a novel.
7. Do not send in messy copy filled with scribbled-in corrections and white out.
8. Always enclose a self-addressed, stamped envelope the size of your manuscript.

Don't type your story on onion skin to save postage. The stuff wrinkles and you can see through it to the next page. It's the most irritating stock in the world, almost as irritating as getting a story all folded up to fit into a tiny envelope. And I'm speaking as an editor now, not as a writer.

When I was the editor of a nationwide men's magazine, I *wanted* to give work to writers. I wanted to find a budding Anaïs Nin or D. H. Lawrence. But I hoped she or he would come typed neatly and enclosed in an 8-1/2 x 11 envelope. If you send any more than five pages, don't fold them at all. Those big envelopes are eleven cents a piece. If my magazine is not worth eleven cents to you, I don't want to hear from you. Get it?

Now is probably as good a time as any to talk about pseudonyms and post office boxes. Many erotica writers use their real names or some cut-up version of same, such as D. H. Lawrence instead of David Herbert Richards Lawrence. Others who are on their way to fame and fortune with their mystery novels, in their father's firm or who teach nursery school, prefer to leave notoriety to a pseudonym. Many writers have several names. Agatha Christie wrote her romance novels under the name Mary Westmacott, to keep her murder mystery fans from stumbling upon them by mistake.

It's as much fun making up names for yourself as it is naming your kids and pets. But cleverness might work against you if you get carried away and choose something no one can remember or wouldn't want to. Porn stars are infamous for making up fun names, since next to none of them work under their real names. Johnny Wadd, Tom Hardon, Harry Reems, Jock Erectus, Tommy La Rock, Richard Long, Beau Jason and Warren Peece, for the guys. Some gals' names are: Chelsea Manchester, Bunny Bleu, Marilyn Chambers, Candy Samples, Honey Wilder, Desiree Cousteau, Cheri Champagne, Annie Sprinkles, Gina Carnale, Cara Lott and Brigite Bordeaux. How they came up with these names is anybody's guess, beyond advertising their attributes or talents as in Candy Samples and Annie Sprinkles. Each probably has a story to go with his or her name.

Georgina Spelvin is an active porn star, but her name goes back to Shakespeare. When an actor played more than one role in a given performance, he or she was given the second name of George or Georgina Spelvin.

I have several names myself. My first was Darien Lynx, which I purposely designed to be erotic. Darien for daring, I imagined. Lynx for the stealthy cat who slinks around. Cats are extremely sensuous creatures. Actually, driving to work on the day that I had to choose a name, I saw a billboard with a big, flashy red Mercury Lynx jutting out of the frame. I wanted to be called Mercury Lynx. A hot name. But too weird. Everyone would know the person didn't exist. So I put what I thought sounded like a real name in front of it. Then I rationalized it later.

My next name was chosen to represent my bisexual self for my lesbian stories. Then I have a male name for those stories told from the male point of view.

You can represent yourself to publishers under your pseudonym, but once the check is written out, you'd better fess up. You don't want Uncle Sam to think you've created a second identity in order to avoid taxes.

Here is how you present yourself:

> Mary Jones
> P.O. Box 4862
> No. Hollywood, Ca

The Devil's Lie
by Darien Lynx

When he flashed his red eyes at me and his fangs began to grow, I became suspicious of him. But it was too late.

The post office box is optional. You'll get on mailing lists and if you prefer to leave junk mail and rejection slips in the post office wastebasket, then go for it. If you're a single woman living alone and you're afraid, then do it. If you don't want your wife to know about your secret writing life, do it. Post office boxes are cheap. Mine runs eleven dollars for six months. Besides, once you have one, you can send for all those things you didn't dare send for at home.

The major drawback is that someone has to go to the post office to pick up the mail. If it's a check you're waiting for, this trip can be a joy. However, if you get into the habit of picking up rejection slips there, you may start dreading the chore.

Writing to Fit

Suppose you send a ten-page story to *Macho* magazine, and it's rejected. Don't throw out your typewriter and go into real estate sales. You're not through with this story yet. Just because one magazine doesn't want it, doesn't mean it isn't any good. Send it to other magazines that use ten-page stories. Once you exhaust those, make it shorter or longer and try again. If you learn that *Sex* magazine takes five-page stories, you can reduce your ten pages to five and send it off again. I know, it isn't always so easy to do. Writers hate to cut. But it is better to cut and print than never to print at all. If it's a good story, it'll be worth it. If it isn't a good story, shelve it and go on to the next one.

Some magazines will cut your work for you, but you want to avoid that if possible. You don't want them to destroy your artistic integrity or mess up your copy either. The editor who changes your closing line may not be as sensitive as you are to your character's dilemma. An even better reason to make it the right length in the first place is that if there happen to be two sensational sex stories on this editor's desk and one of them is the right length (and therefore requires less editing time), guess which one he's more likely to pick?

Say *Sex* has now rejected your five-page story. But you are sure it's just right for *Lust*. Their format calls for fiction twenty pages long. Lengthening is sometimes easier than shortening. Since I've been writing this stuff, I've gotten very good at making things fit. You can make any thought take any number of words to explain. Here's an example:

John knew he'd have to face Mary eventually. She had heard him in the bedroom with Katherine and was waiting for an explanation. Suddenly, he burst through the door and confronted her. She wasn't angry at all. She'd been crying.

Longer:

John wrung his hands and paced the floor. He knew that eventually he would have to come out of the bedroom and face Mary and endure whatever punishment, whatever cruelty, she would have in store for him. She had a right to be angry, he understood that.

Katherine and he had acted badly, with such abandon. Their love had been so overpowering, it had drowned out any thought of guilt or possible danger. And yet they'd known Mary would come home eventually. They knew this and they made no effort to stop what they were doing to listen for her. Now, she'd heard it all, and she was waiting on the other side of that door.

He took a deep breath to quiet his pounding heart, opened the bedroom door, and saw Mary sitting alone on the couch, her head bent down, her hands in her lap. She'd been crying.

Shorter:

John left the bedroom and confronted Mary, who was not angry, but crying.

See how easy it is? Now you want to know what Mary did, right? Well, she forgave him and she and John and Katherine had a threesome and lived happily ever after.

Much of the writing for low-budget magazines you will be doing will have length restrictions. You'll be writing to a character count for the very short bits, a word count for the longer ones, and a pica width for larger type, such as inserts (also called call outs) for photo sets. Come to think of it, all writing has length restrictions. So you might as well learn how to expand and contract your copy.

Knowing Hardcore from Softcore

Another thing you're going to have to learn is just what makes a story hardcore or softcore.

Hardcore uses lots of sex words and softcore beats around the bush. That's the essential difference in terms of writing. In terms of the market, hardcore is whatever can't be sold on a public newsstand and has to be sealed in plastic, kept under the counter, or sold only in adult bookstores. Inside the adult bookstore, hardcore is the stuff that shows men and women having explicit sex together, or men having explicit sex with other men, and softcore adult store material is that which shows single girls alone or with other girls, or single guys alone.

The definition for the purposes of the laws regarding erotic material is somewhat less complex: insertion vs. non-insertion. If the man's penis or anyone's finger goes inside the woman's vagina, it's

automatically hardcore. (The finger, by the way, for some un-
known reason, is allowed to be inserted up to the first knuckle.
Who makes these rules anyway?) Magazines break these rules consistently. Newsstands are justifiably confused and often put hardcore where softcore should go. Any magazine with photographs
depicting sexual activity, rather than pin-up shots, is potentially
hardcore.

One common way to get around what few restrictions are left is
careful positioning of the models so that the actual point of entry
is hidden from view, but there's no doubt in the reader's mind as
to what's going on. A cover shot that way implies that the buyer of
this magazine will see the whole photo inside.

You may have seen photos of a girl supposedly sucking a man's
organ, for example, but she has her hands covering the crucial
evidence. Black stars pasted down to cover insertion or other sex
no-no's, such as nipples on cover girls, have also been known to
work. It's probably a relief to know that writers have nothing to
do with this end of the business. Your copy, as opposed to pictorials, can have all the insertions in it you want, whether the magazine itself is hard- or softcore.

If you're writing for a hardcore magazine, your story will be
definitively hardcore. There's no avoiding it. You can get away
with a softcore introduction if you're very good, but as a beginner,
you'd better know the difference. For a softcore magazine, you'll
want to stay soft. *Playgirl,* for example, will not tolerate the down
and dirty stuff because their readers don't like it.

It's not always easy to tell the difference in the actual copy. So
here is an example of the same story in softcore and hardcore.
Soft:

Mary looked over at her lover in the driver's seat and smiled.
"I can't send you back to the office in that condition," she
said. He laughed and asked her what she was going to do
about it. Just then, Mary slid across the seat and leaned down
onto John's lap, unzipping his fly.

"We're on Main Street, Mary!" he told her but he was still
laughing. When she had his cock out in her hand, he pulled
over to the side of the road, taking a quick glance at the apart-

ment building they'd parked in front of. Mary skillfully took the hard cock in her hand and massaged it to full flower.

Slowly, she came down on it with her warm lips and John pushed his hips up to meet her.

Harder:

Mary's cunt was aching to fuck her lover, but they had no time for that. She looked over at him in the driver's seat and then down at his crotch.

His cock was sticking straight up in his lap, a drop of pre-cum already making a stain on his pants. Mary knew his balls ached and that he'd have a hard-on all day if she didn't do something about it.

"I can't send you back to the office with a stiff rod and blue balls! You'll have all the secretaries coming in their pants."

John laughed and asked her what she was going to do about it. Then Mary slipped down into his lap and started unzipping his fly.

"We're on Main Street, Mary," he said, but he was still laughing. Her small hands grasped hold of his thick, throbbing cock and squeezed the liquid to the top where she caught a drop of it with the tip of her tongue.

She ran her fingers up his shaft, pushing his juices out so she could eat them. John pulled the car over, taking a quick glance at the apartment building they'd parked in front of. He slid his seat back and let her take him full on, lifting his hips to push his cock into her mouth.

She reached into his pants to grab hold of his balls while she deep-throated his prick. Her hot mouth and tight grip sucked out his jism with vacuum force.

In truth, hardcore stories are different from the start. They don't take on a scene in quite the same way. From the onset, words are used to stimulate the reader more quickly, more aggressively. It might be easier to put a hardcore story into softcore than vice versa.

True hardcore:

John had a thick, juicing rod sticking out in front of him straight toward Mary's face. Mary gasped at the size of it.

"You got some fuckpole, Charlie," she said, wondering if she could take it all in.

"Fuck me," he said. "Lemme fuck your pretty face." With those words making her pussy wet, Mary took his stiff dick down her throat in one gulp.

It's in the very nature of the story. In hardcore, the male almost always plays the aggressive role and the female is almost always amazed by his sexual prowess, his virility and the size of his prick. Hardcore is the kind of erotic material feminists object to, not only because there's no tenderness or romance, only dicks and cunts and fucking and sucking, but because it sometimes miseducates the reader. He gets a lopsided view of what sex is all about. Almost all hardcore adult store publications and most home X-rated video productions propagate the myth of male supremacy, female sub-missiveness and an insatiable sex drive in both. The reader/viewer winds up feeling undersexed, underdeveloped in terms of his or her own sex parts, and unsophisticated in terms of his or her own sexual lifestyle.

But that is not your problem. Just remember when you write hardcore that the man is always able to get an immediate and rock-hard erection, the female is always ready with a wet, warm place for him to put it, and nobody ever ends the scene with "was it good for you?" because there's no doubt in anybody's mind, least of all, the reader's.

PART THREE

HOW TO WRITE EROTICA FOR THE SCRIPT MARKET

CHAPTER 9

WRITING FANTASY PHONE CALLS

Script writing is as different from the story writing we've learned about in this book as screenplays are from novels. There are plenty of wonderful novelists who couldn't begin to write a television script and even more TV and feature writers who wouldn't know how to begin to write a novel. So if you can do one and can't do the other, you're not alone. In fact, most of us have a proclivity toward one or the other. A talent for dialogue is as valuable to a writer as a talent for prose. If you're a natural at dialogue, you've come to the right section.

You may have seen ads in newspapers and on television for fantasy phone calls. They started as an entertainment device for heterosexual men. At the time of their inception, the system was much more elaborate and expensive for the customer, as there were few alternatives. Originally, the customer had a conversation with a girl who talked to him about how turned on she was. Now that there are more varied types of phone fantasy services, including taped calls, the live personalized calls have heavy competition. But they are still thriving.

When using these live, dial-a-girl services, a man calls a number listed in the newspaper ad, expecting to hear the voice of the girl in the accompanying photograph. In fact, many girls work the same number. One will ask for his credit card number and then either continue the conversation or turn him over to whoever is on duty. Then the customer is treated to whatever words of love he needs to get off. Having been forewarned as to what his designated time allotment is, it is his responsibility to achieve the desired results within that limitation.

The girl doesn't have to ad-lib. She has a number of scripts in front of her for whenever she runs out of ideas. Someone has to write those scripts.

Other services use recorded messages. The customer is charged directly by the phone company—95¢ to $2 for a 1-3 minute message. He listens to a woman who tells him how great he looks when he's hard and what she's doing to herself because she's so excited about his erection.

The telephone companies, eager to share the profits in these hot lines, began promoting their 976 numbers to anyone who wanted to set up this type of business. This assures them a greater percentage of the income and easier access to the bookkeeping process, since they do it themselves. They bill the customer directly for 95¢ plus tax, plus any applicable toll charges, and then pay the client, or hot line service a percentage of that rate, enough to keep the client in advertising money plus profits and plenty left over for Ma Bell.

The messages and scripts have to be changed at least daily, if not more often, to ensure repeat business. The going rate for these scripts is from $5 to $30 each, depending on the company.

Playgirl magazine got into the action by advertising similar services for women. Their *Dial-A-Hunk* service went over so well that others joined the competition. *Hotwire, The Hot Line, OCS, The Phone Fantasy* and others claimed to make fantasies come true.

Simultaneously, the gay male climbed on the bandwagon. Selling fantasies spoken by men for men proved be as lucrative as selling fantasies spoken by women to men.

A client list of the hetero and gay male lines can be collected by going through your local newspaper. Even free papers, such as the *L. A. Weekly* and *The Reader* have these ads. You can recognize these ads by the references to phone sex. Your town will have them too, if you're near a major city. Ads for female-oriented phone fantasies are popping up in those same publications. If you call one of the numbers, you will often receive an additional phone number at the end of the message to call for "more fun." It will sometimes also connect you with the head office, where script information may be obtained.

In my case, I didn't have to go far to find these clients as three separate phone fantasy organizations came to me. Once you are writing erotica in any capacity, you are likely to get work this way.

Since each of these companies uses scripts at the rate of thirty or more per month, they are constantly burning out their writers and looking for new ones. Once you make a connection, your client will tell you exactly what he's looking for. The following information is about one line in Los Angeles, which is a softcore fantasy phone service for females.

These scripts are about one-and-a-half pages long, typed, double spaced. The speaker will deliver the story slowly, and with properly expressed emotion. Sometimes the client can arrange for a foreign voice or an older voice or whatever you request if you have a story that needs it. But for the most part, the actors are twenty-five to thirty-five years old.

In an amazingly short space of time, you must establish a connection, an intimate connection, between you and your caller. That's number one. Next, you must let her know who your hero is with clues that don't sound too obvious. Then you deliver a fantasy about something that might have happened between the two of them. It has to be believable enough for the caller to get caught up in it, yet fantastic enough so that it belongs in her dreamworld.

First think of our caller, who is probably in her early thirties, has a good job, buys clothes and goes on dates, but could be having a problem finding her Mr. Right. She might call the first time as a gag, for fun, for something to talk about at her morning coffee break. If she likes how she feels about it, she'll call back again. You want to make her happy. Make her feel good that she called your number and not a competitor's. Make her smile, make her feel warm and loved, and entertain her.

Your script should have an entire story in it, complete with handsome hero. I've included two diverse examples here, to show you the scope available to you. You needn't always write about a handsome gentleman complete with raging ocean waves and champagne for two. My fantasies tend to be more accessible. My characters are people I would like to hear from, and they're saying things I would like to hear.

I got an inspiration when the client played a tape for me of one of their actors, who happened to be straight off the boat from Australia. He had a delightfully sexy, foreign accent. So I wrote "Continental Lover" specifically for him. The other character is based on a cute kid from one of my classes, probably not over twenty-three and totally unaware of his sex appeal to the over-thirty female. In my story, he comes of age in the hands of the probably older female fantasy phone-caller.

Continental Lover

Hello! I wonder if you remember me. We had coffee in Paris many moons ago and you told me to look you up when I got back. Actually, we had a great deal more than coffee.

Ah! Americans! I love them. Especially you. You are such a free spirit, a bit like the French, but you do it with style. You did everything with style that night. When I first met you and you struggled with the language (and I let you do it of course), you stood a little too close to me, letting your nipples graze my arm as you pointed to the Eiffel Tower on your tourist's map.

Then we went there together, remember? And found that tiny, dark little place beneath the goliath structure. You leaned against the sooty, blackened wall and lifted your skirt.

It was no problem at all getting into you there, I was as hard as the cobblestones beneath our feet. Remember how we stopped when we heard the chattering of voices, breezing right by us as if we were invisible? And then continued again—that was the best part. *I* continued again, into you, ever so much deeper, up inside of you. . . . Your back against the wall made you come hard against me, pressing your heated flesh into me. . . .

And then you lifted one leg and I sank even deeper into your body and held myself there—*you,* braced against the wall, helpless, impaled upon me—your dozens of muscles tightening their wet grip around my solitary one.

And then you made that little cry I remember, oh so well.

An almost silent whimper in the darkened cave, just enough to let me know you were there, all the way there, with me inside you.

And I moved ever so slightly, a tad deeper, a bit to the side, and *you came*. Oh, my lovely, did you ever come! I felt it myself—a gripping, vibrating, spine-tingling series of contractions massaged the part of me that had entered you and you sucked it all out of me.

You swallowed me, making Paris, the Effel Tower and you utterly unforgettable for all time.

And now I'm wondering, my love, how would you feel about repeating this delightful experience at London Tower this summer? . . . Let me know, will you?

Surf's Up

Hey, hi. 'Member me? It's Eric. Surf's not up today so I thought I'd give you a call and see what you're into these days. I missed you, you know. You shouldn't just float into a guy's life and out again like that. Bad for my young hormones.

And I was just getting into what older women were all about. You told me it'd be better, but lady, you didn't tell me it was *that much* better!

You said it took time for a woman to get seasoned, to learn what really turns a man on. You made me feel like a man, too, from the minute you stripped off my wetsuit till you gave me that awesome bubble-bath.

Since then, I gotta tell ya', I don't even mess with young babes anymore. I keep cruisin' the beach, searchin' for another girl like you. A *woman* like you, I mean. To give me more of that experience you bragged about. 'Specially that *oral* experience. You were right when you said young girls couldn't suck worth beans. Man, I thought I was goin' off to the big wave in the sky right then!

I remember how amazed you were I could get it up again so quick. Guess it's been a while since you had anyone under twenty. Since you left, it's up all the time. Like the surf, waitin' for another good ride.

It's one thing to have a great body, a lotta girls in Malibu got that, but to have a great bod and know what to do with it! That's *primo*. That's you, babe.

Man, I wish I could have a taste of you right now and feel your long fingers between my legs at the same time. Thanks for the lesson on sixty-nine. While I'm at it, thanks for all the lessons.

So when's the next one? I want to watch that trick you do another time, those multiple orgasms. Watch, heck, I want to *feel* it. You don't know what it's like to be inside a woman and feel that happening to her. It's like being inside an erupting volcano or something.

You said you liked my vitality. So prove it. Give me another shot at those golden lips of yours. And I'll give you another three hours of sun, sand, surf and pure young lust. OK?

Seriously, you were totally bitchin', babe. I want some more. Real soon.

Can you see how the character of my hero is expressed by his jargon, and his phraseology. The nineteen-year-old surfer would no more say: "the chattering of voices" than the continental lover would say: "You were totally bitchin', babe." Get your voice right and then stay in that mode until you sign off.

Try to leave the caller with something warm, something that makes her call again. It's like asking for the order in sales copy. She knows this call isn't real, just as our male reader knows the models aren't real, yet she wants to be in on the fantasy anyway, for just a moment. Give her all the help she needs and don't drop the ball until your time is up.

Give the actor as many clues as possible to allow him the best grip on your story. Then hope that the client gives him enough time to go over his lines before the recording session. Then go on to the next one. Unless you produce these in rapid succession, you won't make any money on them.

In a sense, your male caller is easier to please. He just wants to hear a string of dirty words. For example:

Hi, this is Tina. I'm so glad you called. Because I've been so hot and horny. And my pussy's all wet, so wet I can feel it.

What I really need is your big thick hard love rod filling my slit. Oohh. Sink it in there. That feels soo good. Harder baby. Deeper. Go for it, stud. Oohh. Nice. You're sooo big. Move it up and down, side to side. I'm coming. I'm coming. Ooh. Ahh. That was great. For a different message, call back after 3.

Your female caller is more sensitive and you can actually turn her off with strong language. That's why everything is implied rather than specifically stated. You know she had a great time when she made love underneath the Eiffel Tower and that she would like to see her continental lover again. Just as you know the surfer boy gave her a ride for her money. And yet, I never mentioned fucking, sucking, screwing or even making love. Not specifically.

Students in my seminar found this form of erotica the most approachable, perhaps because we all talk on the telephone and most of us know how to turn our lovers on with language. Some of my students have already made sales in this area. You can do it too.

Or, maybe you'd like to hold out for the big time; the video screenplay, outlined in the following chapters.

CHAPTER 10

THE MARKETPLACE FOR X-RATED VIDEO SCRIPTS

Understanding the X-Rated Video Industry

Everyone who has ever rented a blue movie has said to himself or herself, "I could do better than that." Well, so do it. This field is wide open.

With 1,192 X-rated videotapes produced in 1984, and 1,600 in 1985, the home erotic videotape business is booming. Where did they all come from? Some of the early videos began as features, which means they were shot on film for release to the X-rated theater chains, then transferred to videotape for a second market. Pornographic loops, usually fifteen to twenty minutes in length, were patched together to make still more tapes. And not much later, because of the short production time required, brand-new X-rated video stories were completed and on the market before any other subject matter or genre.

Adult filmmakers were the first to realize the potentional of the home video market and their early share represented fifty percent of total videotape sales. Now the figure is a more modest twenty percent, due to the proliferation of Hollywood films. X-rated videos provided the financial support for the opening and operation of thousands of video rental stores across the nation.

While "straight" moviemakers were in a quandary over residual rights in the video sales and rental markets for actors and other talent, adult filmmakers had no such problem. All talent on video productions are paid once, up front. Rarely does an actor or actress receive points (a percentage of net profits) and neither do the writers. Anyway, points only work if you can prove a picture made a profit. And this is as difficult to prove in porn as it is in Hollywood.

Even if you were the writer for *Behind the Green Door* or *The Devil in Miss Jones,* you could still be walking around with holes in your shoes. Whatever your original payment was, whether $500 or $5,000, that's all you should expect to receive.

If your video gets a four-star rating in an adult video review magazine, you can sometimes parlay your success into more money for the next script. However, since video magazines seldom credit writers, it will be up to you to point out your achievements to future clients. Writer credits have just begun to appear on video boxes and on the videos themselves.

This neglect can work in your favor as well. When one of your efforts turns out to be a bomb, you can effectively disown it by failing to mention it. So many things can go wrong with your story after it leaves your hands that you needn't be ashamed of your failures. You can always blame them on the budget, cast and crew—as I do.

There is no way to take your name off a project once it's in progress because the box cover is one of the first jobs completed. This isn't Hollywood, folks. If you have any misgivings about your newest video project, you should probably think up a new pseudonym for yourself.

The first video stories were originally features, shot on film, then transferred to video for home sales. Thirty-eight percent were shot on video by one of the seventy-five (and rising) adult video manufacturers. Even now, when there is plenty of original video product, adult marketers still continue to use films, counting on the recognition factor of the X-rated film stars and of the film titles to boost initial sales. Some collectors prefer tapes that originated on film, because the production values are usually substantially higher.

When researching your market, you will also find distributors listed who do not produce their own videos, but buy packaged goods from manufacturers. Sometimes one of these companies will approach a packager to do a particular video just for them. They'll have a star they want to promote, or a title they're sure will work well in their line, or a theme they want to exploit. So if you don't happen to be on a first-name basis with your local porn producer, but you do know a distributor, it is someplace to start.

An up-to-date partial listing of distributors is on page 275. If you would like more information about what they carry, you may want to send away for one of the X-rated video guides listed in the bibliography. Titles of productions, stars and plot lines are all found in these books. This information can provide valuable assistance when you get ready to write your own script. Also, you'll find out which major themes have been overused and how your story might fit.

Your first step in getting a script-writing job is to find out what's currently going on in the market, and it changes daily. You will have to take a trip to your local video outlet and rent a few tapes. The cost is tax deductible because it's just like buying a dozen *Silhouette* romances before you write one.

Choose your models carefully. If you're on a first-name basis with anyone who's producing videos, look at his work first. Make note of common themes, frequent stars, locations and take a wild guess at his budget. If you don't know which company to aim for, take a sampling of each until you happen upon something that suits your fancy.

After you decide on two or three production houses, look up their work in a video index. Your video store will have one hanging from a chain somewhere (they've lost a few). The more titles the house has, the better your chances are to break in. Make sure you're going to the source of the tape though, not just a distributor.

Make an appointment with a person at the production house, as high up in the ranks as possible. You're aiming for the man who can say yes without having to ask anyone else. Bring your spec script (which we will discuss shortly) and two or three good story ideas, in case he does happen to say yes. And be on time, even though he will be late.

If you are already in the erotica business in any capacity, you can probably get a crack at a video script and work from there into features. One writer-director started as a production assistant, working on "legitimate" films as well as the X-rated set. Another director used to be an actress. Some directors have their production assistants write their scripts because they can exert more control this way.

Script writing is lucrative, creative and an excellent way to learn how to write. Plus, having your work produced and acted out gives you invaluable feedback. Once you listen to your lines being read by a professional, your education will accelerate in megaleaps. Your dialogue will automatically become more crisp and concise, and your scenes will stand as single units as well as parts of a whole.

Many scripts are created, laid out and directed by the producer of the videotape, who isn't even a writer, but there are plenty of producers who don't have the time and wish they knew someone quick and dependable to help out. If you get really good at it, and I'm sure you will since you will have very little competition (and you read my book), you can make some quick and easy money this way.

The first thing you'll need to do after you read this section is study a script. I've given you one on page 246. Notice the format, the scene length, the character development and story line. And pay particular attention to how sex is inserted into the action and how the scene builds up to it.

The next thing you must do is write your own spec script. You will use it to prove to prospective employers that you can write a complete script following the standards of this medium. When you have written (and rewritten) at least one and photocopied a neat draft of it, and you have story ideas for two or three others, you are ready to go shopping for buyers.

Some of your clients—how can I say this politely—want to get off on your script. If your client is into rubber goods, for example, you might want to put some in your script. (You'd be surprised how much you can tell about a person by what kind of story he invents for a sex movie.)

Listen to your employer's words as he describes your assignment. Ask questions, then propose your own ideas based on his concept. If possible, check out some of his previous work and find out what he liked and didn't like about it. Learn what his fetishes and restrictions are, and most important, discover what his goals are in this business: Does he wish to be known as the king of comedy, the leader in black sex films, a promoter of the stars of tomorrow, or what? Maybe he wants a reputation for a high-quality product with the lowest budget in town. These factors are relevant to your on-going relationship.

Remember that you are not pushing one project, but an entire future. Selling one script to one producer and one to the next is far more difficult than selling two to the same guy. Plus, the longer you work with a person, the easier it is to write for him.

If you can't get to the key man and your go-between doesn't give you the information you need, do what you can and learn what he wants by gauging his reaction to your first script.

Notice I keep saying he. Almost all the people on this end of the business are male. There are a few notable exceptions. Svetlana is one. She works with her husband to put out some of the finest erotic full-length features around, such as *Bad Girls* and *Number 8 Fantasy Lane*.

Other women are popping up in New York, Los Angeles and San Francisco, trying to break down the chauvinist doors with some female-oriented product, which will satisfy women's desire for erotic material as well as appeal to their mates. Candida Royalle, an X-rated film star, has released a series called Femme, which illustrates female fantasies. At least they are Candida's fantasy of what she thinks women fantasize. Candida's fantasies have probably gone beyond the modest daydreams of a New England housewife or Wichita grandmother. We're just now learning what women's fantasies are through books like *Pleasures, My Secret Garden,* and *Ladies' Home Erotica*.

One problem which may arise and probably did in Candida's case, is that once the script is out of the woman's hands and into the masculine ones, which produce, direct, market and/or promote the end product, it will likely take on some male influence. After each man adds his ten percent, the resulting production may be a far cry from Candida's original concept.

Another actress who is interested in the future of couple-oriented erotica is Kay Parker. She is working at Caballero, the industry's largest manufacturer and distributor of X-rated videos, designing her own line: *Kay Parker's Romances*. It will be a series of video features aimed toward the new audience for erotica. She expects to direct and produce a high-quality product which will begin to bridge the gap between X-rated and R-rated material, as well as help fill the needs of adult cable television.

It is to our benefit that more women get into this business because the stuff that's out there now is sadly lacking in female sensitivity. It's almost all male-oriented fantasies, like the old "come-on-her-face" scene. That's why it's no fun for women to go to porno movies. Women want to be turned on too but we need our own kind of imagery.

Yet, still, if you are female and you want to get your film produced, go for it anyhow. Yes, you are up against the worst possible kind of male chauvinism. Yes, as things stand now, you can't get it done without male backers—that's how these women are doing it. But your biggest obstacle of all is the almost all-male buyers' market.

Besides blatant sexism, there are other more subtle aspects of adult video which also present obstacles. You will learn that in the cast, females outnumber males. The men in the story will have sex with more than one woman. This situation can be read by a cynic as an underlying message that it's OK for men to have more than one partner, the more, the better. Or, another interpretation would be that the male audience wants to see lots of women take off their clothes and will only put up with a minimum number of men, shown naked as briefly as possible. The actor is in competition with the viewer.

The next not-so-subtle message you get is that girls have to be pretty to have a good sex life and guys do not have to be handsome, or particularly kind to their partners. The physical attributes, beauty, youth and wardrobe of the actresses vastly outrate the actors'. In other words, she's gorgeous, young and dressed expensively; he's more often overweight, unsexy, and wearing ordinary street clothes. I'm exaggerating. But not much. The actor is hired for his ability to perform sexually in front of cast and crew and not because he's a good actor, a handsome devil or has a great body. The actress is hired because she's kittenish and sexy and has a terrific body, which usually means she's young.

Compounding matters, you get the male cameraman and male director who manage to focus on the girl's face and body, and pan away when the man comes on the scene. The only time the viewer gets a shot of the actor's cock is when it's halfway inside of the actress. This leaves the viewer with a subliminal message or two, as well. One, that hot sex happens when the girl is nineteen and gorgeous and when the man is ordinary and two, female parts are more fun to look at than male ones.

Funny thing is, with all the time I've spent in this business, I didn't even notice these things until I saw a gay male video. The men are often better looking, and more muscular than men in hetero films. And there are jack-off scenes with one man sitting alone which can be highly erotic to women. So you women who are tired of looking at those little blondes, rent a gay male tape one night and see if you notice a difference. Try one called *The Outpost,* from Adam and Company (and watch it without your lover).

The VCR business took off so quickly not because people wanted to watch Hitchcock movies or tape baseball games, but because they wanted to go to porno movies and they were timid about sneaking into the Pussycat Theater.

The X-rated home video customer is still more often a man, not a couple, although women are rapidly taking up a small percentage of the market. So you are still marketing to men. The producer is a man. The director is ninety-nine times out of a hundred a man. If you do a story for women, it must also appeal to men. Therefore, you must be very subtle about introducing foreign obstacles such as sex education—most women do not love to eat cum, get tied up or be gang-banged by seven strangers. Put your information in there—lord knows they need it—but be cool. These guys get enough flack from their girlfriends about female sexuality. They don't want to see it blatantly portrayed on their home screen.

There is no scale to determine fair pay in this business. Your fee may range from $150 on up for fixing up a troubled script, or from $50 to $5,000 for writing one from scratch. The most common fee for a video script is $500. Whatever you are paid, you lose control of the script the moment it leaves your hands, if not before. Do not imagine yourself on the set, directing pretty blondes and hunks around the bed. Unless you've got a piece of the action, or you're related to the boss, you're not invited to this party.

Each producer/director is different, but his films and tapes are all the same. They have the same rhythm. They are often based on the proven formula of six sex scenes, four straight (one male and one female), one lesbian (two females), one threesome. For variety he may throw in a shower scene and an orgy. The orgy usually comes at the end and is the grand finale.

When a producer and/or director of a film comes to you with a project, he will already have a concept in mind. He will also have a budget, a list of possible actresses and actors, a location and some situations which must be included in your story. Obviously, these will limit some of your creative flow. On the positive side, it may spur your imagination to new heights if, for example, your boss gives you a castle for your location, complete with dungeon and moat.

Once you've worked with a producer, you'll learn to read his mind and follow his creative bent. The director will also influence your style. Since these things are produced in rapid succession, you'll get plenty of experience in a short amount of time, much more so than in any other filmmaking field. During my first year as a video script writer, I wrote twenty-four scripts, all of which have been produced and are being marketed. How many screenwriters do you know who can say that?

Selling Your Spec Script

Will they buy your spec script? Just as in the feature film and television business, the chances are against anyone buying your spec script, even though it's the best one written since *Devil in Miss Jones.* You're doing all that work to prove you can handle an assignment from them. If someone does happen to buy your script, you can still use it for a spec script. In fact, it's to your credit to have had one go into production. Just make sure you note it somewhere on the property, like this: *Copyright © 1986 by and property of Coast-to-Coast Video.*

Will they steal it? At the current rates, your script is worth less than you are to the producer. He'd be foolish to rip off your work because he'd lose your talents forever, plus any other writers you happen to tell. (And tell *all* of them!) I have never heard of a production house stealing a video script from a writer. But I can't guarantee it will never happen to you. And there's no writer's guild protecting us in this field.

Let's say you've written a great video screenplay and you've found someone who likes your work based on your spec script. He wants to see what you can do for him. So he gives you an idea, a title or a basic theme. Then he says, "Go to work on this and see what you come up with."

Your first question, after you get the specs, is how long he wants the treatment to be. He will say one, two or three pages. He may mention that he prefers a scene breakdown or story outline or leave you to guess. The easiest treatment to read is the story outline (see page 236).

After you've finished your story, you may want to make things easier on the producer by listing for him how many characters you've used and which sets will be required. At this stage of the game, it's best to stick to simple sets that can be put together in a house.

Next, you submit the treatment. If he's eager to start shooting, he'll read it right away and call you about it. Otherwise, the reading may take a week or so. Still, much faster than in the legit business. He may suggest a few changes—such as moving a beach scene to an outdoor swimming pool, for obvious reasons—or make cuts in your design. Do whatever he says—you want to get produced, not guard your artistic integrity—resubmit and get to work on the script. (I am assuming you've settled on a price beforehand. Always know what the pay is before you begin and avoid trouble later.)

When your script is done, call your producer and tell him what changes you've made, if any, and ask how he wants it sent. He may send a messenger for it or ask you to bring it in. If he has time, he'll tell you to mail it. The only one I ever mailed got lost and caused me hours of grief, so I don't advise it.

After he's read it, ask him if he liked it. If everything is OK, mail in your invoice and ask for more work. A good person will pay you within thirty days, or when he needs another script, whichever comes first. A bad person will make you ask for your money, pleading poverty and starving children. Bad people lose their writers. Don't work for anyone who plays games with your check. It isn't worth the grief.

You are entitled to a copy of the finished product, since it probably costs all of six bucks to dupe it, but if no one offers you one free, buy it wholesale. It's worth it to see how they've messed up your blueprint, which is all your script is to the director. Some will adhere faithfully to your design, others will warp it beyond recognition.

In one script I wrote, *Portrait of Lust,* I had included an enigma, a magical ghost which came to the hero out of his wet dreams. My first glimpse of the advertising brochure told me something had gone awry. The star, Traci Lords, my fantasy creature, was blowing dust off a pool cue.

Obviously, the house rented for the shooting of this video happened to have a pool table. Nothing so rare goes unused by the greedy director. Even if it wreaks havoc with your story.

Don't get sentimental over this. You got paid. You got experience. You learned about dialogue and action. Go onto the next thing and when you become the rich and famous author of four hit Broadway plays, you can tell this story at a cocktail soirée and become the life of the party.

Use the addresses from video boxes, look them up in the phone book, use your X-rated video guide or use the list I've provided. Do not mail in your script until someone specifically asks for it, unless you're willing to give it away. Do send writing samples, a resumé if you have one, a list of credits and anything else you think will represent you as a professional writer. Make your cover letter brief and incredibly easy for your prospect to reply to you. A funny postcard with check boxes is sometimes enough.

CHAPTER 11

THE BASIC FORMATS FOR X-RATED VIDEO SCRIPTS

Of the thirty-eight percent of home videotapes which were shot directly on video, about half of them were scripted. This estimate is very rough since producers will call a one-page outline a script when pressed. X-rated theatrical features are harder to break into for the new writer and videos outnumber their production a hundred to one, so we shall concentrate on this area of the market.

The Mini Script

New companies are springing up all over, each producing up to six tapes per month when they're shooting. Where do they get the scripts? Well, I hate to disappoint you, but many of them have no scripts. That's why the actors are always fumbling their lines.

Those that do have scripts come in several types. For the sake of clarity, let's call them mini, midi, maxi and full-length. The most popular kind for the lowest budget video is the mini. It uses minimal copy and is often not typed, but scratched out in barely legible handwriting to disguise the voluminous spelling and grammatical errors. The example following is better written than many you'll find out there. There are several good reasons for using a short script like this one. The main reason is that the actors and actresses often receive the script the day of the shooting. They have no time to memorize lines; they barely have time to get the gist of the story. One video house I'm familiar with uses three-page scripts, maximum, with two to three scenes on each page. It goes something like this:

> Wendy, Becky and Dan are in a bar. He's the bartender. The girls are wearing short skirts, nylons, garterbelts and spike-heeled shoes.
>
> WENDY: I'm sure thirsty.
>
> BECKY: Me, too. I wish I had something to drink besides this whiskey.
>
> WENDY: Yeah. I wish I had some cum to drink.
>
> DAN: May I help you girls?
>
> Dan steps around from behind the bar and shows them his cock.

Well, are you turned on yet? Thrilling, isn't it? I'll bet you can't wait for scene two!

This new generation of home video looks as if it were made at your neighbor's house and in fact, it could have been. It looks as if it was shot in one day, and in fact, it was. Do you think you could write this? For sure.

The trouble is, the director usually writes this type of script himself. It's something he's worked up within the framework of the limitations which have been set up for him by the producer. His acting talent is limited to low-budget performers who are generally not experienced or talented, his set is restricted to the least expensive location, and costuming often means what the actors happen to bring with them. But his most crucial guide is his budget. One director told me he had to shoot a wedding sequence without a wedding dress because his boss wouldn't spring for it. These one- and two-day videos can be shot for $8,000 to $10,000 and usually look it.

In this mini version, there is a short introduction to the characters, minimum dialogue, and then a description of the action, which is extremely vague, leaving room for improvisation. If Debbie wants to be on top instead of on the bottom, the director is not going to fight with her about it.

In a way, the actors are the writers. They move the story along with their own ideas of what is sexy, and they're not bad at it.

The Midi Script

An expanded mini script, which we'll call midi, describes the "set up" in great detail and then allows the director and cast to take over with dialogue and sex. Here is Scene I:

There is a hard rock beat pervading the dressing room of an aerobics work-out studio. Close-ups on the beads of sweat on girls' legs and chests as they get ready to hit the showers.

Miranda, a buxom blonde with lazy brown eyes and painted purple lips, admires herself in the mirror on the locker room wall. Several other girls are in the room, in various stages of undress. Miranda pulls up the leg holes of her lavender leotards which causes the crotch to draw a line up her pussy. She runs her long-nailed fingers up the crease and closes her eyes in shivering satisfaction

Judy, a sultry brunette in the background, is becoming aroused by Miranda. She rubs the tips of her nipples through her red leotard causing them to harden into pointed nubs.

Now we watch Miranda from the back, as if we are Judy. We see her lower the top of her leotard and let two gorgeous full, round globes out. Music up. Heartbeat loud and the sound of Judy's breathing comes in as we walk with her toward Miranda. We see her hand touch Miranda's shoulder and turn her around. Then we see her other hand cup the fullness of Miranda's white breast.

Pan back to see both girls. Music up. Roll titles as the girls get into hot lesbian action, using the benches, mirrors and eventually, the shower room. When the credits finish, Miranda pulls back from Judy and smiles at her, and then says: "Hi. What's your name?" Judy giggles and hugs her.

Notice how "hot" this script is, meaning it is erotic in and of itself. There are other ways to do scripts, but none as effective as making it hot. This way, even if it's already paid for and you have nothing to prove, your reader is already gleaning pleasure from your work. And he or she will remember this when the next job comes along. Besides, it helps his imagination. Just as a comedy script should read funny, a sex script should read sexy.

When you set up a scene for this type of script, you don't have to do much more than tell who is in the room and what the basic sex acts are going to be. You can indicate what you want the actors to talk about in simple statements, such as, *Miranda and Judy decide to give Rod a threesome, but Rod turns them down at first.*

The Maxi Script

The third type of home video production actually does use a bona fide script. We'll call it Maxi, though in fact, by screen writing standards, it's not very long. In X-rated terms, a full-length video script means eighteen to thirty pages (twenty-two is average) for a full-length, eighty-minute story—about half the size of a sitcom script but using the format of a feature film screenplay. An example of one of these scripts is included at the end of Chapter 12. And if you really want to get into scripts, you should probably have a screenplay writing manual in your library, such as Syd Field's *Screenplay* or *The Screenwriter's Handbook* by Nash and Oakey. Get a hold of a script and copy the format or use the regular television script format. Then, when you get an assignment, ask for one of your employer's scripts and use his format. The screenplay format shown in this book is different from a working script.

The Full-Length Script

Feature films are released to the network of adult theaters for a year, then reproduced on videotape and sold to the adult video markets. You might compare it to a hardcover book and its paperback reprint.

Many theatrical features are now being released on videotape. Your old favorites are all available. Some new features are being shot on videotape, but as a rule, what goes to the theaters is shot on film. That doesn't mean you can't crash the feature market with your video script. Often a producer receives a script that is so good, he doesn't want to waste it on a home video. He can make more money by shooting directly on film and releasing it in both markets.

Also, a script that comes in with too many expensive locations will sometimes be rerouted to film. But don't throw in a pre-Victorian palace with a regiment of horse-mounted guards hoping to make the grade. Your employer will tell you ahead of time if he's considering this prospect.

In hardcore moviemaking, the creator of the full-length feature film project is the originator of the story line in most cases. He produces the film, directs the film, hires the artists and collects the credit. He may hire assistants to help on any level with these chores, including the writing.

With the new trend toward cross-over features, however (videos that will reach the cable market and high-budget videos and films that never reach the theater screen but are marketed as videos), I anticipate the feature market to become more accessible to writers. It is already providing employment for technicians, directors, actors, production assistants, make-up artists, caterers, and others, who normally work at legit motion picture and television studios. As we all know, there are more people to fill those jobs than there are jobs to fill. People use the adult video and film production work as a safety net while they try to establish themselves in the legitimate trade. Often, this fact is kept a dark secret since X-rated celluloid is the bastard child of the industry. Legitimate producers deny its existence and seem to have a hard time forgiving workers, even though they realize the experience makes them better at what they do. When some of the social stigma is finally removed from association with the X-rated world, I'm sure more sordid pasts will surface.

There are some other types of hybrid features. These originated not as videos or full-length films, but as loops.

Many so-called features as well as full-length videos are in truth short subjects strung together in much the same manner as loops are connected to make a full-length product. Originally, the little stories, or vignettes as they call them in the business, were sold as units, ranging from fifteen minutes to a half hour in length, and sold at adult stores, or before that, on the black market. If you get an assignment and a handful of vignettes, you'll most likely also get a title, such as *Inside Seka*. In your script, Seka becomes the narrator of her personal experiences, presenting five or six separate stories as one whole.

This type of "movie" requires a writer for the narration, but the material of course is self-explanatory. Your description and depiction of each incident will take on a wanton, lustful attitude, as one not only reviewing an event, but taking added pleasure in remembering each horny detail. Phrases such as "It makes my cunt hot just to think about the thickness of Jerry's rod!" will lace your copy with extra erotic appeal.

And that my friends, is the X-rated screen market as it stands today. Expect growth in the cable TV network for R-rated romances, in serial videos, much like the nighttime TV soaps, such as *Dynasty* and *Falcon Crest*. They'll all need scripts, and so they'll all need writers like you.

Writing to Specifications

Each producer will have his own specifications for the scenes he will require in your script. The following is a list of basics. When you get an assignment, you should clarify as many of these requirements as you can. It will save rewriting later. You can use this list as a guideline, however, when none is provided, and come up with a fairly common specification sheet. Use this outline when preparing your spec script. Remember, these specs may vary with producer and/or budget.

1. Seven to ten scenes, at least six of them "hot" (culminating in hardcore action), including one lesbian scene and one or two threesomes.

2. Two exteriors maximum. Take only two characters to location shootings. Home exteriors, as in swimming pool shots, have no limit on number of characters.

3. Seven set changes maximum. Re-use rooms when possible and the director will shoot those scenes back-to-back.

4. Six to ten characters. Usually seven or eight, mostly female, as in five women, three men. One primary character (the one the story is about) and one secondary.

5. Eighteen to twenty-two page minimum. The average script is twenty-two pages. Don't go over thirty, and pack these with action and dialogue.

Now the going gets rough. It is no simple task to formulate a reasonable story line while moving your characters into and out of those restrictions. But you can do it, right? I'm not through yet.

There are a few other things you should keep in mind. The male viewer is interested in watching girls take their clothes off, so the female characters are more important than the males, in terms of on-screen time.

You must use each character in a sex scene somewhere in your story, because the actors have been paid extra for doing hardcore. These actors are referred to as "working" actors. Be careful though, even superstuds may have trouble doing more than two sex scenes a day. Some producers will allow you a few actors as bit players, or "non-working" actors, to fill out the story, and make it more realistic. In real life, one seldom has sex with everyone she meets, from the bank teller to the paper boy. But concentrate on your "working" characters and only use extras when you must.

Although no one will ever sit down with you and tell you how much each item in your script will cost the company, you should be aware of basic budget restrictions. Some of these are taken care of by adhering to entries on your spec sheet, such as number of sets and players. Others, such as wardrobe, exteriors and location shootings should be obvious to you.

We don't see more period pieces, which would probably sell like crazy, because there is not enough money in the kitty for those elaborate court costumes, castles and horses needed for an X-rated rip-off of *Tom Jones* or *Forever Amber*. If they won't spring for a wedding dress, it's a good bet that an English pub scene, complete with drunken squires, is out of the question.

Most often, your video story will be shot in one house. Exteriors of other houses, office buildings and apartment buildings will be shot by the director and used to imply the indoor action is taking place there. The house will be used to maximum advantage, turning every conceivable space into a living area for one of your characters. The prop people turn dining rooms into bachelor pads, dens into executive offices and patios into outdoor restaurants, and they're very good at it.

Still, with all their magic, there are some things which can't be done. Don't put a gazebo in your script unless you're sure your location has one. They are not likely to rent one for the day or change locations to suit your whimsy. They will more likely cut the scene, or try to shoot it in a Jacuzzi or on a pool table, or whatever they happen to have handy.

When you get your first assignment, ask them if they know where your story might be shot and if that information is available. It may even give you more ideas for the script. Once I was given a location for two stories which included not only a gazebo, and a Jacuzzi, but a private lake with a rowboat. My parameters were much expanded.

Script-Writing Basics

Remember that dialogue must do one of three things: Reveal character, express humor or move the plot along. If you can do all three of these in one line, like Neil Simon does, then you're doing great. Don't waste any lines on "ooohs" and "ahhhs"—your actors will ad-lib them. And by all means, don't put in a bunch of superficial chatter just to fill your twenty pages. It might work once or twice, but you're going to lose your job the first time a producer finds a better writer.

When I first began writing video scripts in October, 1984, most of the sample scripts I was given to read were terrible, really awful. It was clear the writers were just after the money and didn't care a fig about quality, wit or story line. They got away with murder because producers were naive, directors desperate and choices nil. There were few legitimate writers in this field, and those that did have some writing background didn't understand the script format. X-rated feature script writers were not ready to step down into video. And lazy packagers would defend themselves with the argument that the viewer didn't care about the story anyway and the only thing that was important was hiring beautiful girls to have sex.

That may have been true once, but more and more, probably because the competition is getting so thick, it is becoming essential to have as much going for the product as possible. Pretty girls, yes, but also good-looking men, attractive sets, professional costuming, quality acting and a decent script to hang it all on. Preferably one with humor and a strong story line.

In other words, a plot. The same simple plot that is needed for a men's magazine story, only with a few more twists and some additional subplots to make it more interesting, will work. It must have a clearcut beginning which relates in some way to the ending. It must have a situation that has to be solved by the end of the story.

The hardest thing you'll have to do is make your plot work around all those restrictions. How can you explain, for example, if your heroine is in love with the hero, why she's gone off to have a threesome with her roommate and a stranger?

When I first started, I felt like that proverbial centipede who was asked which of his hundred feet he stepped forward on first and fell over trying to think about it. I solved my frustrations by packing all those regulations into my subconscious and then writing my story. After I was finished, I went back over the script with the guidelines in hand, and saw which scenes I'd left out. Then I inserted them. Your first scripts should adhere religiously to your restrictions. After that, when the producer likes you, you might be able to bend the rules a bit, but not much. The formula is a proven one.

Give motivation to all of your characters, make them be somebody and want something. It makes them more real to the viewer. With only twenty-two pages to work in, it is nearly impossible, but at least try. You can express character in very few lines if they're good lines. Action, as you know, tells a long story. Give each character an attitude—she's angry or in love or lonely—then help her solve her problem so that all ends well, which brings up another good point.

If you think of these little stories as comic books and not *Gone With the Wind,* you'll be far better off. Just like romance novels, these sexy tales are not designed to deal with serious issues. There are few chronic alcoholics, drug addicts, murderers or sex offenders in home video. There are no problems that are not solvable by the last scene, no characters who are unredeemable. Everyone is happy, healthy, sexy and glad to be alive.

Television viewers constantly complain that sitcoms (situation comedies) represent problems as something that can be solved in twenty-two minutes and therefore simplify life in a way that can never be achieved in reality. And yet, these same viewers tune in again the following week to watch another simple problem bite the dust. Why is that? Because they aren't tuning in to watch real life; they're tuning out of real life and indulging in a relaxing fantasy.

X-rated videos represent fantasy in its most fantastic form: erotic fantasy. Your viewer, if we were to take a composite, is perhaps a lonely man of about forty-five, who is probably unmarried or married to a woman with whom sex has become routine. But let's also take an unmarried man who is shy, has trouble talking to strangers, and becomes very nervous around women. Occasionally, he has a date and now and then, he may even have sex. In other words, his real life is probably not filled to the brim with teeming, hot sex.

His fantasy life, however, is sizzling with it. He identifies with the stud in your story. And he is right there with you seducing that pretty brunette.

When I was given the title *Older Men with Young Girls* (and yes, there was an *Older Women with Young Boys*), I put in a fairly believable older man. He was recently divorced and was having a difficult time coping with the singles scene. He couldn't get laid. A familiar theme, right?

I felt that my viewers could much more easily relate to this fellow than to a super hunk. And I paid him off with a cute young blonde at the end of the story.

Use reality as a base, add a pinch of fantasy, some humor, string it together with a story line and you'll have yourself a winning recipe.

CHAPTER 12

WRITING A VIDEO TREATMENT, OUTLINE, AND SCRIPT

Outlines and Treatments

Here's where you cross-over people (from "real" script writing to X-rated) will have some problems with terminology. Even in feature film script writing there are some differences of opinion as to what constitutes an outline, a step outline, a scene breakdown and a screen treatment. So, putting aside all those perfectly legitimate arguments for a moment, I am going to give you my personal names for two types of treatment formats, either of which will do the trick: the outline (a scene-by-scene breakdown) and the treatment (a narrative story line).

As you begin working, you will find your producer will have a definite preference for one or the other. One man I worked for needed a scene breakdown in order to visualize the story, another wanted to be told the story in short story form.

I have included examples of a treatment and an outline, both written for the same video screenplay. I had to write the outline to sell myself as a script writer. Since it was my very first script for this company, I chose the longer outline format to ensure that the reader would realize every detail of my concept for her title. That's what I was given to start with, the title, *Portrait of Lust*. That's *all* I was given.

A treatment can be one paragraph to eight pages, the average being four pages. The scene breakdown or outline form should do just that, break the action into pieces.

A sample outline:

Valerie Kelly's Portrait of Lust

Scene I: Eric's bedroom

It is just before dawn. A man is thrashing about in his bed, asleep but restless. It is a hot night and he throws back his sheets to reveal an erection. He is about to have the wet dream of his life. An extreme close-up shows Eric's cock and a woman's hands closing in on it. Her nails are long and painted with high-gloss fire. Her tongue assists her efforts. Her full lips and even teeth moisten and scrape Eric's prick. When he comes, Eric looks up just in time to see her face as she fades away. Eric jumps out of bed and goes, still nude, to his studio.

Scene II: Eric's studio

Eric madly begins mixing colors on his palette. His canvas, a huge horizontal 5 x 10, is already up on his easel and he's looking at it with fire in his eyes. He paints the first broad strokes. We see him working in the pre-dawn light, in mid-afternoon, and after dark. Finally, he steps back to view his work, lights a cigarette and falls into a chair across from the easel. We see it is a portrait of Mirage, the girl in his dream. She is smiling demurely out to him. A white gown is loosely draped over her voluptuous body. Eric is still restless. He throws on some clothes and goes out.

Scene III: A nightclub

Eric is already seated and Fran, a topless waitress, brings him a drink. She bends very close to him and he flirts with her. He watches the stripper on the stage and asks the waitress if she can get her for him. Only if you take me, says the girl. Suddenly he gets a glimpse of the dreamgirl walking across the room, but when he turns her around, it is someone else. Frustrated, he quickly leaves. Later, the waitress and the dancer both arrive at his house.

Scene IV: Eric's bedroom

The three are into it until Eric explodes. Then he sits back, obviously still haunted. He realizes the girls will continue on without him and leaves them there. They get into some unusual positions and are very happy with each other.

Scene V: Eric's studio

When we leave the girls, we find Eric in a trance in front of his painting, as if to penetrate it somehow. The face on the girl has changed—she's got a slight smile now, almost a smirk. The telephone rings and breaks his reverie. It's Guy, asking Eric to go to the beach tomorrow. He says OK, then climbs back in bed with the sleeping girls.

Scene VI: *The beach*

Eric, Guy and Guy's girlfriend Carol are playing on the beach. They get into a good deal of physical contact, then sexual. They wind up in a hidden area of the beach where the three of them make love. Just as Eric looks up from an earth-shattering climax, he sees the dreamgirl again. She's standing not far away, staring straight at him, then she laughs. He gets up and runs after her, almost forgetting to pull on his trunks. But she disappears behind a rock formation and he loses her again.

Scene VII: *Eric's studio*

Eric is still hard, frustrated and crazy with lust for the girl in the painting. He strips down in front of it, as if to defy her to break free. He strokes his erection. Her smile has turned to a seductive "O" and her eyelids are lowered. Eric closes his eyes. When he opens them again, she is in the room with him. She gently leads him to a place on the floor where there are pillows and loose canvas cloths. She lays him down and begins to undrape her incredible body. Then she finds a can of linseed oil (really baby oil) and slicks herself down. Some oil colors are smeared onto her body in the mixture. She looks like a painting herself. (Add body glitter and use colored lights for added effect.) She begins at Eric's toes and makes complete love to him, eventually sliding her pussy down on to his rigid cock. Then he fucks her until her hair is wringing wet and her screams echo through the studio. When Eric finally comes, a slow-motion shot shows his jism shooting up in solid white drops into the black background, then falling, falling, until they hit the canvas. Now the room is empty. A close-up of the canvas shows Mirage and Eric walking off into the distance.

Shades of *Dorian Gray.* The producer and director had two things, a title and an artist who was willing to paint the title portrait. They were enough to inspire the story for me. Many straight stories lend themselves well to erotica with very few diversions.

Notice that this story outline is "hot." It is not only erotic, it is filled with sensual imagery to help the imagination of my reader. As it was the first submitted to this team, I wanted to make sure they caught what I was throwing at them, in all its fine and sensuous detail.

Let's see what the same story would have read like in the story treatment format. The following happens to be ad copy, which means it could double for the boxcover blurb:

Valerie Kelly's Portrait of Lust

Eric is living the life every man dreams of. As a successful painter and confirmed bachelor, he has beautiful women all over him. Yet, still, he is unsatisfied. One night, he has a particularly disturbing wet dream. The object of his dream comes alive in his bed, then disappears.

Desperate to capture her, he runs to his studio to get her image on canvas. Once he's painted her, he finds himself even more frustrated and heads out to his favorite nightclub to get some action. There he meets Tessie and Fran who come home with him.

The next day, Eric is still overwrought and now the image in the painting is haunting to him. A friend asks him over for a day at the beach and there the image appears once again to tease him.

The worst thing is, Eric knows the girl in the painting lives and that she's teasing him, that she wants something. When he finally convinces her to come out of the painting, she changes his whole life.

If you want the producer to have a clear idea of each scene, the scene breakdown is ideal. If he just wants the general idea and trusts you with the details, the above serves just fine. It says there will be two threesomes and several encounters between Eric and his Mirage.

Beginning a Script

OK, so now the producer is convinced you've got the story he wants and it's time to go ahead on the script. He calls and says to move the beach scene to an outdoor swimming pool and go for it. There are many ways to approach a script. After you've done a few, you'll find yours. But basically, you'll need a story, with a beginning, middle and ending.

You could call the beginning Act I. You introduce your key characters, get the audience to root for them, and set up the jeopardy. In the middle part of your play, you'll get the heroine or hero in deeper trouble. A TV producer told me once, "Put your hero up a tree, then throw rocks at him." In Act III the heat is really on and you think the hero is doomed to stay up in that tree collecting bruises, when suddenly a solution appears!

Please don't send for the cavalry. Make your hero find his own way down.

The jeopardy can be very simple. In *Portrait of Lust,* the hero's jeopardy is that his obsession with Mirage, his dream girl, is thwarting his sex life. Sex just isn't as much fun as it was. What could be simpler than that?

In *Older Men with Young Girls,* at the end of this chapter, the jeopardy is that a guy needs to get it on with a girl. My basic theme song. There can be subplots as well, as you can see in this script. Alex and Elaine have some sexual situations to work out, and Chase and Martine do too. But you needn't get that complicated on your first time out.

Subplots in porn scripts serve to satisfy the minimum number of sex scenes. If you show the same weary couple doing it six or seven times, you're going to bore your audience and give your leading man a hernia or worse. So the addition of minor characters (who can come up to the majors easily) gives you something to put on the screen while your main character is working something out (or up).

The first scene of an X-rated video is always hot, which means sex happens in it. Your main character should appear in this first sex scene and his or her dilemma should be established here.

Here is an example of a scene. It happens to be the opening scene of a video, which is convenient because it will show you not only how the first scene works—how to get into sex in three pages or less—it will show you how to tell the audience who everybody is and what they're doing in the story and what the situation is that they have to solve by the end.

Black Baby Dolls
BY VALERIE KELLY

1. *Ext. Monica's mansion—day—Establishing Shot*
2. *Int. Monica's living room—day*

> *Everything is immaculate except Jeremy, the gardener, who sits in his overalls on a couch much too plush for his outfit. Monica is pacing all around the room. She's a nervous wreck. She's mumbling about something and moving vases and ashtrays from here to there and back again. She stops near Jeremy and picks up a small clump of dirt by his shoe. As she tosses it into the fireplace:*

MONICA: Jeremy! I told you not to come in here dressed like that. What's she gonna think?

JEREMY: She's gonna think you got the hots for your gardener, which you do.

> *Jeremy reaches out for her, but Monica is much too nervous. She pulls away and fluffs pillows for a while.*

MONICA: She's never gonna buy it, Jeremy. I don't even buy it. What's an elementary school teacher doin' with a layout like this?

JEREMY (*rising and walking toward her*): Monica, if it's makin' you crazy, just tell her the truth. Tell her you're just house-sitting here because I got you the job and you really live in a two-room apartment in Torrance.

MONICA: Ugh! How disgusting! You make my life sound even worse than it is!

JEREMY (*holding her*): Hey, you got me!

> *Monica brushes dirt off his shoulder and then realizes it's getting on the rug.*

MONICA: Yeah, that's a big help.

JEREMY: Hey, if it wasn't for me, you'd be showing your old high school buddy around a third-floor walk-up.

MONICA: I'm sorry, Jer. I'm just upset.

JEREMY: No shit! Now you got anything else for me to do 'cuz I got chores outside. Maybe you're on vacation, but when my boss gets back, I better be done with my plantin' and weedin'.

MONICA: You mean we don't even have time for a little lovin'?

JEREMY *(shaking his head):* Nope.

MONICA *(rubbing his crotch):* Not even a little oral lovin'?

JEREMY: Nope. You used up all your time with rantin' and ravin'.

MONICA *(throwing a mock tantrum):* Jeremy! You promised you'd help me!

JEREMY: That don't include the services of my trusty ol' cock.

MONICA: But it's the only thing that calms me down, Jer! Come on. Please?

JEREMY: I said no, lady. Read my lips. NO.

MONICA: Mmmm. You're so sexy when you do that. Do it again.

JEREMY: No.

MONICA: That's the shape you use when you go down on my clit. You make a little circle with your lips . . .

Monica begins to get out of her clothes. Jeremy puts his hands deep into his pockets and watches her. He's going to make her work for this.

JEREMY: Ain't gonna work, Monica. I seen that satin bottom a yours plenty a times.

MONICA: And I seen that godzilla cock of yours hundreds of times, but I never get tired of it.

She opens his overalls somehow and pulls his cock out. She's half undressed. Her blouse is open and bra unhooked, her pants are completely off. She is on her knees tugging on Jeremy's balls and sucking him into erection.

They make love to exhaustion, then lie back on the sofa nude to enjoy a cigarette. That's when they hear the car pull up.

MONICA: Oh my god! They're here.

She jumps up and pulls on her clothes all backwards. She throws Jeremy his overalls and such but he's slow. Finally, when she's dressed, she closes off the living room he's in and sees her guest into another room.

One thing you'll notice in these scripts is there aren't a bunch of camera angles and people don't jump around a great deal like they do in the "real" movies. This limitation is again due to budget restrictions. There are two video cameras trained on the actors at all times. One is usually taking a "long shot" and the other is focusing on the action. Other shots are picked up later for close-ups on facial expressions and so on. But basically, your actors' actions are restricted to a small space on the set. It is against all the rules of movie and television drama, so it's one thing you may have to re-learn when you make that transition.

Your main objective in scene I is to get your hero and/or heroine out onto center stage, complete with his or her problem, because the first thing the audience wants to know is who to root for and why. If you wait and introduce your lead character in scene II, you'd better at least talk about him or her and set up the situation.

What to Do and What Not to Do in Your Script

Here are some common mistakes made in scripts.

1. There's no story. Nothing moves the characters from one scene to the next, nor drives them to the ending.

2. There's no hero or heroine. Everyone has equal weight.

3. The sexual situations are fake. Unreal is OK, but fake is out. Make the sex seem like a logical outgrowth of the hero's emotions and/or situation.

4. Dialogue is phony:
   a. It doesn't sound like people talk.
   b. It's too heavy. (Keep it as crisp as possible. People talk in sentence fragments, not paragraphs.)
   c. It's too boring and predictable. This flaw comes from giving everything away immediately. It's no fun.
   d. It lacks attitude. No sense of humor.
   e. All the characters sound the same. The dialogue doesn't

differ from character to character. (I'll give you examples of these in a minute.)

5. The ending comes from left field. Try to make your hero find his own solution. Make it a logical finish, but throw some twists in it along the way.

6. There are no surprises. Every story needs a few surprises.

7. It's not hot enough. Not enough sex going on.

8. The sex comes out of right field. Nobody's talking about it or getting in the mood and all of a sudden, there's a cut to the sex scene. It might work on the screen but it won't wash on paper.

9. Scenes are too long or too short.

Now that I've told you what not to do, let me tell what you must do.

Each scene must have a story point. Something must happen which moves the story onto its next plateau.

Each bit of dialogue must develop character, move the plot along or express humor. And as I said before, it's ideal if you can do all three with one line.

Scenes should have an ending. In sitcoms, they call the final dialogue a "button line," which means nothing more technical than that it buttons up the scene. It does so by making a comment or joke on what just happened and wrapping it up, or providing a clue to the plot, or introducing a hook for the next scene. When you've reached your button line, stop and go onto the next scene. If you're not ready yet, save this line for when you are.

Give each character an attitude. Make them real by having them react to each situation from their own point of view. This will help you with your dialogue too.

Let's take a look at a scene that *doesn't* work and figure out why.

LESLIE: Hello, Harry, I've been waiting here for you all day. Where were you?

HARRY: I was out of the country trying to buy a Mercedes so I could sell it in the states and make enough money so you and I could get it on.

How many rules have I broken here? It's obviously boring,

which is rule number one: Never be boring! But why is it boring? For all the reasons I gave in the rules section. Leslie and Harry are giving everything away. The characters don't have to work to get the information. And there's no time for the audience to guess at the whys and wherefores, something they like to do.

The dialogue is stiff, all exposition, no emotion or attitude and not written the way people talk. You need to create a little banter back and forth as I did in Monica's story.

If this scene above is to culminate in sex, we've got another problem here because Harry just isn't sexy. We need to be set up for it. And, finally, you can't tell the difference between Leslie and Harry, and for X-rated video, that can be a serious problem.

You could take a whole three-page scene to deliver the same amount of information, but if we had the same amount of space, we might have the dialogue go this way:

LESLIE: Harry, I missed you.
HARRY: I've been away.
LESLIE: To buy me a present?
HARRY: In a way, yes.
LESLIE: *(throwing her arms around him)* Oh, Harry, how romantic. What is it?

Whether or not you mention the Mercedes at this point is at your discretion. You might want to save it for your button line to tie up the end of this scene. Daytime soap operas are a great place to learn how to stall, increasing tension before releasing information.

Notice also that in my own small way, I have introduced at least some affection between my two characters, so that if they happen to get it on by the end of the scene, you'll be prepared for it.

I've now told you everything I know about script writing for this genre. But you'll never learn as much from this book as you will from actually doing it yourself. The end product may have looked simple to you once, but now that you know the fundamentals of writing the script and the specifications it must adhere to, you've found it's a little harder than you suspected.

Now here is a full-length X-rated video screenplay, which, in its original format, was twenty-five pages long. Because almost all of it could be shot inside one house, the director was able to include all of the scenes and dialogue. And because he used talented actors and actresses, Joanna Storm, Harry Reems, Nick Random and Bunny Bleu, among others, there was very little wasted footage.

Using this script as a guide only, and remembering to cover all your specifications, write your own X-rated video screenplay.

The character sheet and synopsis, which precede the screenplay, are typed on one page and stapled to each script for actors, wardrobe mistresses, script girls and others. The same sheet is used by casting, often before the script has been completed.

Older Men with Younger Girls
BY VALERIE KELLY
© 1985 by Joint Video Productions

Characters:

Alex—An ordinary guy, nice, sensitive, in his forties or so. Married to Elaine.

CHASE—A suave Romeo. The Cesar Romero of adult video. In his fifties, if possible. Lots of wavy gray hair.

BURT—A dumpy, always-married, bald-headed guy who's just gotten a divorce. He should be funny.

ELAINE—An older woman, late thirties. Very beautiful but naive. Madly in love with her husband, Alex.

CINDY—A wild teenager (but please don't put her in pigtails) who has the hots for anyone over thirty.

MARTINE (pronounced Marteen)—A young girl with love on her mind. Wants to get Chase to settle down.

JENNIFER—A young girl who will sleep with any man, as long as he spends money on her first.

Story Line:

Alex, Burt, Chase and Elaine have a once-a-week poker game to which Chase is seldom on time. He's always busy with his chicklet of the week. One of his lovers, the beautiful Martine, is making love to him right now.

When Chase and Martine finally get to the game, Alex and

Burt have already gone out to look for girls. Chase goes after them, and Martine teaches Elaine a few things about men and sex, by having girl/girl sex.

At the local pub, Alex recounts the tale of how he once went home with Burt's babysitter, Cindy. His memory is extremely vivid and it shows up on the screen. That doesn't help Burt with his problem, however, and he doesn't score, but Chase does, taking home the gorgeous young Jennifer. Meanwhile, Alex goes home to find his wife in heat and when he tries to settle her down, Martine comes out to join the party for a threesome.

The next day, when it seems like Burt will never get laid, he is hit on by his ex-babysitter, Cindy. She takes him to her apartment and ravages his body.

But by the time Chase has convinced Jennifer to go out with Burt, he's sworn off young girls forever. Cindy scared the living daylights out of him.

1. *Ext. The Rolands' house. Night—Establishing shot*
2. *Int. Alex and Elaine Roland's living room. Night*
    There's a card table set up with several decks of cards, a pad of paper and pencils waiting. Chips, dip and beer bottles are on the coffee table. Alex, Elaine and Burt are waiting impatiently for a fourth for poker. Alex is reading the newspaper. Elaine is flipping through a magazine, drinking wine from a glass. Burt is pacing.
BURT: He's never on time. Not once has he ever been on time.
ELAINE: Maybe he hates poker. He's been coming here for four years, every Tuesday night to play poker, but he hates poker.
BURT: In four years, he's *never* been on time.
ALEX: Burt. You've got no room in your heart for love. Chase is a Romeo. He's got things to do.
BURT *(landing finally in a chair):* Yeah, I should have such things. Things that look like this . . . *(he makes shapely lines in the air)* And talk like this: "Oh, daddy, you're such a hunk."
ELAINE: You're just jealous.

BURT: Damn right I'm jealous. Here I've been divorced two whole months and I haven't even got laid yet. You guys got nothin' to worry about. *(to Alex)* You got Elaine, an in-house fox.

ELAINE *(she raises her glass in toast & drinks):* Why thank you, Burt.

BURT: And you got Alex. You don't have to go combing the singles bars.

ALEX: Chase doesn't need to go to singles bars.

BURT: Who's talkin' about Chase? I'm the one who's been cruisin'.

Burt sits down in disgust.

BURT *(continued):* They make it look so easy in those men's magazines.

ALEX: It is easy. You go up to a girl, you say something nice to her, she smiles, you're in.

ELAINE *(getting a little drunk):* Hey, wait a minute. How come you know so much?

ALEX: I've got a great memory.

Alex buries his head back in the newspaper to hide.

BURT *(relaxing somewhat):* I can see him now. Lying in that king-size bed of his, a beautiful fox on his belly . . .

Fade To:
3. *Ext. Chase's house. Night—Establishing shot*
4. *Int. Chase's bedroom. Night*
    . . . where he is indeed lying on his king-size bed with a beautiful fox on his belly. She is Martine (pronounced Marteen) and she is exotic, erotic and in love. She leans down to plant kisses in his furry chest, lower, lower . . . until she gets to his cock where she demonstrates her expertise on his already raging hard-on. She watches his face for changes in expression and moves on cue.

CHASE: Nobody sucks cock like you, Martine.

MARTINE: You're fucking right. And don't you ever forget it.

CHASE: You're almost perfect.

She sinks her teeth into his shaft, playfully of course.

MARTINE: What do you mean *almost?*

CHASE: Sorry.

She sits up and fondles her breasts.

MARTINE: Aren't these perfect breasts? Don't you like the size of them? The shape of them?

CHASE: They're beautiful tits, Martine.

She sits up higher on her knees and crawls toward him.

MARTINE: And what about my pussy, Chase? Didn't you tell me it was the best you ever tasted?

CHASE: I did indeed.

MARTINE: And so tight, you said. Right?

CHASE: So-o-o tight.

With this, Chase moves her back onto his cock and sits her down. She throws her head back, letting her long hair fall sensuously.

MARTINE: Oh, God, Chase. I love the feel of your cock up inside me. I don't think I could live without it.

CHASE: Sure you could, baby. What you couldn't live without is fucking. Fucking is your source of energy.

MARTINE: Fuck me some more, Chase. Don't ever stop fucking me.

Chase rolls her over and does as she says. He brings her to life with his passion.

Meanwhile, back at the poker game:

5. *Ext. Rolands' house. Night*

6. *Int. Rolands' living room. Night*

They haven't moved. Elaine is noticeably drunker.

BURT: He's not coming. I'm going.

He rises and finds his coat.

ALEX *(also rising):* Where are you going?

ELAINE: You can't go. This was my first chance to play poker. I wanted to beat the pants off you.

BURT: I've got to get laid or my cock is going to fall off from atrophy. You know what happens when you don't exercise your muscles. I'm gonna go exercise my love muscle.

Burt heads out. Alex calls after him.

ALEX *(getting his coat):* Wait. I'll go with you.

ELAINE: What?

ALEX: Somebody's got to help Burt out, honey. This is a man in pain.

ELAINE: Oh, I see. And you're willing to make this great sacrifice.

ALEX *(quoting Dickens):* "It is a far, far better thing that I do than I have ever done . . ."

ELAINE: Bullshit! If you're going, I'm going!

ALEX: Honey, how is Burt going to score chicks with you around? They'll think he's married.

ELAINE: Fuck Burt. It's you I'm worried about.

ALEX: Honey, in the twelve years we've been married, have I ever cheated on you?

ELAINE: How do I know?

ALEX: Proves my point. What you don't see can't hurt you. Bye.

He gives her a quick peck on the cheek and dashes out after Burt, leaving Elaine dazed. She flops back onto the sofa, finishes off a glass of wine and pours another, picks up a magazine, puts it down, dials a number on the phone, nobody's home. The doorbell rings.

Elaine rises, weaving slightly, and answers the door to Chase and Martine.

CHASE: Where is everybody?

ELAINE *(pissed):* Where were you? You messed up our game. Sorry, never mind. Don't tell me where you've been. I can guess.

Elaine sits down again. They follow her in.

MARTINE: What's the matter, Elaine?

ELAINE: The boys went out to "score chicks."

MARTINE: Uh oh.

CHASE *(interested):* Uh. Did they happen to mention where they were going?

MARTINE: Why? You want to join them?

CHASE: Well . . .

MARTINE: Chase, you couldn't possibly have one drop of cum left in that old pecker of yours after what we did.

CHASE: Martine, you still know nothing about me.

He kisses her on the nose and departs. Martine is fuming.

MARTINE: Asshole. All men are assholes.

ELAINE: No they're not. *(Martine looks at her.)* They're pricks.

MARTINE: You're right. Pricks. Big ones, small ones, hard ones, soft ones. Just a bunch of cocks.

ELAINE *(pouring drinks for them both)*: Right.

MARTINE *(raising her glass for a toast):* And we're a bunch of cocksuckers.

ELAINE: Speak for yourself.

MARTINE: You mean you don't suck cock?

ELAINE: Never ever ever. Hate it.

MARTINE: Well, you'd better learn to like it or Alex is going to find someone who does.

ELAINE: Bullshit.

MARTINE: I've never seen you drunk.

ELAINE: Alex doesn't like to have his cock sucked.

MARTINE: Now that's the funniest thing I've heard you say all year. There is no man on God's green earth who doesn't like to have his cock sucked. Do you hear me in there?
Martine is trying to get through the muddle of drink.

ELAINE: He likes it?

MARTINE: He *loves* it.

ELAINE: Are you positive?

MARTINE: Absolutely.

ELAINE: Why didn't he tell me?

MARTINE: He probably did. Men don't always say things in English though. Maybe he tugged on your hair or something.

ELAINE: He *does* tug on my hair! That means he wants me to go . . . down . . . there? *(Martine nods.)* Ew. Gross.

MARTINE: It is not gross. It's one of my favorite things to do.

ELAINE: You know *how?*

MARTINE: Chase says I'm the best.

ELAINE: Will you teach me how?

MARTINE *(looking around, playing):* Uh, we don't happen to have one lying around here. Have you got a dildo at least? A vibrator? *(Elaine shakes her head to the negative.)* Well, we'll just have to practice on you. Take off your clothes.

ELAINE: What?

MARTINE: Cocks and pussies aren't all that different. Come on, you want to learn or don't you?

Cut To:
7. *Ext. Nightclub. Night—Establishing shot*
8. *Int. Nightclub—a dark, smoky bar. Night*
   Alex, Chase and Burt are sitting at a table with drinks. Across from them, in the foreground, is Jennifer, a foxy lady sitting at the bar with a drink. She's scanning the room, looking for hot prospects.
   The men are staring at her.
BURT: I don't know. She looks too . . . sophisticated. What's she gonna want with a guy like me?
ALEX: I wanna tell you something. Remember that babysitter of yours? That little blonde?
BURT: We had dozens of babysitters, Alex. They all looked the same to me.
ALEX: Remember that night you asked me to take her home? Well, she was really hot, that one. She jumped me in the car!
BURT: You screwed my babysitter?
ALEX: Yeah.

(Insert Scene)
9. *Int. Cindy's apartment—Night*
   Alex drifts off into memory as we see it on the screen. Cindy, a cute blonde, is all over Alex. There is no dialogue. They just screw in all possible positions.

(Return to Bar)
10. *Int. Nightclub—Night*
BURT: That's fine for you. You're still a young guy. But what about me?
ALEX: Wrong attitude. Young girls like older men. It's a proven fact.
CHASE: They respect us for our knowledge and maturity.
ALEX: And our money.
BURT: So who's got money?
CHASE: Compared to a young girl, you're rich. She thinks twenty bucks is a lot of cash.
BURT: *I* think twenty bucks is a lot of cash.
   POV to show girl still in foreground.

ALEX: Go over there and introduce yourself. Tell her you'll buy her a drink.

BURT: Jesus. I'm getting sweaty palms. Look.

CHASE: Don't shake hands with her.

Reluctantly, Burt gets up, wiping his hands on his pants, and comes up behind Jennifer. He begins to speak several times, framing his first sentence, when she turns around and glares at him.

BURT: Uh, hi.

JENNIFER: Hi.

BURT: Could I buy you a drink?

JENNIFER: No.

BURT: How 'bout a cigarette?

He shuffles out some cigarettes, but loses control as they fall out all over the place. Jennifer backs off in disgust.

BURT: I've got lots of money. At least twenty bucks.

He takes out his cash and starts counting it.

JENNIFER *(shoves him away):* What do you take me for? A hooker?

BURT: No, no, honest.

JENNIFER: Buzz off, old man!

Burt beats a fast retreat to the table, glad to get away from her.

ALEX: Better luck next time, buddy.

BURT: It's just as well. She probably would have eaten me alive anyway.

CHASE: And you would have enjoyed every minute of it. *(He rises.)*

BURT: Hey, where are you going?

CHASE: To show you how it's done.

Alex and Burt watch from a distance as Chase walks up to Jennifer, talks to her for a moment and then walks off with her. Their POV:

BURT: I don't get it. She called me an old man and Chase is three years older than I am.

ALEX: You're looking at natural talent, buddy boy. Let's go home.

They rise to leave.

BURT: That guy must take stud pills.

Meanwhile . . .

11. *Ext. Rolands' house. Night*

12. *Int. Rolands' bedroom. Night*

Elaine is lying back on the bed in her sexy underwear. Martine is in between her legs.

MARTINE: Spread your legs . . . a little more.

ELAINE: Will it tickle?

MARTINE: Probably. See, your pussy's long side lips are just like the shaft of a cock. They get swollen and hard when they're excited.

Martine runs her fingers up and down Elaine's pussy lips as she speaks. Elaine's legs are getting weak.

ELAINE: Let's lie down.

Elaine lies off the end of the bed, her long legs stretching out onto the floor. Martine takes her place between them.

MARTINE: And this little button here, it's just like the knob of the cock. So when I lick it like this . . . *(she does)* It helps the rest of you get excited.

ELAINE *(beginning to get aroused):* So when I get Alex's . . . cock, first I lick the lips, I mean the shaft, and then I come up and lick the knob. Right?

MARTINE: Exactly. Like this.

Martine makes long strokes with her tongue, then puts her mouth around Elaine's clit, coming down on it as she once did Chase's cock. She flicks her tongue on the clit, spreading the pussy lips to get a good angle on it. They keep the lesson going until they forget it's a lesson and get into some girl/girl action. This goes on a long time.

13. *Ext. Chase's house. Night. Establishing shot*

14. *Int. Chase's living room.*

He's helping Jennifer off with her coat.

JENNIFER: You are a wicked, wicked man.

CHASE: How true.

JENNIFER: Who just happens to be a great lay.

He kisses her hands. Moves up to her neck.

CHASE: Right again, my sweet Jennifer.

JENNIFER: Why didn't you tell that guy we know each other?

CHASE: I was making a point.

JENNIFER: You devil, you. So is the point made or do you want me to stay?

He leads her to the bedroom.

CHASE: Silly question.

They begin making love. Jennifer is sliding out of her clothes.

JENNIFER: Darling, why is it you always go after young flesh?

CHASE: I'm attracted to beauty. To exquisite forms *(he demonstrates by running his hand down her bare waist),* to the energy of youth.

JENNIFER: To girls who don't give you a hard time?

CHASE: And who don't ask a lot of questions.

JENNIFER: Know why I like old men?

CHASE *(stops kissing her):* Older men, please.

JENNIFER: Ooops, sorry.

CHASE: And why do you like older men?

JENNIFER: Because you can keep it up longer. And because you're more sensitive in bed. Because you value a woman.

CHASE: And because we spend money on you.

JENNIFER: Right. Younger guys are always broke and when they're not, they still want girls to pay half.

CHASE: Hardly fair.

He lays her down on the couch, takes off the rest of her clothes, and makes long, languorous love to her.

Meanwhile . . .

15. *Ext. Rolands' house. Night*

16. *Int. Rolands' bedroom. Night*

Martine and Elaine are still at it hot and heavy.

Then suddenly, they hear Alex at the door. Elaine feels like she's been unfaithful and panics. She jumps off the bed, kicking the pile of clothes into the closet, then shoves Martine in there too. She leans against the closet door.

Alex enters and instantly knows something's amiss.

ALEX: Elaine. What are you doing?

ELAINE: Doing?

ALEX: You're standing there naked.

ELAINE: Yes. You're right, Alex.

ALEX: Honey, are you drunk?

ELAINE: Yes, I think so.

ALEX: Is that what you've been doing all night? Drinking?

ELAINE: No. Not all I've been doing.

ALEX: Drinking and holding up the closet door?

ELAINE: And also, I've been . . . taking cocksucking lessons.

ALEX *(laughing)*: You what? You hate to suck cock.

ELAINE: Alex. Tell me the truth. The absolute truth.

ALEX: Uh . . .

ELAINE: Do you like having your cock sucked?

ALEX: Well . . . since you ask . . . yes.

ELAINE *(she slaps him playfully)*: You bastard!

ALEX: Elaine!

ELAINE: Lie down!

> *Alex lies down. Elaine starts taking off his clothes. Meanwhile,*

18. *Int. Closet*

> . . . *we see them from Martine's point of view in the closet.*

MARTINE: Oh, my god. She's going to do it.

(Intercut between the two scenes.)

On Alex and Elaine:

> *Elaine has got Alex's pants all tangled on his shoes. Finally she gives up on getting him naked and just leaves everything in a mess, which binds his ankles together.*

ELAINE: OK, now. You just lie still and I'm going to do everything.

> *She picks up his limp cock and tries to make it stand up longways so it looks like a pussy. Then she works on it with her tongue, pointing it upward. Then she puts the head of it in her mouth like a clit. And soon it begins to react.*

In the Closet:

MARTINE: Mmmm. Alex has a big cock.

> *Martine begins to caress herself while watching the scene.*

On Alex and Elaine:

ELAINE: It's growing.

ALEX: I should hope so. Elaine, when did you take this up?

ELAINE: Your knob is much bigger than a clit.

ALEX: Yes, well, it's supposed to be.

ELAINE: I like it. I like the way it fits into my mouth.

ALEX: Jeez. Have you been reading those dirty novels again?

ELAINE *(taking long licks of his shaft):* If you only had a hole I could stick my tongue into.

In the Closet:

MARTINE: Oh no, she's gonna blow it . . . Man, I wish I could have that cock.

On Alex and Elaine:

Elaine is climbing on the bed. Alex takes his clothes the rest of the way off, hopping about.

ALEX: You want to fuck now?

ELAINE: No. I want you to feed it to me. Feed me your cock, Alex, darling. I'm so hungry for it.

This really gets him going. He climbs up and points his rod toward Elaine's mouth, then slides it in. And out. And in.

In the Closet:

Martine is going nuts. She's using a shoe on her clit and she's all aroused but she can't get off. She keeps peering out to see what Elaine and Alex are doing.

Finally, she slides down against the wall and has an orgasm in a pile of clothes and shoes. Her muffled cry is overheard in the bedroom.

On Alex and Elaine:

ALEX: What was that?

ELAINE: Nothing.

Again, Martine moans.

ALEX: Have you got a man in there, Elaine?

ELAINE: No, Alex. I swear.

He rises and shakes his finger at her.

ALEX: If you've got a man in there, I'm going to be really mad at you, Elaine.

ELAINE: Don't open that door!

ALEX: Aha! So you do have a man in there! I should have known when you got so excited. You never get so excited.

Alex slides or swings open the door and Martine all but falls out on the floor, her hand still between her legs.

MARTINE: Hi, Alex.

ALEX: Martine?
He helps her up. She has her eyes on his cock.
ELAINE: I'm sorry, Martine.
ALEX: I don't get it.
MARTINE: You want it?
ELAINE: It's a surprise!
Alex and Martine look at Elaine, stunned.
ALEX: What?
ELAINE *(coming over to them):* It's a surprise. For our anniversary. Martine is our anniversary present.
ALEX: Oh, yeah?
MARTINE: All right!
Martine jumps onto the bed and they have a threesome culminating in massive orgasms for all.
After which, when Alex is drifting off to sleep, he whispers to Elaine:
ALEX: Our anniversary isn't till June.
ELAINE: Who cares?
ALEX: Right. Who cares. I don't care.
He gives both girls a hug (they're on either side of him), switches off the lights, and goes to sleep.
Fade To:
19. *Ext. City street. Day*
Burt is driving. A young girl calls to him from the side of the road. She is Cindy, dressed in cut-offs and a T-shirt, with bright colored socks and flat shoes. (Cindy talks very fast.)
CINDY *(calling to him):* Mr. Grayson! Wait up.
BURT *(he looks at her without recognition):* What do you want?
CINDY: Mr. Grayson. Don't you remember me? I'm your babysitter.
BURT: My babysitter?
CINDY: Or well, I used to be. Your kids must be in college by now.
BURT: Junior high.
CINDY: But don't you remember me? I lived next door to you and Mabel for centuries.
BURT: Cindy? Cindy Taylor?

CINDY: You got it. Hey, Mr. Grayson. You think you can give me a ride? My bike's broke down and I'm super late.

BURT: Sure. Hop in.

Int. car as they drive.

CINDY: I live at the Palms on Lankershim and Second Street.

BURT: I know where that is.

CINDY: I got to like really cram it 'cuz my chem course is crucifying me and my dad says I can't see Cindy Lauper unless I get all A's. He's got me super bummed.

BURT: Cindy a friend of yours?

CINDY: Cindy Lauper? Oh, Mr. Grayson, you're so funny. I only wish she was a friend of mine. She's a big, famous star. She's my idol.

BURT: Oh. And you're going to meet her?

CINDY: No, dorcus. I'm going to her concert. If I get A's, that is. So how have you been doing?

BURT: Oh. So-so. I'm divorced now, you know.

CINDY: You're kidding! That's great.

BURT: Not so great. I'm beginning to wonder if I made a mistake. It's not all that easy out here in the cold. Wait'll you graduate. You'll see.

CINDY: I don't believe that. For a handsome hunk like you?

BURT: Thanks. But not all grown-up women see me that way.

CINDY: I don't know why. I've always seen you that way.

BURT: You have?

CINDY: I've had a crush on you since I was eleven. Didn't you know?

BURT: No. I had no idea. This your place?

Burt pulls the car over and parks.

CINDY: I thought sure you knew. Wow. This is super. You're divorced. I'm eighteen. Now we can do it.

BURT: Do what?

CINDY: Party.

BURT: You want to have a party?

CINDY: No, Mr. Grayson. Party is a verb. It means get it on . . . ball . . .

He still doesn't get it. So she puts her arms around his neck and climbs up into his lap.

CINDY *(continued):* It means we can have sex together.

Fade To:
20. *Ext. Chase's house. Day*
21. *Int. Chase's bedroom. Day*
    He's having Jennifer for breakfast. Or she's having him.
CHASE: About this friend of mine. He's a nice guy.
JENNIFER: Rich?
CHASE: He does OK.
JENNIFER: Tell him if he buys me a mink coat he can see me four times. Is that fair?
CHASE: How about a suede coat for three times?
JENNIFER: What does he do?
CHASE: He's in the furniture business.
JENNIFER: One sleepaway sofa for one night and that's my final offer.
CHASE: Jennifer, you never cease to amaze me.
JENNIFER: I'm about to amaze you some more. Get that rod out and do some more amazing things.
22. *Ext. Cindy's apartment bldg. Day*
23. *Cindy's apartment. Day*
    A one-room apartment with a mattress on the floor and stuff strewn all over the place. She climbs over things, leading Burt inside. She strips as she talks.
CINDY: Oh, God, I can't wait to screw you. I've wanted you for so long.
BURT: Me?
CINDY: Yes, you. I'm crazy about bald-headed men.
BURT: Slightly thinning, not bald . . . Why?
CINDY: They remind me of big cocks. Their whole bodies are these big cocks. And this *(she plants a kiss on his head)* is the head of it. This is what fucks me. I dream about being fucked by bald heads.
BURT: Jeez, Cindy. You're . . .
CINDY: Yeah, I know. Take off your clothes. Hurry up.
    She's already almost naked and he's still got all his clothes on. She pulls at them, trying to hurry him up.
BURT: This is . . . wow . . . I can't . . .
    He's so excited, taking off his clothes is confusing him.
CINDY: Oh, man, do you know how long I've been waiting for you?
BURT: No. Tell me.

CINDY: About eight years. Eight long years.

BURT: I'm glad you waited.

CINDY: Why don't you suck on my pussy?

> *He can hardly believe this. He dives down.*

CINDY: Oh, Mr. Grayson. That's so good. Mmmm, Mr. Grayson!

BURT *(popping up for a moment):* You can call me Burt.

> *Continue . . . Burt and Cindy are still all over the bed. She's maneuvering him into positions he's never even heard of before. She demands to be done "doggy style," then 69, then something else. After they've exhausted all possible ways, Burt shoots off and lies there, spent. He closes his eyes for a minute and when he opens them he sees Cindy standing over him with the largest rubber dildo he's ever seen.*

BURT *(he can't believe she still wants more):* You want me to put that in you?

CINDY: No, silly. I'm gonna put it up your ass . . . Come on. Bend over!

> *She chases Burt all over the bed giggling. He's honestly afraid. He keeps looking at this huge dildo.*

Cut To:

24. *Ext. Rolands' house. Night*

25. *Int. Rolands' living room. Night*

> *The poker game. They're all there, Alex, Burt, Chase and Elaine are playing cards. Martine is bringing food out from the kitchen.*

CHASE *(laying his cards out):* Straight flush.

BURT: You're as lucky at cards as you are with women, Chase, damn you.

CHASE: Speaking of which, that tender young fox at the bar last week would like to get together with you.

BURT: Forget it.

ELAINE: Forget it? Is this the same Burt who lusted after young flesh?

BURT: Elaine, the young girls these days know things about fucking you never even thought about. . . A guy could get hurt!

> *They all laugh as Burt deals out the next hand.*

THE END

EXERCISES TO GET YOU STARTED

Well, we've come a long way, haven't we. We got you out of the gutter and into the mainstream of a potentially acceptable medium. You've learned where to find magazines to write for, how to write a query letter, and how to adapt your story to any format. You've learned who your readers are and what they want to read. You've learned how to take a basically innocuous experience and turn it into erotica. You've learned how to get started in the screenplay business through adult video. And you've even picked up a smattering of sexual politics. You're on your way.

But wait. There's still something you feel insecure about. You're just not altogether sure you can sit down and write your way to stardom quite yet. Well, this chapter is for you. Here are a few exercises to get your Muse aroused.

Exercise 1.   Try filling out this form:

1. Point of view (male or female) _____

2. Name of main character _____

3. Other characters _____

_____

4. Situation (e.g., hero is at a bar and meets girl) _____

_____

5. Problem (e.g., girl is married, not interested) _____

_____

6. Sex angle _____

_____

7. Particulars of scene _____

Weather _____Time of Day _____

Description of Environment _____

Furniture or vegetation _____

8. What are the characters wearing? _____

_____

9. Physical description of each character _____

_____

_____

10. Play around with some adjectives to describe each character, such as, "He had cool blue eyes, a matted red beard and wore a woodchopper's shirt." _____

_____

11. Expected outcome of situation _____

_____

After you can answer all these questions (you don't really need to write them down), you are ready to begin your story. Decide how much space you want to fill (four lines or forty pages), and pace yourself accordingly. Remember you are trying to create real people and a real situation. Even fantasies and fairy tales can be believable.

Exercise 2.   Try a very short story at first, say two pages. You can always use it as an outline for a longer version and it will allow you to test your skill. You might even begin with one of the examples I gave you in this book. Take John and Mary sailing and have them make love in the sun or involve them in an orgy.

Exercise 3.   You can rip off just about any story you're familiar with and turn it into erotica. No one will recognize it and there are only so many basic plots anyhow. But do make a story, with a beginning, a middle and an end. Without a story, there's no tension, no reason for the reader to go on. The story line can be very simple. But something must happen in it. Even sex can be boring.

Exercise 4.   Create a scene between two characters for a video vignette. Have them talk to each other and discover what they want to do by what they say. Imagine you are watching them on television.

Exercise 5.   Take a person from your real life and put him or her into a situation. Or use a character from a television show or a movie and imagine your story with that person's way of speaking and dealing with life. I used Alex and Elaine from the sitcom *Taxi* to get the right sense of humor for *Older Men with Young Girls.* (Older men in adult videos are those over twenty-five.)

Exercise 6.   If you have a problem with dialogue, try saying your lines out loud, even in front of a mirror. You'll catch those corny romantic phrases and blatant clichés this way and you'll learn a good deal about writing the way people actually talk.

Exercise 7.   Describe the objects around you in sensual prose. "The earthenware coffee cup stood in a small puddle marring my ancient desktop. A crumpled napkin lay beside it, the only evidence of my last meal." After you get into the habit of describing such mundane and uninteresting objects, you'll find your fictional ones easier to do.

Exercise 8.   Although your lover will probably hate me for this, the next time you make love, think about what you're doing and measure the response in your partner to each and every action. Think about how you would put your experience into words. Watch your partner carefully for each twitch of an eyebrow, each trace of a frown and listen to the sounds of love-making. Then, whenever it is convenient, try to recreate the scene as best you can. You'll be surprised at how difficult this is at first and how you'll confuse which event happened before the other. But whatever you come away with, it will be excellent foreplay for your career in writing erotica.

Now that I think about it, your lover won't hate me at all. Because one important fringe benefit of writing erotica is that you will become a better lover. Why? The same reason researching and writing a book on fly casting should make you a better fisherman. Writing erotica may not lead you into new avenues of sexual expression (although it could), but it will definitely improve your current ones. And you will appreciate sex more for what it is by paying attention to each aspect of the whole experience.

You're still not ready? All right, I'll take you through the process by the hand.

Go to the newsstand that holds the most magazines in your town. Look for the sex selection. You remember that the easiest way to break into print in this market is through letters, so look for letters magazines. You find a stack of smallish, 5¼" x 8" magazines, usually perfect-bound, with a color cover, and with lots of type, but few photos inside. You see *Forum, Letters, Real Letters, Sensual Letters, Oui Letters, Hustler Letters, Vibrations, Bedside Companion, Couples, Penthouse Variations, Chic* and others. You flip through a few and select one with the most articles and stories in it, or one which concentrates on a subject that particularly appeals to you.

For the purposes of this exercise, I've selected *Penthouse Variations*. One, because I happen to know they pay well, and two, because there are at least four other magazines of this genre which use the same letters format. So if *Penthouse* won't use my manuscript, I can submit it to one of the others.

Penthouse Variations wants 2,500 to 3,500 words for their full-length "articles," but sets no limit for letters. Each letter is a story—a first-person "true" account of an erotic experience.

Buy the magazine and take it home.

Now, you're going to break the magazine down into its elements, looking for clues that will make your story sell before the other guy's. Your first evidence is found on the table of contents page.

I have here the August, 1985, issue of *Penthouse Variations*. The first thing I discover about this book is that it has little or no interest in your regular old guy meets girl and fucks her crazy story. It wants, as its title implies, variations. That means anything but an ordinary sex story. On the table of contents page, I find the following listings: First there is the Variations Advisory, a regular column which features readers' sex problems and the columnist's answers. There is a series of articles including one on foreplay, one on oral sex, another on swinging, a confession of what it's like to live out one's fantasies, some more group sex, one on voyeurism, an experimental story on gay male sex, and one on a big man and a very small girl getting together for spanking and playing. Eight stories posing as articles.

Next, I count twenty-three letters in the various letters sections. I deduce that the odds of getting my letter published are better than the odds on an article.

Now I break down the letters into subjects:

> food & sex
> oral sex
> orgy, swinging, swinger's club (several)
> threesome—two men (two stories)
> threesome—two women
> voyeurism (several)
> office girls spank boss
> submissive male (several)
> bondage (friendly—two stories)
> cross dressing
> sex for money
> dildo
> exhibitionism
> one story with straight sex
> mutual masturbation in car
> spanking

Next we'll study each story in more detail. Who is the story-teller? Male or female, married or single? In this case, I find that most of the stories are told by one half of a married couple. The story is about how they participated in a fantasy experience to-gether—the husband watched from the closet while the wife se-duced a man from the bar. The most popular theme in this book is threesomes. So that's what my story will be about.

Now I'm ready to break down the actual story in order to study its rhythm and movement. After two or three stories, I notice a clear pattern.

Paragraph 1 introduces the subject of the experience and the lead character, the "I" character.

Paragraph 2 elaborates on the experience and the lead character and may bring on the next character.

By paragraph 3 the story has been set up.

Paragraph 4 introduces the rest of the cast of characters.

Paragraph 5 goes into detail about the setting, the environment where the action will take place.

Paragraph 6 begins the erotic detail for the next ten paragraphs, and may introduce complications.

Dialogue can happen anywhere along the line, but most do not have dialogue. When they do, it begins around the third paragraph or so, and is very light, such as: "Do it to me, babe."

Several of these stories have not one, but two story lines, such as, we tried this once at the cabin and once back at home with someone else. The second story always begins after the first is over and done.

The last paragraph wraps up the story with something like: "Now my husband and I go to orgies every weekend and we're loving every minute of it." Or, "Who says a woman can't dominate her own household? I did it and Sam loved it."

After you've done all your preparatory work, your story is practically written for you. All you need to do now is fill in the blanks. Let's say we do this the old-fashioned way and write a story outline.

Paragraph 1: I am a newly married, twenty-two-year-old innocent female and had never had group sex, until recently.

Paragraph 2: My husband is into swinging and he wanted me to enjoy it too.

Paragraph 3: So he took me to a neighbor's house for a night of strip poker and wife-swapping.

Paragraph 4: There I met my new neighbor, Tim. He was so cute and built so well, I knew I was in for a good time.

Paragraph 5: Tim took me into the bedroom he shared with his wife, Elise.

Paragraph 6: Elise joined us.

Paragraphs 7 to 17: We began with three-way oral sex, then

Elise went down on me while Tim sucked my breasts. Then Tim fucked me while Elise masturbated.

Paragraph 18: My husband came in and was angry at first that we were having all the fun. He made me get in the car and go home with him.

Paragraph 19: But after we got home, I was still so turned on, I ravished him. And now that he knows how swinging really gets me going, he takes me all the time. I've learned to love it.

Since the story length of *Penthouse Variations* letters varies from one and a half to five columns, you and I won't be required to adhere to a certain number of pages for this submission. You'll know you've written too much when you start boring yourself. If there is too little detail, it will show up if your friends can't tell what's going on.

Give your story a provocative title. Then give it a subtitle to help the editor see it the way you do. A subtitle is not necessary, but it may help the editor route your story to the right fetish pile if your title is not enough of an indication. Your title and subtitle may be quite simple: "Yesterday's Dream: Anal Sex"; "My First Orgy: Group Sex"; "Embarrassing Erections: The problem with being a voyeur."

Since I can tell you're still not willing to get beyond reading a how-to book and into writing your own story, I'll show you what I did with my outline. This is one lead-in to my story.

Friendly Foursomes
A ROMP INTO THE REALM OF SWINGER'S SEX

I had only been married a few months when my husband Jake suggested we go to a swinger's party. Naturally, I was scared to death. At twenty-two, my only sexual experience was with my husband, unless you count making out in the backseats of cars.

It's not that I never had the chance. As a stacked blonde in a small town, I've had plenty of offers. I'm just conservative. At least I was until last night.

My husband Jake is a good-looking guy. He's tall and kind of hairy and he's got a terrific body and a super thick cock. Of course, up until a while ago, I'd only seen his, so what did I know?

Anyway, last night we went over to these people's house where Jake has gone to swinger's parties before. But no one was there except the hosts, Tim and his wife, Elise. Right away, Tim took hold of my arm and led me off to the bedroom. If he hadn't been such a hunk, I might have protested a little, but I wasn't scared at all.

In fact I was sort of looking forward to it. Sex with Jake had always been terrific, so I figured it would be good with this guy too. Tim was just the opposite of Jake, fair-haired and blue-eyed, with smooth, tanned skin. When he took off his shirt, I saw he had a beautiful chest with hard, brown nipples.

Tim laid me down gently onto the bed, then stood up and stripped for me. When he lowered his bikini briefs, his erection was all ready to go. Tim shoved it down a little, with the palm of his hand over the tip, and I was jealous. I wanted to put my hand there.

Naked, he lay down on the bed beside me and began to unbutton my blouse.

"What about Jake?" I asked.

"Elise will take care of him," Tim said. "Just relax and enjoy yourself." Then he cupped my breast and squeezed it so that my nipple popped up. He licked it, then encircled it with his lips. My body shuddered.

Soon I forgot all about Jake. I closed my eyes and fell into the passion of the moment. . . .

Your story may change from your outline and your format may vary from the paragraph-to-paragraph structure we set up. Don't worry about those things. It's when you're on paragraph four and we still don't know who the main character is, or what the story is about, that you're in trouble.

When you're finished with your story, put it away for a while and go back and read it later to pick up on those stupid grammatical errors we all make. Then type your final draft and send it

in to the editor, at the publisher's address given at the beginning of
the magazine, usually in the indicia.

Put it in the mailbox, then forget about it and go home and
begin your next story. You'll hear from the publisher within two
months. If you enclosed an SASE and your story is not eventually
returned to you, send a letter asking why. If you still don't get your
story back, or better yet, a check or a notification of publication
date, don't send this publisher any more work and advise all your
writer friends not to either. Eventually, they'll get a lesson in business ethics.

Everyone knows something about sex, but not everyone can put
it into words. That's your job as a writer. By expressing the sexual
experience well, you'll be providing your audience with the stimulation they desire and the information they need. Look at it as a
public service. On the other hand, your ulterior motive is that you
will be paid for your efforts, sometimes quite well. Your income
can escalate quickly in this business and you can make a living in a
relatively short period of time.

One thing you should know is you never have to write anything
you don't want to. Whatever you won't do, some other writer will
pick up, and some subjects are off-limits to all of us. Most adult
houses will shy away from bestiality, sex connected with violent
acts, rape, child seduction and incest. These subjects are not acceptable and the publishing house is running the risk of being
closed down if it deals with them. Writing about anyone under the
age of eighteen in a sex magazine is illegal, although for some
reason I don't understand, it is permitted in paperbacks where
there are no illustrations. Borderline subjects include water sports,
drug-related sex acts and scatological references. Don't be afraid
to say no if an editor tries to persuade you to bend your rules a
little. Writing about something disgusting to you is not what you
became a writer for and it isn't necessary. There are plenty of markets available for ordinary sex stories.

Throughout this book, you have found examples of many types
of erotic material you may be asked to write. Read them slowly, as
your reader would, and you'll catch on very fast. It's easy—most
of these stories are first drafts. If I can do it, you can do it too.
There is a reading list in the appendix which will help you keep
your facts straight, as well as provide you with new ways to do

familiar things. When I was hired to write a series of masturbation stories, I ran out of positions after about twelve. I found a whole lot more in *The Hite Report* to flesh out my stories.

You may want to make a shopping trip to your local paperback bookstore to pick up some research material, and you'll need to visit your local newsstand and video store to find your potential clients. Even if you never sell any of your sex stories, this whole adventure into erotica can be an exciting, stimulating, creative kick in the pants for your writing, and for your love life too. You'd be surprised how many people share your interest in sex.

The glossary at the back of this book may also be helpful to you. When I first got started in this business, I wished there were such a thing in existence. I knew the traditional words for body parts and a few raunchy ones, which I rarely used, but I hadn't an inkling as to what a "dominatrix" was, or even a "daisy chain."

Whatever you do, for heaven's sakes, have fun. Enjoy your new career in sensual writing and all that it brings you. And remember, sex is whatever you make it. It only has as much power as you allow it to have. If some of your friends feel sex is dirty and writing about it is shameful, that's their problem. You and I know they're missing out on something altogether pretty darn wonderful. As Shirley MacLaine says in *Terms of Endearment,* it's fan-fucking-tastic!

Write to me at the publisher's address if you have any questions. Be sure to enclose an SASE. Let me know about your successes and sales. And thanks for joining me in this adventure into the world of erotica. I wish you the best success with your career as a writer.

MAGAZINES THAT PUBLISH EROTICA

This list includes monthly and quarterly magazines that are sold on newsstands and that contain sexually oriented material. It is not a complete listing. Magazines go in and out of business, change titles and owners. A market list of men's and adult magazines, including confession and romance, detective and mystery magazines, is available from The Writer, Inc., 120 Boylston Street, Boston, MA 02116, for $2. There are additional publications listed in this year's *Writers Market*. You will probably find an extensive collection by visiting your local newsstand.

In any case, it is wise to look through a given magazine before attempting to write for it, to make sure your story fits its format.

Adam Film World (articles)
Knight Publishing Corporation
8060 Melrose Avenue
Los Angeles, CA 90046

Cavalier (articles and fiction)
2355 Salzedo Street
Coral Gables, FL 33134

Chic Letters (letters and
   articles)
Stewart Communications, Inc.
18455 Burbank Boulevard,
   Suite 309
Tarzana, CA 91356

Eidos
Brush Hill Press, Inc.
P.O. Box 96
Boston, MA 02137

Eros (articles and fiction)
351 West 54th Street
New York, NY 10019

Erotic Fiction Quarterly
   (fiction)
P.O. Box 4953
San Francisco, CA 94101

Firsthand Magazine (gay-male
   articles and fiction)
P.O. Box 1314
Teaneck, NJ 07666

Forum (articles, letters and
   humor)
1965 Broadway
New York, NY 10023

Gallery (articles and fiction)
Montcalm Publishing Corp.
800 Second Avenue
New York, NY 10017

Genesis (articles, fiction and
   letters)
Cycle Guide Publications
770 Lexington Avenue
New York, NY 10021

Gent (bust-oriented articles
   and fiction)
2355 Salzedo Street, #204
Coral Gables, FL 33134

Gentleman's Companion
   (articles and fiction)
Hudson Communications
155 Avenue of the Americas
New York, NY 10013

High Society
801 Second Avenue
New York, NY 10017

Hot Male Review (gay male)
MagCorp Publishing Company
8467 Beverly Boulevard, Suite
   200
Los Angeles, CA 90048

Hustler (articles, fiction and
   letters)
2029 Century Park East, 38th
   Floor
Los Angeles, CA 90067

Juggs (bust-oriented fiction)
155 Avenue of the Americas
New York, NY 10013

Leg Show (leg-oriented fiction)
155 Avenue of the Americas
New York, NY 10013

Letters Magazine (fiction and
   letters)
P.O. Box 1314
Teaneck, NJ 07666

Mandate (gay male articles and
   fiction)
155 Avenue of the Americas
New York, NY 10013

Mr. Male Review (gay male)
MagCorp Publishing Company
P.O. Box 15608
North Hollywood, CA 91615

On Our Backs (gay female)
P.O. Box 421916
San Francisco, CA 94142

Oui (articles, fiction and
   letters)
300 W. 43rd Street
New York, NY 10036

Oui Letters (articles and
   letters)
300 West 43rd Street
New York, NY 10036

Penthouse (articles, fiction and letters)
1965 Broadway
New York, NY 10023

Penthouse Variations (articles and letters)
1965 Broadway
New York, NY 10023

Playboy (articles and fiction)
919 North Michigan Avenue
Chicago, IL 60611

Players Magazine (black-oriented articles and fiction)
8060 Melrose Avenue
Los Angeles, CA 90046

Playgirl (letters)
3420 Ocean Park Boulevard, Suite 3000
Santa Monica, CA 90405

Screw (articles and letters)
116 West 14th Street
New York, NY 10011

Skin (gay male fiction)
MagCorp Publishing Company
P.O. Box 15608
North Hollywood, CA 91615

Stag (articles and fiction)
888 Seventh Avenue
New York, NY 10106

Swank (articles and fiction)
888 Seventh Avenue
New York, NY 10106

Turn-Ons (fiction)
313 West 53rd Street
New York, NY 10019

Video View
P.O. Box 15608
North Hollywood, CA 91615

VIDEO DISTRIBUTORS/ PRODUCERS

Here is a partial listing of video companies that create and distribute their own videos. For more information on the productions, their quality and story lines, please refer to one of the two video guides listed in Appendix C: Recommended Reading.

For an instant update on the latest releases, plot lines, stars and production companies, consult these two publications: *Adult Video News,* P.O. Box 14306, Philadelphia, PA 19115; and *Video Insider*, 223 Conestoga Road, Wayne, PA 19087.

Adult Video Corp. (AVC)
18121 Napa Street
Northridge, CA 91325

Ambassador Video
21540 Prairie Street C
Chatsworth, CA 91311

Arrow Films
85 East Hoffman Avenue
Lyndenhurst, NY 11757

Bizarre Video Productions
12812 Garden Grove Boulevard
Garden Grove, CA 94109

Blue Video
3615 Carnegie Avenue
Cleveland, OH 44115

Caballero Control Corp.
7920 Alabama Avenue
Canoga Park, CA 91304

California Dream Machine
1705 North Highland Avenue
Suite 653
Hollywood, CA 90028

Cal-Vista Corp.
6649 Odessa Street
Van Nuys, CA 91406

Cinderella Distributors
8021 Remmet Avenue
Canoga Park, CA 91304

Class X Video
Box C
Sandy Hook, CT 06482

Command Video
1540 Broadway
New York, NY 10036

Creative Image
P.O. Box 38307
Hollywood, CA 90038

Diverse Industries
7651 Haskell Avenue
Van Nuys, CA 91406

Essex Video
8841 Wilbur Avenue
Northridge, CA 91324

Excalibur Films
424 West Commonwealth
Fullerton, CA 92632

Gold Stripe Video
P.O. Box 180
Nesconset, NY 11767

Gourmet Video
13162 Raymer Street
North Hollywood, CA 91605

Hifoca-Hollywood
   International Films
1044 South Hill Street
Los Angeles, CA 90015

International Home Video
   Club
220 Shrewsbury Avenue
Red Bank, NJ 07701

Key Video
3529 South Valley View
   Boulevard
Las Vegas, NV 89103

Love Television
495 Ellis Street, #38
San Francisco, CA 94102

Media Home Entertainment
5730 Buckingham Parkway
Culver City, CA 91304

Mitchell Brothers
895 O'Farrell Street
San Francisco, CA 91409

Now Showing Video
P.O. Box 560
Fulton, CA 95439

Orchids International
1460 F. Monterey Pass Road
Monterey Park, CA 91754

Quality X Video Cassettes
430 West 54th Street
New York, NY 10019

Select/Essex Video
P.O. Box 1055
Northridge, CA 91324

Super Video Productions
Super Sight & Sound
28853 Orchard Lake Road
Farmington Hills, MI 48018

Susan's Video
P.O. Box 759
Frederick, MD 21701

TGA Video Ltd.
8821 Shirley Avenue
Northridge, CA 91324

Uschi
P.O. Box 663
Walnut Creek, CA 91789

VidAmerica
235 East 55th Street
New York, NY 10022

Video Company of America
   (VCA)
9333 Oso Street
Chatsworth, CA 91311

Video Tape Enterprises
P.O. Box 34037
Coral Gables, FL 33134

Videotape Exchange
1440 North Crescent Heights
   Boulevard
Los Angeles, CA 90046

Video Vista
90 Golden Gate Avenue
San Francisco, CA 94102

Video X Pix
430 West 54th Street
New York, NY 10019

Vision Video Productions
Box 25669
Los Angeles, CA 90025

Visual Entertainment
   Productions
16134 Covello Street
Van Nuys, CA 91406

Wizard Video
5303 Sunset Boulevard
Los Angeles, CA 90077

X-Tra Vision
6616 Eleanor Avenue
Hollywood, CA 90028

APPENDIX C

RECOMMENDED READING

One or more of these books in your reference library will give you a deeper understanding of human sexuality. This is just a small sampling of what is available in the field of sexology. The case histories included may serve as inspirational material for your fiction.

Sexology and Reference

Barbach, Dr. Lonnie. *For Yourself: The Fulfillment of Female Sexuality.* New York. Doubleday. 1976. Case histories of women talking about their sexuality with comments from the author.

———. *For Each Other: Sharing Sexual Intimacies: Women's Sexual Experiences.* New York, Doubleday. 1983. More of the same, plus how to become sexually satisfied.

Barbach, Dr. Lonnie, and Linda Levine. *Shared Intimacies: Women's Sexual Experiences.* New York. Bantam. 1981. More of the same, including what women do to satisfy themselves.

Califa, Pat. *Sapphistry.* Tallahassee, Florida. The Naiad Press. 1983. Exploring the lesbian relationship.

Friday, Nancy. *My Secret Garden.* New York. Pocket Books. 1973. Women's sexual fantasies.

———. *Forbidden Flowers.* New York. Pocket Books. 1975. More sexual fantasies.

———. *Men in Love.* New York. Dell Publishing Company. 1980. Men's sexual fantasies.

Hite, Shere. *The Hite Report—A Nationwide Study of Sexuality*

(Women). New York. Dell Publishing Company. 1976. All aspects of the sex lives from a survey of hundreds of women. Good reference for unusual masturbatory techniques and positions for intercourse.
————. *The Hite Report—On Male Sexuality*. New York. Ballantine. 1982. Men answer questions about their sex lives and share fantasies.

Kronhauser, Drs. Phyllis and Eberhard. *Erotic Fantasies: The Study of the Sexual Imagination*. New York. Grove Press. 1969. Wild fantasies regarding fetishism, homosexuality and everything taboo.

Loulan, JoAnn. *Lesbian Sex*. San Francisco. Spinsters Ink. 1984. How to be a lesbian or talk like one, including fragments of case histories and dialogue.

Martin, Del, and Phyllis Lyon. *Lesbian Woman*. New York. Bantam. 1972. Finally, the truth about being lesbian from women who know. An important book for dispelling popular myths.

Rimmer, Robert. *The X-Rated Video Guide, Revised and Updated*. New York. Crown Publishers. 1986. Hundreds of synopses and reviews of adult videos.

Segal, Dr. Jay. *The Sex Lives of College Students*. Pennsylvania. Miles Standish Press. 1984. A survey of 2,400 college students which included their complete autobiographies and revelations of their early sex lives.

Wolfe, Linda. *The Cosmo Report: Women and Sex in the Eighties*. New York. Bantam. 1982. Advertised as hotter than the Hite Report. More survey data.

Vassi, Marco, editor. *The Wonderful World of Penthouse Sex*. New York. Warner Books. 1976. A collection of articles on sexual trends.

Erotica

Barbach, Dr. Lonnie. *Pleasures: Women Write Erotica*. New York. Doubleday. 1984. Thirty-one women share their true erotic stories and poetry.
————. *Erotic Interludes: Tales Told by Women*. New York. Doubleday. 1986. Women writers weave fiction out of fantasy to explore their sexual and sensual cravings.

Nin, Anaïs. *Delta of Venus*. New York. Harcourt Brace Jovanovich. 1977. A sensuous woman's approach to writing erotica for a man. Male fantasies from a female point of view.

―――. *Little Birds*. New York. Bantam. 1979. A continuation of Nin's erotic stories.

―――. *Aphrodisiac*. New York. Crown Publishers. 1976. Excerpts from the erotic literature and diaries of Anaïs Nin, with line drawings.

Lawrence, D. H. *Lady Chatterley's Lover*. New York. Bantam. 1971. A novel seething with sex. In his own words: "This is the real point of this book. I want men and women to be able to think sex, fully, completely, honestly, and cleanly."

Rampling, Anne. *Exit to Eden*. New York. Dell Publishing Company. 1985. A novel about what goes on inside an exclusive sex club.

Roquelaure, A. N. *The Claiming of Sleeping Beauty*. New York. Dutton. 1983. A fairytale revamped S&M style by an artist of erotica.

The Kensington Ladies' Erotica Society. *Ladies' Own Erotica*. Berkeley. Ten Speed Press. 1984. Tales, recipes, poems and other mischiefs told by older women, not all of them "real" writers.

Just for Fun

Adler, Pat (of the Kensington Ladies' Erotica Society). *The Erotic Companion*. Berkeley. Ten Speed Press. 1985. A little book with lines in it accompanied by erotic cartoons on subjects such as foreplay, love, nude beaches, and so on, to inspire you.

Books about Writing

Barnhart, Helene Schellenberg. *Writing Romance Fiction for Love and Money*. Ohio. Writer's Digest Books. 1983. Not just how to write romances, but how to write a good story.

Corbett, Edward. *The Little English Handbook: Choices and Conventions*. Illinois. Scott, Foresman and Company. 1984. An easy guide to punctuation and grammar problems.

Falk, Kathryn. *How to Write a Romance and Get it Published*. New York. Crown Publishers. 1983. Short articles by prominent romance writers on every phase of writing.

Field, Syd. *Screenplay*. New York. Dell Publishing Company. 1982. Script formats, diagramming a story, tips on building character, jeopardy and drama.

Meredith, Scott. *Writing to Sell*. New York. Harper and Row. 1977. How to write with your market in mind—from concept to print.

Movsesian, Ara John. *Pearls of Love*. Fresno. The Electric Press. 1983. How to write love letters and love poems.

Nash, Constance, and Virginia Oakey. *The Screenwriter's Handbook.*
New York. Harper and Row. 1978. More tips on writing and selling
scripts.

Spears, Richard A. *Slang and Euphemism.* New York. Signet. 1982. A
dictionary of oaths, curses, insults, sexual slang and other words and
expressions often not found in your regular dictionary.

Strunk, William, Jr., and E. B. White. *The Elements of Style.* New York.
MacMillan Publishing. 1972. A must in any writer's library.

1986 Writers Market. Writer's Digest Books. A listing of publishers and
their requirements, with addresses and editor's names, and often including payment and terms.

A P P E N D I X D

SENSUAL WORDS

White perusing the dictionary, I made the arbitrary and purely personal decision that these are the sexiest words in the English language, either in themselves, or from the images they produce. If you're stuck on a story, reading this list may inspire you. The sexiest letter is "S," which is not surprising since sensual, sexy and sensitivity all begin with S. Stories with S-words are sure to be successful.

ablaze	breezy	crazy	enrich
adventurous	brooding	dancing	erotic
afterglow	bronze	dangerous	eternal
alive	bulge	daring	ethereal
allure	bursting	decadent	evoke
ample	calm	decent	evocative
ambiance	capricious	delicate	expose
animal	caring	demure	exuberance
animated	carouse	desire	eyelash
anxious	ceaseless	diffident	fabric
artistic	chasm	dreamy	facile
attain	cherish	drowsy	familiar
aural	cherubic	dwell	fantasy
awaken	chiseled	easily	fascinate
bed	coarse	eager	fathom
bite	compatible	earthy	feathery
blazing	constant	ecstatic	feisty
blend	content	effusive	feline
blithe	contortion	electrify	fickle
blowing	covert	enfold	fidgety
bosom	cram	enigma	figment

finesse
fleshy
flirt
florid
fluid
foamy
frenetic
frisky
frontal
furtive
fury
fuse
gait
gallant
gap
gentle
glad
glimmer
glimpse
glitter
gloomy
glorify
glorious
gorgeous
great
greedy
groan
groin
grope
guarded
guide
gush
habit
hair
haven
hazy
heady
headstrong
heart
heavy
hidden
hiding

hollow
hope
hug
humid
hunger
husky
hysterical
icy
idealistic
illuminate
illusion
image
imagination
immense
impish
impulse
incendiary
incite
indecent
in-depth
indiscreet
infinite
inflame
inflate
infuse
inhibit
innocent
insistent
intense
interval
interpersonal
intimate
intoxicate
irascible
itch
ivory
jam
jaunty
jealous
jiggle
jubilant
juicy

jut
keep
kinky
kind
kindle
lacy
languid
large
laugh
laze
layer
leak
lightly
limber
lingering
like
lipstick
liquefy
liquid
listen
livid
lonely
loose
love
lovely
lubricate
lucky
lunge
luster
macabre
mad
magnetize
maintain
majestic
marital
masterful
maze
meadow
memory
mere
merge
mesmerize

miracle
mirage
mirror
modest
moderate
moisture
moment
moon
motivate
mutual
mystify
mythical
naked
natural
nerves
niche
nude
nurse
nurture
nympho
odor
oily
ooze
opalescent
opiate
oral
organ
overcome
pace
pacify
pale
palm
partake
passionate
pause
peek
penchant
perceptive
pervasive
pet
petal
petulant

pillow	romantic	skimpy	submit
pique	rosy	sky	succulent
please	rowdy	sleepy	suffer
pliant	ruffle	slender	sulky
plunge	satiate	slim	sultry
plush	satisfy	slip	sumptuous
poke	saturate	slot	sun
polish	saucy	slowly	surf
pout	savage	smolder	surge
pretty	scamp	smooth	surreal
private	scanty	sober	surreptitious
probe	scent	sopping	surrogate
provocative	scheme	sordid	svelte
provoke	scintillate	soul	swap
pudgy	scorching	sparkle	sweetheart
pulchritude	secluded	spicy	swept
quake	secret	spiritual	sweet
quality	selective	spoil	swell
quantity	sensational	springy	swim
qualm	sense	squirt	take
quiver	sensuality	star	tame
rave	sensuous	stare	tan
ravish	sentimental	starlight	tangy
radiate	serious	starry	taper
rare	sexy	startle	taste
real	sexual	stay	tawdry
realize	shadow	steal	tear
rebel	shady	steamy	tell
recline	shallow	stiffen	tenacity
redolent	share	stimulate	tantalize
refreshing	sheer	sting	tender
release	shell	stir	tense
relax	shoot	stormy	thrill
reluctant	show	straddle	throes
renew	shy	straight	tight
repose	sight	strip	tingle
replete	silky	strive	titillate
restrain	silhouette	stroke	tongue
ride	silvery	stun	touch
rise	simulate	subconscious	true
rock	sinewy	sublimate	trustful
roll	sincere	submerse	tumultuous

unbelievable
undulate
understand
unfamiliar
vacant
vacuous
vain
valley
value
vapid
vaporous
variant
variety

vast
veil
velvet
venal
venture
verve
vibrate
violate
virginal
virtue
virtuous
virulent
viscous

vision
vivacious
vocal
volcano
wake
wanton
watery
wet
whimper
whisper
wild
wind

winter
wistful
worthy
writhe
X-rated
yacht
yearn
yield
zany
zealous
zest
zone

GLOSSARY

For our purposes, some of these familiar words and phrases have taken on new or expanded definitions. I'm sure you know more words than are listed here, but just in case, here are some definitions which may not be in your home dictionary.

Abandon *n*. freedom from self-imposed constraint.
Aberration *n*. deviation from the norm.
AC/DC *adj*. a person who swings both ways, who is sexually attracted to both males and females.
Action *n*. an event or series of events; a sexual adventure.
Active or sexually active *adj*. one who has sex often, more than once a week.
Adultery *n*. having sex with someone when married to someone else.
Affair *n*. a prolonged sexual liaison, often a love relationship.
A-hole *n*. anus; the orifice in the backside.
À la mode *adj*. anything with ice-cream on top, e.g., cock à la mode.
All the way *adj*. making love to completion; not stopping before intercourse.
Amour *n*. love, or a lover.
Anal *adj*. referring to the anus.
Anal coitus *n*. anal intercourse.
Anal erotic *n*. someone who is sexually aroused when stimulated anally or someone who prefers anal sex to other varieties.
Anal fetish *n*. a proclivity toward things involving the anus.
Anal intercourse *n*. inserting the penis into the anus.
Androgynous *adj*. having both male and female qualities.

Anus *n.* the orifice in the backside.

Aphrodisiac *n.* a substance that arouses one's sexual desire, like Mandrake Root or Spanish Fly. Love is the best aphrodisiac.

Aphrodite *n.* The Greek goddess of love or someone who looks like her.

Areola *n.* the darkened area around the nipple which becomes harder and darker during sexual arousal and causes an erection in the nipple.

Around the world *adv.* making love to someone without missing an inch; kissing, touching and caressing every part of a person's body. Can't be done in less than twenty minutes.

Arouse *v.* to increase one's sexual desire; to get someone sexually excited.

Arse *n.* archaic for ass; not useful unless you're reading Samuel Pepys' *Diary*.

Asexual *adj.* someone who has no interest in sex at all; not our customer.

Ass *n.* bottom, backside, rear end, derrière, buttocks, etc.

Asshole *n.* the orifice in the backside.

Ass man *n.* a man who is most interested in this part of another person's anatomy.

Auto-eroticism *n.* arousing oneself sexually; masturbation.

Auto-fellatio *n.* kissing one's own penis. Ron Jeremy, the porn star, is the only one I know who can do it.

Auto-flagellation *n.* whipping oneself when no one else is around to do it or wants to; popular with masochists and the Rev. Mr. Dimmesdale, Hester Prynne's beau.

Available *adj.* always ready to have sex.

Avaricious *adj.* a vicious appetite; always hungry for sex.

Backside *n.* ass, butt, buttocks, bottom, rear end, etc.

Back door *n., adj.,* euphemistic phrase meaning rear entry; having anal sex.

Back road *n., adj.,* same as above.

Balls *n.* testicles; the two glands that hang in the scrotum.

Ball-buster *n.* something that takes the macho out of a man, like a humiliating experience or a woman who is out to break his spirit.

Bang *v.* to fuck, make love or have intercourse with.

Bare assed *adj., adv.* naked.

Bawdy *adj.* obscene, but in a humorous way.

Beat off *v.* to masterbate, jack off, jerk off.

Beat the meat *v.* same as above; usually refers to male masturbation.

Beefcake *n., adj.* a sexy man, a hunk, a guy with a great body.

Ben Wa Balls *n.* an oriental device for keeping a woman in a constant state of arousal. It consists of two balls, slightly smaller than ping-pong balls and connected with a string, which fit inside the vagina and stay there all day long.

Bestiality *n.* having sex with animals (yes, I thought it was "beastiality" too).

B-girl *n.* a bar waitress who receives commission on the drinks she sells.

Bidet *n.* a small, low bowl, like a toilet, plumbed for washing private parts. Also good for soaking socks and nylons.

Bi-lingual *adj.* a person who has sex with males and/or females with little or no preference.

Bi-sexual *adj.* same as above.

Blow *v.* holding someone's genitals in one's mouth; not blowing really, but sucking, kissing and so on.

Blow job *n.* doing the above to the point of orgasm.

Blue *adj.* anything off-color; an adult movie is blue.

Blue balls *n.* the state of a man's testicles after too much foreplay without orgasm; very painful and unadvisable for good sex.

Boff *v.* to fuck, have intercourse with, make love to. This word is not in popular use just now.

Bondage *n.* tying up a sex partner with rope or wire or leather for the purposes of increased sexual enjoyment. A popular activity among sado-masochists and some gay males, and a frequent, unlived fantasy.

Boner *n.* an erection, an erect penis, a hard-on ready for action.

Boobs or boobies *n.* breasts, tits, especially women's.

Bordello *n.* a place where sexy women congregate and wait for their dates, who pay them for their sexual expertise and entertainment.

Bottom *n.* yet another word for ass or butt.

Box *n.* the vagina, cunt, pussy, etc.

Breasts *n.* the two beautiful globes that adorn a woman's chest; tits, boobs, bust, etc.

Bring off *v.* to take to orgasm; to cause an orgasm.

Broad *n.* derogatory term for woman unless said in jest, such as, "She's a feisty broad."

Brothel *n.* same as bordello; a place where one can go for a good time if he brings his money and leaves his inhibitions home.

Bugger *v.* to fuck in the ass, usually by one male to another.

Bum *n.* bottom, British style.

Bummer *n.* a bad trip, an awful experience.

Bumps and grinds *n.* what strippers do to music and lovers do while fucking.

Buns *n.* bottom; the cute seater on a man or a woman; always used in the favorable way, such as, "He's got cute buns!"

Bundling *v.* what our parents and grandparents did instead of necking or making out, which amounts to the same thing.

Bunghole *n.* asshole.

Bush *n.* the hairy area around the pubis; the muff.

Bust *n.* a set of breasts on a woman.

Butch *n.* a homosexual female who nearly always plays the male role and tends to dress in men's clothes.

Butt or buttocks *n.* yes, more asses and bottoms.

Button *n.* the clitoris; the tip of the female erection.

Buzz *n.* a rush or thrill from somthing sexual.

Buzz words *n.* words which are designed to produce a particular reaction in the reader, and which invite a sensual response.

Call girl *n.* a woman with whom one can make an appointment for a date who will have sex without asking for a permanent commitment, provided one pays the going rate and doesn't misbehave. Usually, she has a manager who acts as a go-between.

Camp *n., v.* something which is "in" which this word is not; when a gay male behaves in an overly feminine manner for the purposes of entertaining his friends.

Can *n.* yet another word for bottom.

Carnal *adj.* relating to sexual matters, objects or desires.

Casanova *n.* a man who keeps many lovers going at the same time and is always in active pursuit of new conquests. A drag if you're married to him.

Cat house *n.* a bordello or brothel.

Cavalier *n.* same as Casanova.

Celibacy *n.* the state of total abstinence from sex; what people practice (either temporarily or permanently) when they've had disagreeable sexual experiences or who confuse the bodily function of sexuality with a moral issue.

Cervix *n.* a soft place at the top of the vagina which marks the opening to the womb; very tender and reachable in certain sexual intercourse positions.

Chauvinist, male *n.* a person who actually still believes in male supremacy and a complete bore at an N.O.W. rally.

Chaste *n.* virginal, without sexual interest or pursuits.

Cheap *adj.* easy to come by sexually; attainable without much effort.

Cheat *v.* having sexual relations with a person other than one's main squeeze, usually in secret. It's called cheating because you're giving away sexual energy that belongs to your #1.

Cheesecake *n.* a woman or women who are sexually interesting. An attractive woman with a good body, especially in the leg department. Also used as an adjective when referring to posters or calendars with bathing beauties on them.

Cherry *n.* the hymen; a thin membrane covering or partially covering the vaginal opening in a virgin. When one pops a girl's cherry, he takes her virginity and ends her maidenhood.

Chick *n.* a youngish female, prime for dating.

Chicken *adj., n.* young sex objects. A "chicken" film is one made with underaged actors and is illegal.

Chippy *n.* a young girl who is leaning toward prostitution as a possible career.

Circumcision *n.* the cutting away of the male foreskin; a tradition in some religions and societies, which has fallen off slightly in popularity. There is now an operation available whereby men can restore their foreskins.

Cleavage *n.* the crease between the breasts; décolletage.

Climax *n.* orgasm; the peak of excitement in sex when men and some women ejaculate, and when tension pent up during foreplay is released.

Clitoral stimulation *n.* manipulation of the clitoris to excite sexual interest.

Clitoris *n.* the female muscle located on the roof of the vagina, the tip of which protrudes from beneath a tiny foreskin at the top of the vaginal opening. It becomes hard during erotic stimulation.

Closet queen *n.* a homosexual man who has not publicly announced his sexual preference.

Cock *n.* the penis, prick, rod, staff, dick, love stick, joystick, etc.

Cockring *n.* a ring made of rubber, metal or leather which fits at the base of the cock as decoration or to help maintain erection by keeping the blood in the shaft.

Cocksman *n.* a man who is very good at fucking and proud of it, and who usually has a reputation for having a big one.

Cocksucker *n.* a person who enjoys fellatio; a woman who has no trouble getting a man to go to bed with her a second time.

Cock teaser *n.* a person who pretends to be interested in having sex but never goes through with it.

Cohabit *v.* to live with another person to whom one is not married.

Coitus *n.* intercourse.

Coitus interruptus *n.* intercourse which is interrupted at the last moment so as to prevent pregnancy. Be careful though—that's how my little brother was conceived.

Come *v.*, *n.* to have an orgasm or climax; what comes out when you ejaculate, aka "cum."

Come shot *n.* the part of a pictorial layout or screenplay where the man ejaculates.

Concubine *n.* a woman who is financially supported by the man she has sex with, not counting housewives.

Concupiscence *n.* a very strong sexual desire; a high sex drive.

Condom *n.* a cute little jacket for the penis, usually made out of rubber or sheep gut, and more fun if the woman puts it on the man and the man forgets his hang-ups and those old jokes such as, "Wearing a rubber is like taking a shower with a raincoat on." Aka rubber.

Constrictor Vaginae *n.* just like it sounds, the muscles in the vagina which constrict during sexual excitement to produce a sucking sensation on the item inserted, and which are utilized when a woman is doing her Kegel exercises. *See Also* pubococcygeus, or *PC*, muscles.

Contraceptive *n.* any device or aid used to prevent pregnancy; birth control pill, I.U.D., condom, etc. Not mentioned much in erotic literature because it interrupts the action (much as it does in real life).

Copulation *n.* the act of intercourse; fucking.

Cosset *v.* to cuddle or stroke as in petting, to pamper.

Courtesan *n.* A woman who trades her sexual favors for a position in the King's court, or more recently, a prostitute who works especially for rich men.

Cradle robber *n.* a person who chooses sex partners who are much, much younger than he or she is.

Cross-dressing *n.* the act of wearing clothes of the opposite sex. Transvestites are cross-dressers.

Crotch *n.* the place between a person's legs where the genitals are located.

Cuckold *n.* a man whose mate is having an affair with someone else and he's the last one to know.

Cunnilingus *n.* oral sex performed on a woman; kissing, licking and sucking the female genitals.

Cunt *n.* female genitals; vagina, pussy, slit, twat.

Daisy chain *n.* a row or circle of people having sex with the person before and after; a popular activity at orgies, but a shocker at a Tupperware party.

Debauch *v.* to make use of another person sexually and exploit that person for selfish purposes.

Degenerate *n.* a person whose sexual needs are base and disgusting and which deviate from the norm.

Derrière *n*. French for bottom or buttocks but frequently used in English.

Deviate *n*. same as degenerate; deviant.

Diaphragm *n*. a contraceptive device which fits inside of the vagina and caps the entrance to the womb; usually made of rubber.

Dick *n*. penis, cock, prick, etc.

Dildo *n*. a phallic-shaped device, usually made from rubber, plastic or metal, and which sometimes contains a battery for use as a vibrator; a substitute hard-on for lovers and masturbators.

Discipline *n*. a sexual act which includes one person dominating the other and making demands of him. A popular activity among masochists requiring another to act out the dominant role. Sometimes includes costumes, leash, collar, whips, etc. Often goes with bondage and is referred to as B&D.

Dog fashion or doggy style *adv*. having intercourse where one partner, usually the female (or the male homosexual who plays the "female" role), is on hands and knees, and the other enters from behind.

Domina or Dominatrix *n*. a woman who takes the dominant position to the extreme, often wearing costumes made of latex or leather with collar and cuffs and spike-heeled boots. The Domina act is reportedly the second-most popular request made of prostitutes. (Guess what is #1?)

Don Juan *n*. like the cavalier and the casanova, a man who is obsessed with the desire to seduce as many women as possible with little interest in sustaining relationships.

Drag *adj., n*. cross-dressing, usually pertaining to male homosexuals and usually referring to the extreme. When a man is in drag, he's dressed to the hilt in female clothing.

Drag queen *n*. a male homosexual who loves to dress up like a female and who usually has extremely feminine characteristics in manner and behavior.

Dyke *n*. the female homosexual who prefers to take the masculine role and tends to dress in men's clothes; butch.

Easy *adj*. easily had sexually.

Eat *v*. to perform oral sex.

Effeminate *adj*. having female attributes, gestures or qualities; tending to be more female than male.

Ejaculate *v., n*. to emit jism, sperm or cum from the penis or vagina; the liquid emitted.

Emission *n*. a quantity of milky liquid which seeps or squirts out of the penis.

Erection *n.* when the penis or clit is engorged with blood and hard to the touch.

Erogenous *adj.* pertaining to those zones of the body that respond to sexual stimulation or to material that produces a sexual response.

Eros *n.* the Greek God of love

Erotic *adj.* pertaining to material, objects or people which have sensual appeal and produce a sexual reaction in those who respond to it; sexy; a turn-on.

Erotica *n.* literature and pictorial or screened material that depicts the sexual act in a loving or sensual way, and arouses its audience sexually. It comes from "Eros," the name of the Greek god of erotic love.

Erotogenic zones *n.* same as erogenous zones; those areas of the body that respond to sexual stimulation.

Erotomania *n.* extreme and obsessive sexual desire.

Eunuch *n.* a man who has been castrated.

Excite *v.* to stimulate sexually.

Exhibitionist *n.* a person who enjoys performing erotic acts in front of an audience; exhibitionists make good porn stars and strippers.

Exotic dancer *n.* a performer who dances to music while taking off his or her clothes; a stripper.

Fag *n.* a male homosexual; also, faggot.

Fairy *n.* same as above but usually refers to the very effeminate variety.

Falsies *n.* a pair of breasts made from rubber or plastic foam that are inserted into a bra or bodice to imitate real breasts.

Family jewels *n.* testicles and their contents.

Fanny *n.* affectionate term for the backside or bottom.

Feel up *v.* to touch someone's genitals, esp. to reach inside for the purposes of causing sexual excitement.

Fellate *v.* to suck cock; to perform fellatio.

Fellatio *n.* making love to a penis, and to kiss, stroke, lick and otherwise fondle it.

Female domination *n.* where the female is always the aggressor. Sometimes includes costumes.

Female impersonator *n.* a man who dresses up as a female for the purposes of entertainment, usually on stage. Not always a homosexual.

Femme *n.* the female homosexual who prefers to play the female role and is feminine in manner.

Femme fatale *n.* a sexually enticing woman who lures men into dangerous places.

Fetish *n.* a proclivity or obsession toward one particular sex act, object or anatomical part.

Finger *v.* to manipulate something with one's fingers; to stimulate sexually with fingers.

Fixed *adj.* referring to a person who can no longer conceive or cause conception to occur because of a surgical operation; a 100% safe form of birth control recommended for lovers who are through having children but are highly active sexually.

Flaccid *adj.* the state the penis is in when it is not erect. However, you don't see many flaccid organs in erotic literature. Men don't find it flattering.

Flagellation *n.* beating, whipping or abusing.

Flagrante delicto *n.* having sex; used as part of the phrase "caught in flagrante delicto," meaning caught in the act.

Flesh peddler *n.* a person who makes his living selling people or pornography; one who manages prostitutes.

Floozy or floosie *n.* a woman who has no sexual devotion to anyone and doesn't care about maintaining a good reputation.

Fool around *v.* to make love, mess around, make out or to take a sex partner who is not your mate.

Foreplay *n.* anything that happens before intercourse. Kissing, caressing, even talking to each other can be part of foreplay.

Foreskin *n.* the layer of skin that overlaps the head of the penis before circumcision in men and that covers the clit in women.

Fluffer *n.* a person who stays off stage and "fluffs up" the actor's cock between scenes. Usually a female, she gives the actor a blow job to help him keep his erection for the next scene.

Fornication *n.* love-making; the act of having intercourse.

Free love *n.* the philosophy that love and the sexual expression of it should be given freely without considerations of prior commitments and obligations. The option of spontaneous choice.

French kiss *n.* a kiss where the tongue probes the other person's mouth.

French postcards *n.* small, postcard-size photographs usually of women in lingerie, taken in the early days of photography. The women assume erotic poses. A predecessor of pornography.

French tickler *n.* a device, often made of rubber, which usually fits on the end of a condom and is designed to increase a woman's pleasure when inserted into her vagina.

Freudian *adj.* referring to Freud or to underlying motivations or sexual innuendos in one's actions.

Frig *v.* inserting one's fingers in a woman's genitals.

Frigidity *n.* once thought to be a physiological disease in women that prevented them from experiencing orgasm. Men who were bad lovers often blamed their inadequate sex lives on their partner's frigidity. Now we know the blockage is from choice or emotional resistance, or because of inadequate performance by the lover.

Fuck *v.* to have intercourse, make love, screw, stick, make it, get it on, copulate, etc.

Fur *n.* the hair around the pubic area or on a man's chest; on a woman also known as a muff or bush.

Gang-bang *n.* several people, usually male, having sex with one person, usually female, in a series or all at once.

Gash *n.* vaginal slit; the line which separates the labial lips.

Gay *adj.* being homosexual; preferring one's own sex to the intimate company of the other. Esp. male.

Genitalia or genitals *n.* the sexual organs.

Get fixed *v.* to be rendered by surgery incapable of conceiving or bearing children.

Get it off or get off *v.* having sex to the point of orgasm.

Get it on *v.* to have sex with a partner; to make love.

Get it up *v.* to get an erection.

Get laid *v.* to have intercourse, usually in the passive; to pick someone up and get fucked by him or her.

Get off *v.* to be enthusiastic about something almost to orgiastic proportions; to have an orgasm.

Get your rocks off *v.* to have an orgasm; to come.

Gigolo *n.* a paid, professional male lover.

Give head *v.* to perform fellatio or cunnilingus.

Glans *n.* the very tip of the clitoris or penis.

Glory hole *n.* the asshole, when referring to anal sex.

Go all the way *v.* to take something to its finish; in sex, to have intercourse.

Go down on *v.* to perform fellatio or cunnilingus.

Golden shower *n.* a sex act that includes urination.

Grafenberg spot or G-spot *n.* the paraurethral gland, a spongy tissue inside the vagina on the underside of the front wall. Found on a woman, probably by a woman, but named after a man. Some women ejaculate when their G-spot is stimulated.

Greek love or the Greek way *n.* making love anally.

Group sex *n.* sex with more than two people involved, as in a threesome or orgy.

G-string *n.* a tiny piece of fabric covering the genital area, required by law in some states when stripping in a public bar.

Hand job *n.* making love with the hands only, to oneself, or to a partner, as in mutual masturbation.

Hard-on *n.* an erection.

Harlot *n.* a woman who makes her living selling sexual favors.

Head *n.* oral sex; the knob of the erect penis.

Hedonism *n.* the philosophy that we're all here to have a good time and everything else comes second.

Hermaphrodite *n.* a person who was born with genitals of both sexes; a transsexual in process.

Heterosexual *n.* a person who prefers to make love to members of the opposite sex; a "straight" male or female.

Hole *n.* any orifice suitable for fucking, usually the anus or vagina.

Homophile *n.* a person who has a fondness for members of the same sex. The relationships formed are not always sexual in nature.

Homosexual *n.* a person who prefers to make love to members of his or her own sex.

Hormones *n.* for our purposes, when one's hormones are up, he or she is more inclined to be sexually active. Hormones also alter one's sexual tendencies, as when transsexuals take them to become more female or more male, or post-menopausal women take them to maintain their normal levels.

Hook and hooker *v.,n.* to procure customers who will pay for sex; a prostitute, usually a female.

Horny *n.* the state of being aroused sexually with not enough outlets for the sexual energy. Turned on.

Hot *adj.* eager to have sex, same as "hot to trot"; ready for a sexual adventure at any time.

Hot box *n.* a woman's vagina that is particularly easy to arouse sexually; a good fuck.

House of assignation *n.* popular in Madame Bovary's day, these were buildings with separate apartments that could be rented out by the afternoon, day or week, and in which lovers, usually married to others, would spend an intimate time together. Baths and meals were supplied. A far cry from today's version: adult motels.

House of pleasure or house of prostitution *n.* a place where a man can get a cold drink and a hot date for one small price at the door.

Hump *v.* to fuck; to dry fuck, as in going through the motions while still fully dressed.

Hung *adj.* refers to a man whose penis is of enormous proportions, enough to astound his friends. If a guy is "well hung," that's a compliment.

Hunk *n.* a man with a great physique, usually on the macho side, and often with a handsome face to match.

Hustle or hustler *v., n.* to walk the streets or patronize bars in order to find customers for sex; a person who hustles.

Hymen *n.* the thin membrane that sometimes covers or partially covers the vaginal opening in a virgin. It is broken on the first insertion or beforehand.

Illicit *adj.* immoral, illegal or outside the realm of the norm.

Immoral *adj.* contrary to the morals of whoever is judging it.

Impassioned *adj.* filled with enthusiasm for something; terribly excited about something.

Impotence *n.* the inability to maintain an erection, temporarily or permanently, in a male. Often caused by emotional or psychological problems and can sometimes be cured with sex therapy and a patient sex partner.

Incest *n.* having sex with a member of one's immediate family.

Intercourse *n.* sex, love-making, screwing, fucking, inserting a penis into a vagina.

Jack off *v.* to masturbate; to manipulate one's clit or penis to the point of orgasm.

Jail bait *n.* a sex partner who is under the legal age of consent, usually eighteen, but in Denmark, fourteen.

Jerk off *v.* same as jack off.

Jism *n.* the fluid that spurts from the penis during orgasm; a white, milky, viscous substance which sometimes contains sperm.

Jock *n.* a man who is into sports and lets everybody know it. Often wears Adidas shirts and Nike shoes to parties and carries a basketball.

John *n.* the name a prostitute gives to a customer to keep him anonymous.

Johnson or Mr. Johnson *n.* a penis, as in "playing with Mr. Johnson."

Joint *n.* a penis, cock, prick. Also, a marijuana cigarette.

Joy stick *n.* a penis.

Kama Sutra *n.* originally a book that included information about sex, and illustrations of sexual positions. Now usually refers to one position where the man sits on a flat surface and the woman sits on his lap facing him, his penis inserted into her vagina. A fun way to make love if you like looking at each other.

Kegel exercises *n.* a form of muscle contraction and expansion that a woman does using the inner walls of her vagina to improve tone and ensure tightness. These contractions occur involuntarily during orgasm. Named for Dr. Kegel, who "discovered" them.

Kept woman *n.* a woman, usually a mistress, who is housed, fed and clothed by a patron who uses her for sexual purposes (not counting housewives). Usually a surreptitious arrangement.

Kinky *adj.* contrary to the established way of doing things; something that you or I wouldn't do but that might be interesting to read about. Making love in gorilla suits in the ladies' john at city hall, would definitely qualify as kinky.

Kiss *n.* the touching of one's lips to another surface, preferably a body part belonging to another person; the tongue may also be employed to produce such interesting variations as the French kiss and cunnilingus.

Knob *n.* the head of a penis; the hard, round tip that looks like a door knob.

Knockers *n.* a set of breasts, usually large ones.

Labia majora *n.* the outer lips of the vagina.

Labia minora *n.* the inner lips of the vagina.

Lay and laid *v.* to have sex with or to have had sex with.

Lascivious *adj.* usually goes with the word "behavior"; arousing someone's prurient interest; lusty, lewd.

Lecher *n.* a person, usually an older man, who is obsessed with the seduction of women, usually very young women; a lech.

Lesbian *n.* a woman who prefers other women for sex partners and companions; a homosexual woman.

Lesbo *n.* slang for lesbian.

Lewd *adj.* boistrous, sexual, bawdy, usually referring to language or behavior.

Lez or lezzie *n.* slang for lesbian.

Liaison *n.* a joining together, a bonding or connection, as in a sexual relationship.

Liberate *v.* to make free; to set free of former obligations.

Libertine *n.* someone who believes in freedom and does not restrain his or her behavior morally or sexually.

Libido *n.* underlying sex drive or instinct.

Licentious *adj.* sexually unrestrained.

Lick *v.* to stroke and moisten with one's tongue.

Lingerie *n.* underwear for females, usually very feminine, lacy, silky and sexy. Includes stockings, garters, bras, panties, slips, teddies and nightgowns.

Lips *n.* the beautiful, pinkish protrusions of muscled skin at the mouth of the face and the mouth of the vagina, which are capable of sensual delights.

Load *n.* often refers to an amount of ejaculate as it spurts forth, as in "he shot his load."

Lothario *n.* a man who seduces in a charming manner, and who typically loses interest after conquest.

Love button *n.* clitoris, also known as pleasure button.

Lover *n.* a paramour; a person with whom one has a sexual relationship; a boyfriend or girlfriend; a "main squeeze."

Lubrication *n.* the thick, creamy moisture that is secreted by the vagina during sexual excitation.

Lubricous *adj.* sexually wanton, horny, already oiled and ready to get it on.

Lust *n.* sexual desire.

Machismo *n.* That special something that makes a man "all man," and which sometimes is off-putting in its exaggerated state.

Madam *n.* a woman who runs a house of prostitutes, and sort of a mistress of ceremonies and bookkeeper rolled into one.

Maidenhead *n.* hymen or "cherry."

Maidenhood *n.* the state of virginity.

Make *v.* to get someone to bed; to take him or her sexually.

Make it *v.* to make love, to go all the way.

Make out *v.* to neck, pet, cuddle, kiss and hug each other.

Mammary glands *n.* the glands in the female breasts that secrete milk when the woman is lactating.

Mary *n.* a male homosexual who always plays the female role and who often emphasizes his feminine characteristics.

Masher *n.* a man who is overly aggressive when seeking female companionship, often going after innocents.

Masochism *n.* the desire to want to be hurt or to hurt oneself, to be in pain or to be punished.

Master/slave *n.* a game played where one (usually the female) is dominant and the other (usually the male) is submissive. Often accompanied by paraphernalia. Slaves are kicked, beaten, whipped and urinated on, which gives them a sexual thrill.

Masturbation *n.* manipulating one's own sex organs to orgasm; stroking the clit or penis to erection and then to orgasm; jacking off, self abuse, playing.

Meat *n.* a real hunk of man; a male organ as in "beating the meat"; a woman who belongs to one man, as in "that's his meat." Also, white meat is a white woman who goes with a black man and black meat is a black woman who goes with a white man.

Member *n.* the male sex organ. Discreet term.

Menage à trois *n.* a threesome; a sexual liaison among two women and a man or two men and a woman. In this case three is not a crowd and is often more stimulating than two.

Mess around *v.* to fool around, get sexy and maybe do something, but maybe not; to play with the idea.

Missionary position *n.* the man lies face down on top of the woman (who is face up) while they are making love; the most popular and traditional position. If a couple only knows one love-making position, this one is usually it.

Mistress *n.* a woman who lives in a house or apartment provided by a married man, eats and sleeps with him, makes love to him and spends his money, but is not married to him. She is often kept without the lawful wife's knowledge and without the respectibility normally given to lawful wives. Also, a dominatrix. A woman who serves as master for S&M tricks. Also called a top.

Moll *n.* a woman who belongs to a gangster; a tough woman.

Mons *n.* the fleshy mound, covered with hair, over the pubic bone of a woman's genitals.

Mouth *n., v.* the orifice through which we take in food, sexual parts and tongues, and which also helps us form love words; to caress with the lips.

Muff *n.* the curly pubic hairs surrounding the vagina, and a soft place to fall asleep.

Multiple orgasm *n.* having climaxes one after the other, usually in rapid succession. Women are very good at this; men are still learning.

Mutual masturbation *n.* when two people are stroking each other's genitals; stroking one's own genitals while watching the other do the same; love-making when neither party is interested in the other, and only reaching for his or her own climax.

Narcissism *n.* self-love to the extreme, as when one loves his or her own body and makes love to it lovingly. If this person is ever attracted to someone other than himself, it is because he's found a mirror image.

Naughty *adj.* nasty, risqué, off-beat, not generally accepted behavior.

Neck *n., v.* that beautifully sculptured pedestal which holds the head erect and is a great place to kiss. Orientals and cats consider the back of the neck the most erotic place on the female body. To make out, pet, hug and kiss without coming.

Necrophilia *n.* making love to the dead. Since that's nearly impossible these days, a person with this fetish will ask his partner to take a cold bath, then lie perfectly still and not make a sound while he ravishes her body. We're talking kinky now, folks.

Nipples *n.* the pretty pinkish or brownish tips to breasts on males and females which love to be sucked, gently pinched and licked, and which become erect with the arousal of sexual desire.

Nubbins *n.* breasts, usually little ones.

Nude *adj.* naked.

Nudie magazines *n.* magazines that have at least one layout of a naked person, usually a female alone.

Nympho and nymphomaniac *n.* a woman who can't get enough sex. Once considered a disease, but now hailed as a positive attribute.

Obscene *adj.* something disgusting or lewd. A very subjective determination. A naked woman is obscene to some people while war is obscene to others. Refers to behavior, language, literary material, art, etc.

Oedipus complex *n.* a psychological condition in which a man wants to make love to his mother or at least greatly admires her, and often seeks love/sex relationships with older women.

Ogle *v.* to gawk shamelessly; to look at flirtatiously

Old dirt road *n.* the ass, the anal passage.

Old-fashioned way *n.* intercourse in the missionary position.

One-night stand *n.* making love to a person one just met and never seeing that person again.

Oral intercourse *n.* fellatio; making love to or with one's mouth; inserting the penis into a mouth or the tongue into the vagina.

Organ *n.* for our purposes, another euphemism for penis.

Orgasm *n., v.* the culmination of sexual activity where muscles tense up and then release pent-up sexual energy; when the penis ejaculates fluid and the vagina secretes juice and clamps down on whatever's in there to squeeze out the last drop of satisfaction. To come, climax, peak, get off, etc.

Orgy *n.* a party where three or more people get together to have sex with more than one partner at a time.

Oversexed *adj.* a judgment usually made by someone who is irritated by another's higher sex drive. Oversexed can mean anything from wanting it three times a day to wanting it once a month. Purely subjective.

Over the top, to go *v.* to have an orgasm; to bring past sexual excitement to satisfaction.

Pair *n.* a set of breasts on a woman.

Pander *v.* to set up a sexual liaison, usually with the intent to make money.

Pansy *n.* male homosexual.

Paramour *n.* a lover; a person one makes love to regularly; a "main squeeze."

Passion *n.* lust, craving, deep desire, excitement and enthusiasm for some particular thing, activity, person or chocolate chip cookies.

Passive *adj.* playing the submissive role; allowing something to happen rather than instigating it.

Pasties *n.* little glued circles, stars or patches that fit over the nipples of an exotic dancer.

Pearl diver *n.* a person who loves to suck clit; a man who can always have a second date.

Pecker *n.* penis, cock, prick, rod, staff, dick, etc.

Pecker checker *n.* a person who is always looking at men's crotches, ostensibly to guess the size of the cock.

Pederasty *n.* a sexual act between two males, particularly when one is much younger.

Pedophiliac *n.* a person who is sexually attracted to very young children.

Peel *v.* to take off one's clothes in a seductive manner; to strip them off slowly, exposing a bit at a time.

Peep show *n.* an erotic projected film that is for your eyes only, and which could cost a quarter or more for each segment. A more recent variety features a live model behind a glass window to whom one can make requests. Each request adds to the bill.

Peeping Tom *n.* a man who hides in the bushes to catch a glimpse of a woman taking off her clothes; a voyeur.

Penis *n.* the organ which hangs between a man's legs in repose and stands up to attention when aroused, and is capable of impregnating, fucking or otherwise giving pleasure; a cock, prick, rod, staff, dick, etc.

Perform *v.* to give good sex; to make love in varying degrees of proficiency. If you can't perform, you can't get it up. If you're worried about performing, you may jeopardize the performance.

Perversion *n.* some behavior that goes too far; a good thing taken past its limits. A subjective determination.

Pervert *n.* a person who practices perversions.

Pet *v.* to stroke and caress.

Phallus and phallic *n., adj.* the erect penis or anything resembling its shape.

Philanderer *n.* a man who can't remain sexually faithful to one woman at a time, who is always cheating and has no conscience regarding promises broken and lies told.

Pick up *v., n.* to make a connection with a stranger for the purposes of having sex; a person who is easily picked up.

Piece *n.* sex, usually quick.

Pillow book *n.* a sex manual, which in oriental cultures is given to a couple on their wedding day to help them exercise creativity in their love-making. It is said that some geishas take a pillow book with them in their suitcase, which is filled with dildos and other erotic paraphernalia.

Pimp *n.* a man who sells the sexual services of his workers for a percentage of the take, usually more than he deserves.

Play around *v.* to make love; to cheat on one's lover.

Play with *v.* to manipulate genitals, or whatever else is handy, with the fingers.

Poke *v.* to fuck, either with a cock or some fingers.

Pole *n.* a penis in its hard state.

Pop shot *n.* where the male ejaculates on a female so the viewers can see it's all for real; come shot.

Pornography *n.* literature, art or photography meant to arouse prurient desires in its audience. Usually less artful than degrading. Original definition came from words which meant the writing of prostitutes.

Premature ejaculation *n.* when the penis ejaculates before it gets inside the vagina or soon after. Quite common in young or inexperienced men, and in men who are afraid of or intimidated by women. Very common on the first night with a brand-new partner because of increased excitement and/or performance anxiety. If it becomes a chronic problem, it can be cured with patience and a few hints from Masters & Johnson.

Priapism *n.* a disease where the penis is continuously erect. (Not as much fun as it sounds.) Lewd and lascivious behavior.

Prick *n.* penis, cock, dick, staff, rod. etc.

Prick tease *n.* a person, usually female, who gets a guy excited and then doesn't let him fuck her; cock tease.

Privates *n.* genitals; male and female sexual parts.

Pro *n.* a prostitute; a person who is very good at sex.

Profligate *n.* a person who is really into sex in a serious and obsessive way, and who overly indulges in sexual pleasures.

Promiscuity *n.* the state of indiscriminately choosing, and having many, sex partners.

Prophylactic *n.* something which obstructs conception; a device that interrupts the flow of the sperm to the egg; usually refers to a rubber or condom, but could be a diaphragm or anything used for birth control.

Proposition *n., v.* a suggestion of sex play; an offer to have sex; to make a verbal advance regarding sex.

Prostitute *n.* a person, usually female, who works late nights but has no trouble getting up in the morning. She is often mistaken for a criminal because men pay her for her sexual services and sometimes those men are from the vice squad.

Prurient *adj.* having to do with sex and sexual arousal.

Puberty *n.* the point in time where boys and girls begin to become men and women, where their genitals expand, grow hair and crave attention.

Pubic *adj.* referring to the area around the pubis or genitals.

Pubococcygeus or PC muscle *n.* a muscle located inside the vagina of the female, from the pubic bone to the coccyx, which contracts involuntarily during orgasm and voluntarily during Kegel exercises. Frequent exercise will produce a tight vagina. Men also have this muscle, and through exercise can achieve multiple orgasms for themselves as well as their partners.

Pudend or pudendum *n.* the pubic mound.

Pull the pud *v.* to masturbate; the term applies to males only.

Pussy *n.* vagina, including mound and pubic area; cunt, box, cock heaven. A soft name for a soft spot.

Put out *v.* to have sex.

Queen *n.* a homosexual male who is extremely effeminate and often loves to give parties where he is the center of attention. He may love to wear women's clothes too.

Queer *n., adj.* a homosexual, usually male.

Quickie *n.* having sex on the run, like in the bathroom of an airplane or in the stairwell of the theater just before the movie lets out. Usually more satisfying in its spontaneity and the state of danger than it is physically.

Quiff and quim *n.* Very old words for vagina, pussy or cunt.

Randy *adj.* horny; to be in a state of sexual arousal with no solution in sight.

Rape *v.* to take someone sexually by force without their desire or permission.

Ream *v.* to have intercourse anally; to jam an erect phallus in hard and fast.

Rectum *n.* asshole; anal opening.

Red light district *n.* no, they no longer sport red lights, necessarily, but they do still exist. You can find them near streets lined with massage parlors, cheap motels and adult bookstores, and recognize them by the abundance of pretty girls walking back and forth in high-heeled shoes and short, tight skirts who almost always carry a purse with a shoulder strap.

Ribald *adj.* indecent or vulgar or just slanted by a sexy sense of humor.

Rim *n.* the opening to the anus.

Rim job *n.* licking all around the opening to the anus.

Risqué *adj.* daring, maybe sexy too, perhaps a tad wicked, and usually lots of fun.

Rod *n.* slang for penis, usually in its erect state.

Romeo *n.* a lover; a man who charms women, one after the other.

Rump *n.* another word for bottom.

Sadism *n.* a desire to produce pain in others.

Sadist *n.* a person who desires to produce pain. It requires a masochist partner. Often relates to sex in some psychological and mysterious way.

Salacious *adj.* sounds like delicious to me—or a combination of salivate and luscious—but to some it has a negative connotation, as in vulgar or obscene.

Sappho *n.* the Greek poetess who wrote poetry about women loving women.

Sapphist *n.* a woman who loves women.

Satanism *n.* A cult that worships the devil instead of God and employs sexual activities in its practice.

Satisfy *v.* to render sated or satiated; to bring a woman to so many climaxes, she's lost count, or to bring a man to such an incredible orgasm, his legs are weak and he's promising to love you forever.

Satyr *n.* the male nymph, half man, half goat, who played the flute and ran after women with lust in his heart and under his fur.

Satyriasis *n.* a condition where a man is always horny.

Scatological *adj.* having to do with excrement.

Screw *v.* to have intercourse, make love, fuck, have sex with.

Scrotum *n.* the cute little sac that holds the male testes and which tightens up when the man is aroused and which loves to get licked and scratched.

Seat *n.* do we really need another word for bottom?

Seduce *v.* to interest someone in having sex; to flirt, cajole, caress and manipulate until the person agrees to make love.

Self abuse *n.* masturbation; a very old way of saying it.

Semen *n.* the fluid which is emitted from the male organ upon orgasm.

Sensual *adj.* having a scintillating and tantalizing feeling; being of a sexual nature.

Sensuous *adj.* same as above.

Sex aids *n.* anything that has the potential to make sex even more fun than it already is; dildos, massage oils, vibrators, erotic literature, photographs of people making love, etc.

Sex appeal *n.* that special something that makes you more attracted to one person than the next. It doesn't need to have anything to do with physical beauty but usually relates to personality and charm.

Sex education *n.* the fundamentals of sexual contact, arousal, intercourse and orgasm. May be an in-school or extracurricular subject. Most students learn mainly from their lovers.

Sex object *n.* a person who is thought of mainly as an instrument for sexual intercourse.

Sexology and sexologist *n.* the study of sexual habits and behavior; the person who does this.

Sex pot *n.* a person who is sexy beyond belief, who exudes her sexuality like fragrant perfume.

Sex therapy *n.* psychoanalysis and treatment for sexual disorders and dysfunctions and usually includes sex education and work with the partner.

Sexual act *n.* anything to do with a sexual experience, from foreplay to climax.

Sexual deprivation *n.* the state of not having sex.

Sexual intercourse *n.* inserting the penis into the vagina for the purposes of physical gratification and/or to increase intimacy between two people.

Sexual organs *n.* the penis and the vagina.

Sexual orgasm *n.* is there any other kind?

Sexual tension *n.* that driving intensity that might begin at the back of your neck but always centers in on the groin and builds until it needs to be released, most often through orgasm, but some repressed people prefer volleyball and a cold shower.

Sexy *adj.* reminding one of sex; a person with attributes and attitudes that make all who come in contact with him or her begin to have sexual fantasies. Clothing, literature, movies and Woody Allen can all be considered as sexy. Anyone who loves to make love usually comes across as being sexy.

Shack up *v.* to live with a person with whom one had sex without benefit of marriage. Usually temporary.

Shoe fetish *n.* the proclivity toward sex acts involving shoes. Very popular with male homosexuals and sado-masochists, although different shoes are used.

Shoot off *v.* to have an orgasm.

Short hairs *n.* those cute little curlies in the pubic area, usually referring to the male's.

Simultaneous orgasm *n.* when the male and the female come at precisely the same moment. Was once considered the only way to do it right. Now with sex education and a little comon sense, we know it is even more fun to feel the woman clamping down on the man's cock in her orgasm and to feel the man's juices squirting up during his. It's much harder to feel the other's orgasm if you're busy concentrating on your own.

Sixty-nine *n.* the position for love-making that puts the lovers upside-down, with the man's face in the woman's crotch and vice versa. A good position for oral sex but rather awkward otherwise.

Skin flicks *n.* movies with lots of skin in them; porno movies.

Sleep with *v.* implies having sex with as well. If a man asks you to sleep with him, you can leave your P.J.'s and toothbrush at home.

Slit *n.* the crevice between two vaginal lips.

Slut *n.* a promiscuous female; one who fucks around and gets caught, or who plays fuck and tell.

Smooch *v.* cartoon language for kissing up on someone.

Smut *n.* garbage; lewd literature with or without pictorials which degrade and disgust.

Snake *n.* the male sex organ; what sexually repressed men and women have nightmares about.

Snatch *n.* vagina; female sex organs.

Social disease *n.* any form of disease that is transmitted sexually, such as herpes and gonorrhea. Not a good theme for your story.

Sodomy *n.* Usually refers to anal sex or bestiality, but technically describes any noncoital sexual activity.

Spanish fly *n.* a drug that is purported to increase sexual desire.

Spasm *n.* the quick contraction or series of contractions that occur within the vagina or penis during orgasm.

Sperm *n.* cute little tadpoles which swim around in male ejaculate hoping to become children, but often wind up in a rubber lifeboat.

Spermatozoa *n.* same as above.

Sphincter cunni *n.* the muscles inside the vagina which are so clever at squeezing out a man's jism.

Spoon style *adj.* a way of sleeping together situated like spoons in a drawer, nesting with one person's rear in the other one's groin. Also a nice way to make love.

Square *n.* a person with little or no sexual experience and even worse, no interest in getting any. A real downer at an orgy.

Stacked *adj.* refers to women who have tremendously huge breasts, who are "really built."

Stag *n.* a man alone; a man who comes to a party or bar alone.

Stag party *n.* a party where only men are invited, usually because they're going to show porno movies and there's a stripper hiding in the cake.

Stick *n., v.* a hard penis; to fuck.

Straight *adj.* a person who has no homosexual tendencies at all, or at least hasn't bothered to investigate long enough to find them; a person who is rather prudish about sex. Straight sex implies only traditional intercourse, no improvisations or extra participants.

Streetwalker *n.* a prostitute who walks the streets looking for customers.

Stripper *n.* an exotic dancer; a person, often female, who gets up on the stage and takes her clothes off in time with the music.

Striptease *n.* the dance that the stripper performs. It was given this name because it tends to arouse the men in the audience and tease them into getting hard-ons.

Stud *n.* a male who is a very good lay.

Sublimate *v.* to redirect certain impulses, especially sexual ones, to some other activity. Like going jogging when you'd really rather make mad, passionate love to that new neighbor.

Succubus *n.* someone who comes back from the dead to have sex with the living. A kind of sexually depraved ghost.

Suck *v.* to take another person's genitals, fingers or flesh into one's mouth.

Suck off *v.* to do the above until the person climaxes.

Sugar daddy *n.* a man who takes care of a much younger woman and buys her lots of expensive things. Not counting real fathers and husbands.

Sultry *adj.* hot with sexual desire, seductive and heated up for action, but in a lazy, sensual way.

Surrogate *n.* a person who is employed as a sex partner for another person who needs someone to practice on. Regarded as a legitimate profession because of its nobility of cause, though it smacks of prostitution. Surrogates get a higher minimum wage too.

Swing *v.* to be sexually active, often with more than one partner at a time or involving mate-swapping.

Swing both ways *v.* to make love with equal interest in males or females; AC/DC; bi-sexual.

Swinger *n.* a person who swings.

Sybarite *n.* a person devoted to pleasure, like a hedonist only more specifically sexually inclined.

Tail *n.* ass, usually female and also implies a sexy one.

Take *v.* to make love to; to make.

Talk dirty *v.* using sexy words for the purposes of arousing one's partner in foreplay. Phrases such as, "I just love to suck your gorgeous, thick cock," can do wonders for a limp erection. And it never hurts to tell a woman she has the most beautiful breasts you've ever kissed.

Tart *n.* an archaic word for whore.

Tease *v.* to provoke sexual reaction by being coy, flirtatious, seductive and cute. Great for foreplay but can get annoying if you take it too far.

Tit banger *n.* a guy who loves to place his cock between two voluptuous breasts and slide it up and down until he comes.

Tits *n.* breasts, knockers, boobs.

Tongue *v.* to lick something with that red muscle in your mouth; to flick against, encircle and otherwise make love with one's tongue.

Top *n.* a dominatrix or mistress.

Tramp *n.* a woman who sleeps around.

Transsexual *n.* a person who feels he or she was placed in the wrong body and has an operation to rectify the error. A man becomes a woman by having his penis removed and a vagina built from the skin, and he grows a set of hormone-developed breasts. A woman becomes a man by having a penis made from her skin and taking male hormones. This procedure is very difficult and expensive and involves years of counseling and adjustment.

Transvestite *n.* a person who likes to dress in clothing more suitable to the opposite sex. Not necessararily a homosexual, but probably.

Troilism *n.* a threesome, sex with three people at the same time; menage à trois.

Trollop *n.* another archaic word for tart.

Turn on *v., n.* to get yourself or someone else excited sexually; the thing that turns you on.

Twat *n.* vagina, cunt, pussy, slit.

Uterus *n.* the female sex organ, which tries to collect the man's sperm and connect it with the ovum or egg.

Vagina *n.* the female genitals; the frontal opening between her legs, which gobbles up whatever's handy, such as tongues, fingers, dildos, cocks.

Vamp *v.* to seduce; to persuade using sexual means.

VD *n.* veneral disease, gonorrhea, herpes; sexually transmitted diseases. Off limits in erotica.

Venus *n.* The Roman goddess of love; someone who looks like her.

Voluptuary *n.* a person who can't get enough sexual stimulation, who's always thinking about it, doing it or fantasizing about it.

Voluptuous *adj.* an erotic-looking person; an extremely sensual female.

Voyeur *n.* a person who'd rather watch than do it; one who gets sexually excited by witnessing a sex act and goes out of his way to arrange such a thing.

Vulgar *adj.* lewd or obscene; gross.

Vulva *n.* female genital lips.

Wanton *adj.* sexually hungry, lustfull.

Water sports *n.* a sexual activity which includes urination. Used more for humiliation than for sport.

Wazoo *n.* a penis or cock; or breasts if referring to a pair of wazoos.

Wet dream *n.* a dream that triggers a sexual response causing the dreamer to wake up with either a hard-on or a wet spot on the sheets.

Whack off *v.* to masturbate, usually for males.

Wham-bam-thank-you-ma'am *phrase.* Aka Slam-bam-thank-you-ma'am. The way some men still (sadly) make love. They get it in as soon as possible, without foreplay, and get it off and get it out just as fast, then get dressed and don't always say thank you, ma'am.

White slavery *n.* the practice of kidnapping young girls and shipping them to places all over the world to be used as sex objects. Yes, it still exists, and no, the girls aren't always white.

Whoopie *v.* as in "making whoopie." Used primarily by game show hosts to elude censorship and embarrass contestants.

Whore *n.* a sexually indiscriminate woman who sometimes does it for money.

Wife swapping *n.* the party game where two or more men trade wives for the night. These are the same groups who once met to play bridge but finally realized sex was a lot more fun than cards.

Work up *v.* to get up for sex; to become aroused.

X-rated *adj.* not to be seen by juveniles; contains sex and/or violence and adult themes. When we figure out why "they" put sex and violence together like this, we may have our first clue regarding how it became immoral to enjoy sex, lustful to seek it out and shameful to exhibit tenderness and affection in a public place.

ACKNOWLEDGMENTS

I would like to thank *Parliament News, Inc., Video-X, Lipstick* and *Playgirl* magazines, for permission to reprint my articles and fiction as support material for this book, and *Joint Video Productions* for permission to reprint video script materials.

I would also like to thank the first person to believe in the project, Melvin Powers, and the second and continually supportive person, Joan Bambeck of *Writer's Digest* magazine. A special thanks has to go to Esther Mitgang, of Harmony Books, for having the foresight and the courage to accept the manuscript for publication when no other publisher would dare to take the chance. And a very special thanks to my editor Doug Abrams for helping put together a brand new kind of how-to-write book, even though he had a good time doing it.

I N D E X

abortion, 12
absurdity, sex and, 6
AC/DC, 131, 175
active vs. passive voice, 156-159
actors and actresses:
  fantasy phone calls and, 211, 212, 214
  interviews with, 83-85
  profile of, 83-84
  pseudonyms of, 200
  video residual rights and, 216-217
  "working" and "non-working," 232
  in X-rated videotapes, 221-222, 226, 227, 232, 246
Adam Film World, 86
adjectives, use of, 169-170, 171, 172-173
adult marketplace:
  author's experiences in, 18-21
  for erotic fiction, 25-67
  opportunities for new writer in, 5-6
  place of residence and, 20
  referrals in, 20
  as training ground, 5-7
Adult Video, 86
Adult Video News, 86
advertising, sex in, 13
advertising copy, 80-83
  for magazines, 80-81
  for sexual paraphernalia, 80
  for videotapes, 80, 81-83, 239
agents, 21
Alyson Publications, 99-100
American Booksellers Convention, 99, 112
anal sex, 188
anti-pornography activists, 9
architecture, sexual depictions in, 4
Aristophanes, 3-4
art, erotic, 3-4
articles, 68-75
  case histories and, 68-69
  example of, 69-75
  for public relations, 83-85
  style of, 68-69
Ass Parade, 89
ass publications, 89, 95-96
autobiography, 100

baby-boom generation, 12, 59
Baby Doll, 90
Bad Girls, 220
B&D (bondage and discipline) publications, 93, 101, 102
Bantam Books, 59
Barbach, Lonnie, 5
Barnhart, Helene, 61
Bartlett's Familiar Quotations, 163

Beach Blondes, 92
Bedside Companion, 25, 265
Behind the Green Door, 217
Berkley Publishing Group, 59, 60
bestiality, 9, 270
Best Little Whorehouse in San Francisco, The, 78
Beta-Max, 29, 30-31
Big Boobs, 89, 91
Big Mama, 42, 91
Black & Lusty, 90
"Black Baby Dolls," 241-243
Black Mama, 90
black publications, 90
Black Satin Dolls, 90
Blank, Joani, 111
Blueboy, 46, 100
Bondage Life, 93
Bondage Parade, 93
bondage (B&D) publications, 93, 101, 102
bookstores, adult, 9, 39
    flack escaped by, 10
    miscellaneous material for, 93-94
Bottom, 89
breast publications, 89, 94
breasts, 39
    in humorous tale, 35-39
    in milk publications, 92
    permissible terms for, in romance novels, 62-63
Bright, Susie, 112
Buf, 94, 195
Bust Parade, 39, 43
button line, 244
buzz words, 169-170, 171

Caballero Control Corp., 220
California, pornography in, 8-9, 196
call outs (inserts), 203
Candlelight Ecstasy, 59
Candlelight Ecstasy Supreme, 59
Captive Woman, 57
Carrier Pigeon, 99
casual sex, 12
category romance novels, 60, 66

Cavalier, 48
cave drawings, erotic, 3
character count, 203
characters, 130-138
character sheet, 246
Cheri, 46, 48, 94, 195
Chicago Manual of Style, 162
Chic Letters, 32
child pornography, 9, 57
Christian romance novels, 66
Christie, Agatha, 200
Chubby Cheeks, 89, 91
Chunky Asses, 42
Cinema X, 86
climax (literary and sexual), 139
close-out magazines, 80
Close Up, 195
"cock fantasies," 90, 112
collateral material, 85-86
come shots, 48, 139
"coming out" novels, 100
"Confessions of a Breast Erotic," 35-39, 89
confession-type stories, 101
Consumer's Electronics Show, 85-86
"Continental Lover," 212-213
Corbett, Edward, 162
Cosmopolitan, 5
couple-oriented erotica, 10-11, 168-169, 220-221
Couples, 25, 265
cover letters, 49, 197-199, 225
Crack!, 92

daisy chain, 271
Dell Publishing, 59
Delta of Venus (Nin), 5
denouement, 141-146
Devil in Miss Jones, The, 217
Dial-A-Hunk, 210
dictionaries, 162-163
dirty word market, 2
dirty words, 139-140
    reasons for use of, 2
divorce, no-fault, 12
dominance/submission, 103, 112

Dominatrix, 92, 271
Down There Press, 111
Dreams Die First (Robbins), 5

Easy Rider, 94
editors, 145-146, 161, 198, 199-200, 202
EFQ (Erotic Fiction Quarterly), 99
EFQ Publications, 99
Eidos, 98
Electric Press, The, 67
Elements of Style, The (Strunk and White), 162
emphasis, 161
encyclopedias, 163
Eros, 48
erotica:
    animals in, 57
    answering critics of, 1-5
    author's first experiences with, 14-18
    early evidence of, 3-4
    pornography vs., 4
    responsibilities in writing of, 4
Erotic Fiction Quarterly (EFQ), 99
erotic novels, *see* novels, erotic; novels, erotic romance
Esquire, 6
ethnic publications, 90
euphemisms, 62-63
exercises, 262-271

Falk, Kathryn, 61
fantasy phone calls, 209-216
    actors and actresses in, 211, 212, 214
    charges for, 210
    customers for, 209-211
    female-oriented, 210, 211, 212, 214-215
    gay male market for, 210
    male-oriented, 209-210, 214-215
    script markets in, 209-211
    script payment rates for, 210
    telephone companies and, 210
    types of, 209-211
    writing scripts for, 211-215

fat girl publications, 91
female-oriented erotica, 10, 98-99, 100
    defined, 11
    fantasy phone calls as, 210, 211, 212, 214-215
    male interest in, 11
    male-oriented erotica vs., 129-130
    romance novels as, 58-67
    sample scripts for, 212-214
    X-rated videotapes as, 220-221
feminism:
    pornography as viewed by, 7, 206
    sexist words and, 3
feminist publications, 100, 111
fetish markets, 88-97
    adult store publications in, 43, 80, 89-94
    categories of fiction and articles for, 88-95
    examples of writing for, 95-97
    newsstand publications in, 94
fiction, erotic, 25-67
    erotic novels, 56-67
    letters, 25-39
    long short stories, 48-56
    poetry, 67
    short-short stories, 39-48
Field, Syd, 229
Firsthand, 68, 100
flats, 42, 43
Forum, 21, 25, 46, 68, 197, 265
freelance writers, 20, 94, 197
free love, 12, 13
French postcards, 8
Friday, Nancy, 5, 190
"Friendly Foursomes," 268-269
full-length scripts, 229-231, 245-261
"Full Service Pump," 103-110

Gay and Lesbian Press Association (GLPA), 100
gay female market, 111-117
    characteristics of fiction in, 112-113
    example of writing for, 113-117
    payment in, 111

publications in, 111-113
publishers' requirements in, 112
sources of materials in, 111-112
see also homosexuals; lesbians
gay gothic novels, 100
gay male market, 99-110, 111
example of writing for, 103-110
fantasy phone calls in, 210
locating publications in, 99-100
newsstand vs. adult-store magazines
in, 100-101
payment in, 100, 102
publishers' specs for, 101-102
types of magazines in, 102-103
writing requirements for, 100-102
X-rated videotapes for, 222
see also homosexuals
Geisha Girls, 42
Gem, 195
gender gap, reading habits and, 58
Genesis, 46, 48
Gent, 48, 94, 197
Gentleman's Companion, 197
girlie magazines, 8, 9, 195
Girls Loving Girls, 90
glossary, 286-310
GLPA (Gay and Lesbian Press Association), 100
Goldstein, Al, 85
Gomez, Jewelle, 112, 113-117
Good Vibrations, 111
gothic romance novels, 60, 66
gothic-type heroine, 58
Greece, ancient, sex in arts of, 3-4
Greene, Gail, 5
G Spot, The, 111

hardcore pornography:
in erotic novels, 56-57
men as best writers of, 47
negative imagery in, 10
sensitivity absent in, 11
softcore vs., 203-206
hardcore publications, softcore vs., 46
Harlequin Romances, 59
Harper's, 85

Hayes, Leeanne, 69-75
Heavy Hangers, 89
Hefner, Hugh, 8
hermaphrodites, 93
Hers & Hers, 44, 90
High Society, 25, 68, 94, 182, 196
historical romance novels, 59, 60, 66
Hite, Shere, 5, 190
Hite Report, The (Hite), 190, 271
Holmes, John, 85
homosexuals:
defamatory terms for, 3
publications for, 46, 47
see also gay female market; gay male
market, lesbians
Honcho, 100
Horny Housewife, 57
Hot Line, The, 210
Hotwire, 210
"How to Get Laid," 69-75
*How to Write a Romance and Get It
Published* (Falk), 61
How to Write Erotica (Kelly), 111,
163
humiliation, 102
pornography and, 4
humor, sexual, 6
ancient, 3-4
in short story, 35-39
as turn-off, 35
Hustler, 46, 94, 195, 196, 265

Impulse, 46
India, sexual depictions in, 4
incest, 9, 31, 102, 270
father/daughter, 57
sexual depictions in, 4
insertion, 46, 90, 112
non-insertion vs., 203-204
inserts (call outs), 203
In the Wind, 95
In Touch, 46, 100
Iron Horse, 94

"Jennifer," 150, 154-55
Joint Video Productions, 78-79

Jong, Erica, 5
Joys of Erotica, Volume 4, 77
Juggs, 46, 94, 197

"Keli's Bath," 39-41, 89, 141
Kelly, Valerie, 236-237, 239, 241-243,
    246-261
  early experiences with erotica, 14-18
  professional career of, 16-20
  see also Lynx, Darien

Ladies' Home Erotica, 220
Latin Lovers, 90
Lawrence, D. H., 190, 200
leather and latex publications, 92, 101
Leggs, 89
legislation, 9, 196, 203, 270
leg lovers, 42
Leg Parade, 42
leg publications, 89
Legs & Lingerie, 42, 43, 89
Leg Show, 197
length restrictions, 201-203
Leonard, Gloria, 84, 85, 182
Lesbian Lovers, 42, 49, 90
"Lesbian Love Story, A," 49-56, 90
lesbians:
  publications on, 90, 100, 111-113
  in stories, 44-46, 49-56, 189
  see also gay female market;
    homosexuals
Letters, 46, 265
Letters Magazine, 31
letters magazines, 25-26, 31-32, 46,
    265-268
  categories sought by, 32
  unsaleable material for, 32-35
letters to the editor, 25-35, 93, 94
  by assignment vs. "on spec," 31
  payments for, 31-32
  story elements in, 26
lingerie modeling, 43-44
lingerie publications, 89
Lipstick, 69
Little English Handbook, The (Cor-
    bett), 162

Long & Lovely, 89
long short stories, 48-56
  example of, 49-56
  length of, 48
  payment for, 48-49
  writing "on spec" for, 48
loops, 76-77, 216, 230-231
Los Angeles, 8-9
Los Angeles Times, 16
Loveswept, 59
Lynx, Darien (Valerie Kelly), 35-39,
    89, 121,122-129, 200, 201
Lysistrata (Aristophanes), 3-4

McCall's, 5
macho hero, 58
macho males, 11, 95, 130, 193
MacLaine, Shirley, 271
Mademoiselle, 6
magazine dealers, separating hardcore
    vs. softcore publications by, 46-47
magazines:
  advertising copy in, 80-83
  articles and fiction in, 9-10
  close-out, 80
  girlie, 8, 9, 195
  movie reviews in, 86-87
  nudist, 8
  re-covers, 80
  sex and politics in, 7-14
  video, 46
magazines, adult store, 39, 100-102
  dealers' positioning of, 46-47
  print runs for, 42
  sexually oriented, list of, 272-274
  titles of, 43
  writing to photographs for, 39,
    41-43, 44, 47
magazines, newsstand, 39, 94,
    100-101, 195-196
  dealers' positioning of, 46
  print runs for, 42
Magcorp, 101-102
mailing lists, adult, 85
male-oriented erotica:

fantasy phone calls as, 209-210, 214-215
female-oriented erotica vs., 129-30
Male Sexuality, 111
Mandate, 46, 100
manuscripts, publication of, 195-206
marriage:
  returning popularity of, 12-13
  singleness vs., 13, 192-193
maxi scripts, 229
Mayfair, 195
Melons & Mounds, 89
Men in Love (Friday), 190
midi scripts, 228-229
Milking Mama, 92
Milk Maids, 92
milk publications, 92
Milky, 92
mini scripts, 226-227
misinformation, 188-194
  in male-oriented videotapes, 222
models, photographic, 39, 43
"Monica," 150-154
"moral majority," 12
Morris, J. B., 101, 103
"Mothers Need Love Too," 26-29
motorcycle magazines, 94-95
movies, erotic:
  advertising copy for, 82
  as loops, 76-77, 216, 230-231
  public relations for, 83-85
  reviews of, 86-87
  see also videotapes
movies theaters, adult, 82
Ms., 98
My Secret Garden (Friday), 190, 220
mystery novels, 100, 200

Naked Nymphs, 90, 95
Natividad, Kitten, 84, 85
Neolithic age, erotic sculptures in, 3
Newsweek, 85
new trends, 98-99
New Zealand, sexual depictions in, 4
Nin, Anaïs, 5, 57-58, 162
nonfiction, erotic, 68-87

advertising copy, 80-83
articles, 68-75
collateral material, 85-86
paperback cover copy, 79-80
public relations material, 83-85
reviews, 86-87
video box cover copy, 75-79
Norton, Bill, Sr., 158
novels, erotic, 56-67
categories of, 57
cover copy for, 79-80
hardcore, 56-57
mainstream fiction and, 56
payment for, 57-58
novels, erotic romance, 58-67
books on, 61
course of passion in, 61-62
dramatic undercurrents in, 63-66
as female-oriented, 58
growth in, 58-59
hero in, 59-60, 61, 66
heroine in, 59-60, 61-62, 66
magazine sex vs., 61
markets and formats for, 60
names in, 62
pre-marital sex in, 60
publishers' tip sheets for, 60, 66
publishing houses for, 58, 59-61, 66
straight sex stories vs., 56-57, 58, 61, 63, 65
typical details in, 66
vocabulary in, 61, 62-63
writing sex scenes for, 66
nude centerfolds, 8, 58, 94, 102, 196
nudist magazines, 8
Number 8 Fantasy Lane, 220

OCS, 210
Older Men with Young Girls, 235, 240, 246-261
onion skin paper, 199
On Our Backs, 111-112
orgasms, 190
  male ego and, 11
  in written fiction, 139, 141, 149
orgies, 191-192

Oriental Lust, 90
Oui, 94, 195, 197
Oui Letters, 25, 265
Outlaw Biker, 95

pacing, 159-160
paperback cover copy, 79-80
  aim of, 79
  example of, 80
  payment for, 79
paperback market, 58
"Parisian Lay-over," 121, 122-129,
  130, 131, 188
Parker, Kay, 84, 85, 220-221
Pearls of Love, 67
Penthouse, 10, 25, 46, 48, 94, 195
Penthouse Variations, 6, 46, 265-267
personal experiences, writer's use of,
  174-188
Pet Pussy, 90
Phone Fantasy, The, 210
photographs:
  come shots, 48, 139
  for hardcore magazines, 47
  writing stories to, 39, 41-43, 44, 47
pica width, 203
picture books, 103
"Piece of Time, A," 112, 113-117
pill, the, 12
Pillow Talk, 68
Playboy, 8, 9, 10, 46, 58, 94, 195
Playgirl, 25, 46, 94, 102, 145, 150,
  196, 204, 210
Playguy, 100
Pleasures: Women Write Erotica (Barbach), 111, 220
plot:
  in print erotica, 121-130
  in video scripts, 233-235
poetry, erotic, 67, 98, 99, 112
point of view, narrative, 139-141, 148,
  149, 150
  in gay erotic fiction, 101-102
  in romance novels, 66, 149
Pond, Lily, 67, 98
Ponicsan Darryl, 5

pornography:
  child, 9, 57
  feminist objections to, 7, 206
  hardcore vs. softcore, 203-206
  legislation on, 9, 196, 203, 270
  male market for, 8
  need for new form of, 13
  politics of, 7-14
  rapid growth of, 8-9
  sex crimes and, 4
  understanding of, 1
  see also hardcore pornography
Portrait of Lust, 225, 236, 237-238,
  239, 240
postcards, French, 8
post office boxes, 200-201
pregnant publications, 91
pretty girl publications, 91-92
pro-family groups, 12
prostitution, pornography compared
  with, 7
pseudonyms, 200-201, 217
Pub, 195
public relations material, 83-85
  getting interviews for, 83
  porn stars in, 83-85
  publishers' needs and, 84-85
publishing industry:
  regulation of, 9
  sexual attitudes of, 7-9
pull-outs, 42
pulp, 195

query letters, 197-199
Quotable Woman, 163

Random House Dictionary, 162
*Random House Dictionary of the En-
  glish Language*, 163
rape fantasies, 193
reader research, 59
readers, 58, 59, 61, 149-150
  couples as, 168
  erotic romance novels and, 58, 59,
    61, 62, 66
  identification with heroine by, 66

personal characteristics of, 62
sex with strangers and, 187
writer's knowledge of, 147-148
re-covers, 80
Redbook, 5
Reems, Harry, 85, 200, 246
reference materials, 278-281
regency romance novels, 60, 66
reviews, magazine, 83
Ridings, Sean, 103-110
Robbins, Harold, 5
"Robyn's Nest," 96
Roget's Thesaurus, 163
Roommates, 90
Roth, Philip, 5
Royalle, Candida, 220
rubber apron fetish, 92
rubber baby pants, 92

sales brochures, adult, 85
S&M (sado-masochism), 9, 92-93,
   101, 112, 193-194
San Fernando Valley, 9
Sappho, 42, 90, 189
"Sarah," 141, 142-145
Satin and Lace, 89
scene breakdown, 224, 236, 239
scene description, 170-173
Screenplay (Field), 229
Screenwriter's Handbook, The (Nash
   and Oakey), 229
Screw, 46, 197
sculptures, erotic, 3
Second Chance at Love (Berkley), 59,
   60
Secret Lust (paperback blurb), 80
seductive writing, 164-166
Seka, 85
sensual imagery, 166-169
Sensual Letters, 265
Sensual Review, The (Lynx), 17
sensual words, 282-285
sentence structure, 159-160
"Serena: Car Wash Cookie," 130,
   131-138, 183
setting, 138-139

sex:
   absurdity and, 6
   in erotica vs. pornography, 4
   multiple partners in, 13
   salutary effects of, 6-7, 14
sex crimes, pornography and, 4
sex education, 11, 222
sexism:
   in video industry, 220-222
   in words, 3
sex newspapers, 195-196
sexology, 91, 278-279
Sexology, 21
sex toys, 85, 111
sexual equality, 7
   sexual inequality vs., 11-12
sexuality:
   children's 14
   as personal issue, 14
   theories of, 13
sexual revolution (1960s), 12
Shannon, 93
shoe-fetish stories, 101
short fiction, market for, 6
short-short stories, 39-48
   examples of, 39-41, 43-46
   length of, 39
   model's name in, 39
   one-paragraph personality, 43-44
   photographs with, 39, 41-43, 44, 47
Silhouette, 59
Silhouette Desire, 59
Silhouette Intimate Moments, 58, 59
Silhouette Romances, 59
Silk, 89
Silky, 89
Simon & Schuster, 59
sin, 2, 14
single-girl adult magazines, 39-44
singleness, 13, 192-193
situation comedies, 234-235, 244
Skin, 46, 101, 102, 103
socially redeeming characteristics, 9
softcore erotica:
   for beginners, 47
   defined, 10-11
   hardcore vs., 203-206

softcore publications, hardcore vs., 46
"Sophie," 96-97
spanking publications, 92
Special Edition, 59
special markets, 88-117
  fetish, 88-97
  gay female, 95, 111-117
  gay male, 95, 99-110
  new trends in, 98-99
spec scripts, 218, 219, 223-225, 231
Spelvin, Georgina, 200
Stag, 48
Stallion, 100
state rulings, 46
stereotypes, sexual, 11
Stewart, Keli, 39-42
"Stood Up," 44-46, 90
stories, *see* long short stories; short fiction; short-short stories
Strip Tease, 43
Stroke, 101, 102
suburban housewife, 9
Supercycle, 95
Superromance (Harlequin), 59
Superromance (Worldwide), 59
support material, 85-86
"Surf's Up," 213-214
Svetlana, 220
Swank, 48
Swinger's Digest, 46
swinging, 44
Synonyms and Antonyms, 163
synopsis, 246

Tatelbaum, Brenda, 98
tear sheets, 26, 31, 48, 49, 112, 197
teen romance novels, 66
Temptation, 59
tense, verb, 148-155
Terkel, Studs, 191
Terms of Endearment, 271
Thomas, D. M., 5, 67
threesomes, 44, 131, 266
tip sheets, 60, 66
Tip Top, 42, 89
tongue-in-cheek stories, 35

"Transsexual" letter, 32-34
transsexuals, 93
transvestite (TV) publications, 93
True Letters, 25
TV International, 93
TV (transvestite) publications, 93
TV Tricks, 93
20,000 Words (Leslie), 162
type specs, 42

Ultra, 17

"Valene," 43-44, 89
"Valentine Affair, The," 174, 175-182
Valley Girl, 9
Vanity Fair, 85
vase painting, erotic, 3
venereal diseases, 12
vibrators, 111, 112
video box cover copy, 62, 75-79,
    82, 146, 225, 239
  examples of, 77-78
  loops and, 76-77
  parameters of, 75
  payment for, 75, 76, 77
  running time and, 77
  as sales pitch, 77, 78
  vocabulary for, 76
video distributors/producers, 275-277
"Video Foreplay," 29-31
video guides, 218, 225, 279
video index, 218
video magazines, 46, 86, 217, 274
video rental stores, 216
video scripts, 216-261
  basic formats for, 226-235
  budget restrictions and, 226-227,
    231, 232, 243
  common mistakes in, 243-244
  examples of, 227, 228, 237-238,
    239, 241-243, 246-261
  full-length format of, 229-231, 245
  mailing of, 224, 225
  market for, 216-225, 226-231
  maxi format of, 229
  midi format of, 228-229

mini format of, 226-227
necessary elements in, 244
outline format in, 236-239
payment for, 217, 222, 224
plot and character in, 233-235,
    240-241, 243-245
producer/director and, 218-221,
    222-225, 227, 230, 231, 236
residual rights for, 216-217
scene settings in, 232-233
selling of, 218-220, 222-225
specifications for, 231-233
spec scripts and, 218, 219, 223-225,
    231
stealing of, 223
treatment format in, 236, 239
viewer profile and, 235
writer credits for, 217, 223
writing procedures for, 236-261
writing terminology in, 236
X-rated video industry and, 216-223
videotape blurbs, see video box cover
    copy
videotapes, 85-86, 93
    actors and actresses in, 221-222,
        226, 227, 232, 246
    advertising copy of, 80, 81-83, 239
    distributors of, 217-218, 275-277
    gay male, 222
    industry, 216-223
    manufacturers of, 216-221, 275-277
    market for, 6, 216-225
    movies as, 217, 229-231
    production costs of, 81, 226-227,
        231, 232, 243
    reviews of, 86-87
    serial, 231
    sexism and, 220-222
    writer credits for, 217, 223
Video X, 26, 86
vignettes, 230
violence, 112, 196, 270
    pornography and, 4
voice-overs, 76

water sports, 9, 196, 270

Webster's New World Dictionary, 162
White Hotel, The (Thomas), 67
white slavery, 57
women:
    appeal of romance novels to, 58
    career vs. family role of, 12
    girlish qualities of, 3
    monogamy and, 13
    pornographic treatment of, 7, 189
    as sexual objects, 8, 11
    as video producers, 220-221
word count, 196, 203
words:
    defamatory, 3
    "dirty," see dirty words
    freedom in use of, 2
    inventive use of, 2-3
    sensual, list of, 282-285
    sexist, 3
Working (Terkel), 191
Worldwide Library, 59
Writer, Inc., 272
writer credits, 217, 223
Writers Market, 272
writing erotica, print, 119-206
    active vs. passive voice in, 156-159
    adjectives in, 169-170, 171,
        172-173
    avoiding misinformation in,
        188-194
    basic formula for, 121-146
    buzz words in, 169-170, 171
    character in, 130-138
    climax in, 139
    creating emphasis in, 161
    creating sensual images in, 166-169
    denouement in, 141-146
    description of scene in, 170-173
    editors' cuts in, 145-146
    finding material for, 174-194
    focusing in, 160-161
    hardcore vs. softcore in, 203-206
    knowing the reader in, 147-148
    manuscript preparation and,
        199-203
    pacing in, 159-160

writing erotica, print, (*cont*)
    personal experiences as material for, 174-188
    plot in, 121-130
    point of view in, 66, 101-102, 139-141, 148, 149, 150
    query and cover letters for, 197-199
    seductive approach in, 164-166
    selecting publishers for, 195-196
    selling of, 195-206
    setting in, 138-139
    sexy elements in, 164-173
    stereotypes in, 170-171
    telling the story in, 147-163
    verb tense in, 148-155
    writing and reading in, 161-163
Writing Romance Fiction for Love and Money (Barnhart), 61

X-rated films, *see* movies, erotic
X-Rated Movie Handbook, 86
X-rated video scripts, *see* video scripts
X-rated videotapes, *see* videotapes

Yellow Silk, 67, 98
young girl publications, 89-90, 95-97
Young Innocent Female, 57